Campaigns with
the Field Train

Campaigns with the Field Train

Experiences of a British Officer During the Peninsula and Waterloo Campaigns of the Napoleonic Wars

Richard D. Henegan

Campaigns with the Field Train: Experiences of a British Officer During the Peninsula and Waterloo Campaigns of the Napoleonic Wars
by Richard D. Henegan

Originally publishd under the title
Seven Years Campaigning in the Peninsula and the Netherlands 1808 ~ 1815

Published by Leonaur Ltd

Text in this form copyright © 2007 Leonaur Ltd

ISBN: 978-1-84677-390-7 (hardcover)
ISBN: 978-1-84677-389-1 (softcover)

http://www.leonaur.com

Publisher's Note

The opinions expressed in this book are those of the author and are not necessarily those of the publisher.

Contents

An Unfortunate Start	7
The Field Train	9
The Supplies Set Out	13
Henrica & Antonio	21
The Trouble with Carts	27
The Pursuit of Boats	31
Disaster at Oporto	42
Fire on the Powder Ship	51
The Murder of Prisoners	55
To the Scheldt	59
Pestiferous Walcheren	70
To Iberia	74
The Spanish in Arms	78
Barossa	94
The Defence of Tarifa	106
To England	109
Return to Portugal	114
Scandals!	122
To the Front	130
Into Spain Once More	140
Towards Vittoria	147
The Battle of Vittoria	152
After the Battle	162
San Sebastian	175
The Escape	184
San Sebastian Falls	188
The Death of a Lady	194

The 95th at the Bridge of Vera	199
The Crossing of the Bidassoa	204
Battle of the Nivelle	214
St. Jean de Luz	221
Fighting After St Jean de Luz	236
A Tragedy	240
Murillo's Spanish	244
Bayonne	248
Toulouse	255
To England	268
Ordered to America	273
To Belgium	281
Hard Fighting	288
Waterloo	295
The End of My Military Life	309

Chapter 1
An Unfortunate Start

When the ambition of Napoleon Buonaparte had succumbed before the obstacles presented to his project of adding England to the list of nations he had conquered, the whole phalanx possessed the resources that Spain and Portugal stood most in need of; and yet she lacked one thing—*rulers to direct and wield her strength to advantage.* Old habits, principles, and precedents governed, whilst a new state of affairs, and novel exigencies demanded the adoption of a new routine of public arrangements, the expediency of which the ill-success of so many previous expeditions might in itself have suggested.

Our statesmen at that period seemed only anxious to force their names upon the page of history, without reference to the means by which glorious results were to be obtained. Ever ready to enter into any project submitted to their notice, they were equally averse to employing other than petty means to attain it. No sooner was it in progress, than they began to hesitate, assistance was withdrawn, and an inevitable failure brought with it no experience for the future. Witness the expeditions to the Elbe, Ferrol, Buenos Ayres, and the individual *there* chosen for directing operations.[1] The unnecessary effusion of blood caused by employing too small a naval force in the capture of the Spanish Treasure Galleons in 1804;[2] the arma-

---
1. General Whitelock.
2. To seize the valuable treasures with which these four Spanish frigates were freighted, and at a moment when it was of the utmost importance to wrench these sinews of war from the French, our Government sent out an equal number of frigates to intercept the Spanish Admiral. The result was a most disastrous loss of life, which would have been avoided had a larger British force been employed, in as much as the Spanish Admiral might have surrendered with honour under such circumstances to an armament he was incapable of resisting, and it would also have been, on our (continued)

ment sent in 1808, unasked, to assist Sweden, and unaccepted when arrived there; and finally the miniature force sent in the same year under the command of Major-General Sir Arthur Wellesley, to chase the French from Portugal, which force, originally intended for some undefined object on the coast of South America, was thus blown in a contrary direction by the ever-veering breath of the ministry. No sooner had it left the Cove of Cork, than it was wisely remembered that only a Major-General had been placed in command, and that nothing short of the dignity of a Lieutenant-General could uphold the honour of the British name. Who was the nearest at hand? became the question. Sir Harry Burrard. That Lieutenant-General was accordingly forthwith dispatched to supersede the Major-General; but this was not all. Scarcely had he set sail for his destination, when it was remembered that there was a senior Lieutenant-General to Sir Harry Burrard, and one therefore still better qualified to take the command. In consequence, another vessel was dispatched to carry off from his Governorship at Gibraltar, this senior Lieutenant-General, Sir Hugh Dalrymple, and land him on the coast of Portugal. But here fortune did for England what her own wise rulers did not, and wafting Major-General Sir Arthur Wellesley first on shore, gave him an opportunity of giving Marshal Junot a sound thrashing before the arrival of the two Lieutenant-Generals.

Sir Harry Burrard was the next to land. The action was nearly over, and as the smoke cleared off, the optics of the Lieutenant-General could discern the French running away, and the Major-General pressing on to the pursuit. But here the Lieutenant-General assuming his authority called out:

"Halt, Major-General, I have in my pocket the warrant which gives me the command over you, and as I have scarcely recovered from sea-sickness, the men may rest until to-morrow."

Before the morrow came, the arrival of the senior Lieutenant had completed the trio of Commanders and Sir Hugh Dalrymple thus swallowing up the dignity of Sir Harry Burrard, as he had previously swallowed up that of Major Wellesley, the troops were ordered into inactivity, until new surveys of the ground, and fresh information had enlightened the mind of the latest arrived Commander-in-Chief.

Hence the Convention of Cintra!

---

side, more politic to have placed a matter of such high import beyond the chances that attend an engagement at sea between vessels of equal strength and numbers.

CHAPTER 2

The Field Train

It was in August 1808, that the army under Sir John Moore, to which I was attached as Military Commissary in the Field Train,[1] anded at Marceira on the shores of Portugal.

The Field Train was a corps attached to the Royal Artillery, whose officers wore the uniform of the Royal Artillery, and held comparative rank in the army, according to their respective grades in the department. The Ordnance Commissary at its head held the rank and received the allowances of a Lieutenant-Colonel commanding.

On the Field Train devolved the duty of preparing the Battering Trains, and Field Brigades of Artillery, and delivering them over in a state of complete efficiency for action. During the protracted war in the Peninsula, the assistant of this department was fully developed, in as much as on its Officers devolved the laborious duties of disembarking the Battering Trains from the Transports—mounting the guns—equipping them for the Batteries—keeping up the necessary supplies during the progress of the different sieges, and, after the termination of each, collecting the captured guns and organizing the whole for future service.

The author, as Ordnance Commissary at the Head of this department during the active and brilliant Campaigns of 1813 and 1814, received his instructions from the Board of Ordnance, and was held by the Board of Ordinance responsible for all ammunition and stores, placed under his charge for the public service. To him the Commanding Officers of Artillery and Engineers looked for the requisite supplies and equipments for their respective corps

---

1. To those who are unacquainted with the nature of the Field Train, It may not be uninteresting to specify the duties that belonged to that department on Foreign Service.

and on him also fell the duty of supplying the entire Anglo-Portuguese army, amounting at the period above named to *seventy thousand men,* with all the small arm ammunition required for its use in the field.

The performance of these duties demanded not only a thorough knowledge of the various proportions of ammunition for Battering and Field-Artillery, but also a scrupulous attention to every changing feature of a battle field—especially during a long contested engagement, when the least delay, or the issuing of a wrong calibre of ammunition, might have produced fatal results to the most important military operations.

Many distinguished and experienced Artillery Officers have considered the Field Train to be an indispensable branch of the army, and certain it is, that during the many years we were engaged in war on the Continent, no Military Expedition was undertaken without a full compliment of Field-Train Officers, who, upon every occasion displayed the greatest self-devotion and zeal. Egypt—Monte Video—the Peninsula and the Netherlands witnessed their indefatigable exertions.

In thus alluding to the merits of the Field-Train, the Author feels pride in the recollection that during the most brilliant period of the war, he served at the head of this meritorious department.

In the preceding May, the same army, under the same Commander, formed the expedition sent to the assistance of Sweden, when threatened with an attack by the combined forces of Russia, France, and Denmark. A misunderstanding finally terminating in an open rupture between the Swedish Monarch and Sir John Moore, caused the latter to convey his troops to England, from whence, immediately afterwards, without disembarking, we sailed for Portugal. On the 24th of August, the fleet ran down close in-shore, between Oporto and Mondego Bay. The weather was beautiful, and the animated appearance of the coast was joyously responded to by hearts that bounded at the magic words of *foreign service.*

The white quintas peeping out from the green foliage that enclosed them; the church spires, almost as numerous as the quintas; the peasantry in their gay costume, flocking along the beach to gaze on our gallant ships; the country boats pressing round us, manned by the dark natives, holding up their tempting grapes, wine, fish,

&c, for purchase. Officers and men grasping with one hand the alluring eatables, with the other parting with their good English coin, wondering meanwhile how its value could be already so well understood and appreciated. All this gave a zest to the first glimpse we obtained of Portugal.

On anchoring in Mondego Bay preparations were made for the disembarkation of the troops, but the heavy swell upon the bar rendered the attempt too hazardous, and the fleet consequently stood out to sea that night. The following morning we anchored in Marceira Bay, and the landing commenced. Most of the transports had been provided with flat bottomed boats, into which the men, in heavy marching order, were transferred. A rapid succession of these boats, closely packed with human beings, went tumbling through the surf, discharging on the beach their living cargoes, with little damage beyond a complete drenching. But as the day advanced, the surf increased, and each succeeding boat encountered increasing difficulties in reaching land. At one moment upwards of twenty boats were struggling with the waves, and an awful anxiety for their fate was experienced on board the .ships they had left, and by those who awaited them on shore. The sea had grown higher and higher, and the foaming billows broke furiously over the beach, raising a cloud of spray along its margin. Some of the boats were raised high upon the mountain waves, and dashed by them in safety on the shore; but others, less fortunate, came broadside and the next moment were floating bottom upwards.

The soldiers, encumbered with their heavy packs, could make but feeble and ineffectual efforts to save themselves, and drowning men, in all the horrors of unavailing struggles, were seen in all directions convulsively buffeting with the waves. Some were picked up by the lighter and better managed craft of the men-of-war; others were saved by the intrepid endeavours of their comrades on shore, who, disencumbering themselves of their kits, plunged through the boiling surf to the rescue.

The foremost in this enterprise of danger was a young Scotch gunner, in Captain Drummond's company of artillery, of the name of McNeil. Three times he had returned to land in safety, bearing at each return an exhausted comrade in his arms. Another boat upset in bounding through the dangerous whirlpool; McNeil heard the cry of despair from the crew, and although his strength was subdued by great exertion, threw himself into the raging element, to return, alas! no more. The noble fellow had grasped the arm of one of the imploring suppliants, when the prow of a ship's launch, impelled by a heavy sea, struck him a fatal blow upon the head. He sank, and towards evening the tide left his inanimate body on the shore. It was interred the same night, the funeral service being read over it by one of his own officers.

So terminated, with a loss by drowning, of upwards of sixty men, a disembarkation ominously prophetic of the after calamities that attended Sir John Moore's unfortunate campaign.

The dripping soldiers stood upon the beach, but not even the beautiful and varied scene around them, could dispel the gloom caused by the mournful fate of so many of their comrades. And yet the scene was well calculated, from its novelty and animation, to chase away care from a soldier's mind—it spoke of *foreign service!*

On one side stood the men drenched to the skin adjusting their knapsacks and accoutrements—officers mustering their companies—and regiments already put in marching order, winding slowly up the narrow defiles of the high mountains beyond on the route towards Vimiera. Peasants were pouring in from the neighbouring hamlets, with grapes, chestnuts, figs, wine, pumpkins, &c, for sale, while fat friars, mounted on mules and asses, bearing large umbrellas to protect their shorn pates from the sun, mixed among the soldiers, offering congratulations, and dispensing benedictions on the new comers. Here and there were groups of soldier's wives, with canteens and haversacks slung across their shoulders; some wrangling about the payment for the articles they had purchased; others indulging in copious libations of wine, to celebrate their recent escape from the water.

When to these varieties are added the terrors of a tremendous thunder-storm, which burst from the mountains, at one time enveloping every object in darkness, at another throwing a lurid and sulphurous light over sea and land, there remains little more to say of the first footing gained by Sir John Moore's army on the soil of Portugal.

Chapter 3

The Supplies Set Out

The first orders I received in Portugal were to proceed with a party of gunners to the fortress of Belem, which had been evacuated on the preceding evening by the French, who had embarked on board our transports for their own country, in accordance with the Convention of Cintra. This service occupied three days, during which we waged a most unsuccessful warfare against a countless host of enemies, in the shape of fleas. Nothing can possibly give an adequate idea of the myriads of these active imbibers of human blood, found in the sleeping apartments of the French soldiers. In the daytime our white trousers were changed to a bronze hue by their unwelcome presence, and during the hours of darkness these nimble gentry so completely anticipated any future assistance we might require from the *phlebotomist,* that when subsequently a fever and dysentery broke out among the troops, it was perhaps from this cause that neither myself or men suffered, thanks to the reduced temperature of what our sanguinary enemies had left us.

We were not a little glad to quit a fortress garrisoned by so unsubduable a force, and we finished this inglorious campaign by returning to Prazzo d'Arcos, where the artillery was encamped, and there making a report to the Commanding Officer, Colonel Wood, of one hundred and twenty brass guns, mounted upon garrison carriages, a very considerable quantity of ammunition, and an innumerable multitude of French fleas, prisoners of war, being in a serviceable state in the Fortress of Belem.

The circumstances connected with the appointment of Sir John Moore to the command of the army to be employed in Spain, and the preparations made at Lisbon for the march of that army through Portugal, have been repeatedly the subject of description and animadversion. It is, therefore, only necessary here to observe, that the Portuguese authorities at Lisbon showed a contemptible ignorance of the topography of their country, and the state of its roads; and as Sir John Moore was under the necessity of forming his plans for the march of his troops, in a great measure, on this erroneous information, serious evils necessarily resulted.

Without specifying in detail the movements of the army, it will suffice to say that its strength was divided. The artillery and cavalry, with a division of infantry, under the command of Sir John Hope, took the road of Elvas and Estremadura, while the rest of the infantry, under Generals Beresford and Frazer, proceeded in a northerly direction to Almeida—the divided divisions to concentrate at Salamanca.

When these movements were decided upon, I was appointed, at Lisbon, to organize the reserve ammunition for this army under orders for Spain. It consisted of two millions, five hundred thousand rounds of ball cartridges, and a large supply for the artillery. The stores were to be conveyed, in the first instance, by water from Lisbon to Abrantès, in fifteen boats, provided by the Regency, of about forty tons each, and such was the clumsy negligence, or want of proper information, on the part of the authorities, that instead of reaching Abrantès, it was found impracticable to ascend the Tagus in large boats beyond Santerem, not half the distance. The river, even long before that point, loses its majestic breadth, and narrowing into an insignificant stream, becomes only navigable for small craft, propelled by poles.

This unexpected circumstance threatened evils of serious import, by causing delay in the operations of the army. Fast a-ground in large boats, with shallow water before us, we had no alternative but to lay a forcible embargo on every small boat that passed up or down the river. It was a cruel necessity to stop the peasants as they plied backwards and forwards with fruit and other perishable articles, forcing them to discharge their little cargoes on the banks of the river, for the purpose of re-loading their boats With our heavy stores; but in this manner we laid strong hands on one hundred and ninety-eight small craft, into which, after tedious labour, the transfer of the Ordnance stores was effected by the thirty-second regiment, which had been selected as escort to this valuable convoy, and we proceeded onwards to Abrantès.

From Abrantès the convoy of ammunition was conveyed on bullock wains, over rugged mountains and wretched roads to Castello Branco, by the route of Nizza, and the almost impassable defile of Villa Velha, where a flying bridge was thrown over the Tagus. The wet season had commenced, and should any of the gallant fellows of the thirty-second be still alive, they will not have forgotten this first breaking in to the hardships of a soldier's life, of eleven days exposure, without intermission, to a drenching rain.

At Castello Branco I received orders to halt the convoy. The thirty-second then moved onwards into Spain, and after recruiting the exhausted transport, one half of which had broken down on the march, six companies of the Buffs, under Colonel Drummond, replaced the thirty-second regiment as escort, and we continued our march towards Salamanca.

On the night of the 26th of December we arrived at Ciudad Rodrigo, after a long and harassing march from Castello Branco. The weather was wet and cold, and the tedious operation of packing the ammunition wains in the great square of the town, subjected the men to a lengthened exposure to its severity. Having, however, concluded these duties, we retired to our respective billets for the night, but long before the dawn of day, the beating to arms of the Spanish garrison announced that something had taken place to disturb the tranquillity of the city. We were quickly on foot, and found that a Spanish officer had arrived with the intelligence of a French column being within a few hour's march. With all the animated and stirring spirit that characterizes the Spanish character when under the influence of excitement, the inhabitants declared they would shed the last drop of their blood in the defence of their homes. Women and children were to be seen busily lending their aid to the preparations making on the ramparts to oppose the enemy, while groups of monks, with their long brown robes tucked up, to give more freedom to their movements, appeared on the batteries, exhorting their countrymen to defend themselves to the last against the foe.

Amid these warlike preparations, it may naturally be supposed that our small band were looked upon by the Spaniards as staunch and certain allies, in this hour of need; and their unsuspecting reliance on our valorous intentions in their favour, had caused them to raise the draw-bridges that connected the town with the country; never contemplating the possibility of our requiring to make a sortie. The astonishment they felt, when orders were given for the opening of our march, was expressed in the most unequivocal language, and they boldly refused to allow us egress from their walls, for what they denominated a base desertion. And here it may not be out of place to add, that there were many among us, who warmly shared the feelings of the Spaniards, and would gladly have avoided a movement that looked very much like running away.

Nor did it require much depth of wisdom to perceive that if our precipitate departure were only to insure the safety of the ammunition, that object was more likely to be achieved by keeping it within the walls of a fortified city, than by exposing it on the high road to an open attack of the enemy; however, in military matters, one head rules the many, and so it was in this case, for Colonel Drummond had no means of obtaining information of what was going on, and was entirely influenced by the advice of Colonel Roche, an English officer in the service of Spain.

After a stormy conference with the Spanish Governor upon the necessity of the ammunition falling back upon Almeida, the "open Sesame" of the gates was pronounced, but the inhabitants were so strongly incensed against us, that, as we slowly moved along the streets of the city, with the cumbrous and creaking wains that bore away the ammunition, our progress was interrupted by the clamours of the crowd, loudly expressing indignation at our departure, and applying to us the epithet of *Ladrones,* with other choice expressions, for thus deserting them in the moment of danger.

The snow lay thickly on the wide plain that extends between Ciudad Rodrigo and Almeida, increasing in appearance its vast extent. Our progress was slow, often retarded by the breaking down of the ammunition wains, and it was late when we arrived at Fort Conception, a distance of about three leagues, where we bivouacked for the night.

The day's march had been tedious and monotonous, and my anxiety for the safety of the large convoy of ammunition, under my special charge, was not diminished by the corroborative reports that met us on our route, of the enemy's proximity. No sooner, therefore, had slumber visited the weary members of our little camp, than I proposed to an officer of the commissariat department, who accompanied us—and who, from a previous campaign in South America with General Whitelock, had acquired it perfect knowledge of the Spanish language—that we should mount our trusty steeds, and under cover of night steal forth in quest of information respecting the movements of the enemy.

My proposal was met with corresponding zeal, and accordingly, when silence reigned around, we mounted our horses, and sallied forth on our expedition towards the banks of the Agueda.

The night was piercingly cold, but cloudless, and the several hamlets through which we passed gave no signs of animated life, save the barking of the dogs, as our horse's hoofs fell heavily on the frozen earth. Towards midnight we approached a village called Sisermo, situated on the banks of the Agueda. Here we halted, and after reconnoitering the houses it contained, we knocked at the door of one whose inmates we thought most likely to afford us the information we sought, and refreshment for our horses. For several minutes our summons for admission remained unheeded, but as we became more urgent, a stir within announced that we were heard.

The door was cautiously opened, and two figures, wrapped in large brown cloaks, demanded our business. My companion, who was spokesman, briefly answered that we were English officers requiring refreshment for ourselves and horses; and we were accordingly ushered into a long gloomy apartment, at the extremity of which glimmered a solitary lamp. Our conductors left the room, and as we threw off our cloaks and disencumbered ourselves of our swords, we mutually agreed to proceed very cautiously in search of the information we required, and on no account to give circulation to the reports we had heard that morning at Ciudad Rodrigo.

A man now entered the room dressed in the religious garb of the country. He was still in the prime of life, of broad and athletic make, and in few words introduced himself to us as the master of the house.

I particularly remarked the expression of his countenance as he inquired, with an air of mock gravity—looking at the same time earnestly at our uniforms—if we were aware of the French being already on the opposite banks of the Agueda. My friend, having previously determined on bridling his tongue, was taken all aback by the suddenness of the question, and evinced so much hesitation in his answer, that our host, after one more scrutinizing glance at our appearance, hastily quitted the room.

The chance of obtaining correct information of the movements of the enemy appeared as distant from us as ever, and we were consulting on the best means to adopt for the purpose, when the sound of approaching footsteps, with the murmur of many voices met our ears, and before we had time to express our surprise, our host re-entered, accompanied by a train of ferocious looking fellows, who wrapped in their ample cloaks, stood regarding us with grim and lowering visages. My companion's knowledge of Spanish left us but a brief space in ignorance of our perilous position.

The house which we had selected as the most promising for our purpose, belonged to the Padre of the parish, an individual, who, like all others of his calling in those eventful days, had neither, by precept nor example, trained his flock in the paths of peace.

The Spanish clergy, fierce in the defence of a religion that gave them unlimited influence over a credulous and imaginative people, were ever the first to raise the banner of war, and to rouse their devoted followers to a sense of vengeance against the despoilers of their country.

The name of Frenchman was an abomination to the Spaniards, and no sooner had our host perceived the obnoxious blue of our uniforms, than he hastened to announce to his quickly assembled countrymen the joyous news of our capture, never once suspecting the possibility of English officers being otherwise attired than in the well known, and easily recognized, red coat. In vain did my companion set forth our condition, and our errand. A savage grin of exultation was the only answer vouchsafed, and was reflected in the countenance of every one present, ourselves excepted, when the Padre concluded an animated and high wrought picture of the wrongs of Spain, by condemning us both to be hanged as enemies to her children and her soil.

Loud *viva's* applauded the decree, and an unusually villainous-looking rascal stepping forward, the Padre honoured him with directions to hang us on a certain tree he named, overlooking the Agueda, that we might be advantageously placed to hail the first approach of our countrymen. With fiendish looks, several of the Spaniards quitted the apartment to assist in the preparations for our summary execution, and the others dropping off, one by one, we were left to the comfortable indulgence of our own reflections.

The suspense in which we were left was horrible. To perish on the battle field is the chance of war, and even the pang that rends the mother's heart for the fall of an only son, so perishing, is susceptible of one faint gleam of consolation when memory retraces the cause in which he fell. Our doom was to be widely different. No tear of sympathy would be shed for our untimely fate—a fate that would probably never even be revealed to those we left behind; besides, the blood of youth danced high and joyously in our veins. Hope then held out so many bright visions of happiness, which maturer age has found to end in disappointment; but in youth they at least possess the charms of reality, and to see them all engulfed at one swoop. Oh, it made a century of a moment!

With feelings of desperation, produced by the agonizing excitement of the hour, we looked around us in the hope of finding some means of escape—but in vain. The only pass to the outer entrance was guarded, and our own rashness, in laying aside our swords, had deprived us of the last hope of satisfaction in selling our lives dearly.

An awful pause ensued, the length of which might have been timed by the bumping of my companion's heart, as it struck audibly in this moment of hopeless despair. Nor was my own, perhaps, less tranquil; but it was holding silent converse with my brain, and as the village bell ushered in the first hour of another day, the thought came rushing madly, that this opening day, my last on earth, was by a strange coincidence the anniversary of my birth.

At this awful crisis the door opened, and the Padre reappeared, followed by an important looking personage, and several armed men. Advancing a few steps towards us, the newcomer, whose official dignity of Corregidor we guessed at by his self-important mien, addressed us in the mock heroic style habitual to Spaniards.

Enlarging upon the enormity of our offence in seeking, as spies, to betray the hospitable hearth, he enacted in his own person the offices of judge and jury, by sentencing us to be forthwith removed from his august presence to immediate execution.

The countenance of my companion bore testimony to the sufferings of his mind, and as my look of despair was turned upon him, he drew from his breast-pocket a handkerchief to wipe away the large drops that stood upon his brow.

In this simple action lay our deliverance. A letter fell to the ground. The Padre threw himself on the prize, concluding that its contents would lead to some important intelligence, and withdrew to the dim lamp already mentioned to examine it. Our anxious eyes sought in those of the reader for one relenting look. His grim followers were grouped around him, eager to participate in the treasonable intelligence our letter was supposed to contain; when "*Santa Maria!*" burst from the lips of the Padre. His eyes dilated—his cloak gradually unfolded—he rapidly approached us, and before we had time to wonder, we found ourselves alternately hugged and embraced with an ardour impossible to describe, and half smothered by the vapour of garlic and tobacco smoke that poured forth from the astonished throng.

"My friends," exclaimed the Padre, "these are indeed English officers, and known to my revered patron, the faithful Don Francisco."

His words solved the mystery of so sudden a transition in our favour, and proved how weighty matters may be outweighed by trifles light as air. The officer who accompanied me had been stationed at Ciudad Rodrigo for the purpose of furnishing supplies to the troops, as they arrived on their march into Spain; during that time he was quartered in the house of a wealthy *hidalgo*, who entertained much friendship for him. On the evening preceding the rumoured approach of the French, this nobleman had quitted the city, having previously caused to be placed in his guests apartment a brace of richly ornamented pistols, accompanied by a letter, praying his acceptance of them, as a mark of his esteem and regard. In the hurry of the moment, this letter had remained forgotten in the pocket of my friend, until it fell from thence as already related.

To this circumstance we were indebted for our lives, and for an excellent supper of well seasoned *ola,* and a *borracho* of potent wine, in which we drowned the recollection of our previous terror.

Chapter 4
Henrica & Antonio

Late on the succeeding evening we arrived at Almeida, and found that the same rumours which had caused our precipitate departure from Ciudad Rodrigo were in circulation there.

The whole frontier was agitated by reports of the rapid approach of the French army towards it, and the several detachments that had been left in the rear, as guards and escorts, were concentrated under the command of Brigadier-General Cameron, who with the seventy-ninth regiment, and Colonel Drummond's division of the Buffs, made a vain attempt to join the main body of the army in Spain by crossing the Douro at Moncorva.

Thus left without escort of any kind, the responsibility of the vast supply of ammunition rested exclusively on myself and party, which consisted of only twenty-three gunners of artillery. I remember being one day in close conference with Colonel Guard, the Commandant at Almeida, on the best means to adopt for the transport of this ordnance depot, when a letter was brought to him from Sir Robert Wilson, strikingly characteristic of that gallant officer, but smacking so much of the chivalric valour of the Knight of La Mancha, that the gravity of the conference was altogether disturbed.

Sir Robert Wilson had raised and organized a corps of Portuguese bearing the name of the three L's—or the Loyal-Lusitanian Legion.

It is true that some of our wags had honoured it with another appellation, less sonorous to the ear; but notwithstanding this, the three L's appertained to a tight little band that did good service under its distinguished commander. Indeed, at the moment of which I speak, the movements of Sir Robert Wilson in advancing towards the enemy formed a refreshing contrast to the zig-zag marches of all our detachments in the opposite direction. But to return to his letter to Colonel Guard: "They say," wrote the gallant chief, "that the roads are impassable for my artillery; 'but I say that zeal, skill, and oxen will accomplish wonders.' They say that the French are approaching, 'but I say fear not, for my invincible legion will hover on your flanks and protect you.'"

We drank a bumper that evening to the supremacy of "Zeal, Skill, and Oxen;" and another to Sir Robert Wilson and his "invincible Legion."

Some idea may be formed of the difficulties to be encountered in removing a convoy of ammunition consisting of two million rounds of ball cartridges, besides a large proportion for field artillery. To our army, the safety of so large a supply was of the utmost importance, while, on the other hand, the circumstance of its falling into the hands of the enemy was to be avoided at all risks. I had perceived a disinclination on the part of Colonel Guard to take upon himself the responsibility of giving any directions respecting a branch of the service with which he considered himself unconnected. In this perplexity of affairs, I, therefore, took upon myself to apply to the Portuguese authorities, in the hope that their knowledge of the country's resources would assist me in the views I had formed for the transport of the ordnance depôt.

The Governor of Almeida strongly recommended that the ammunition should be removed to a place on the Douro called Arueda, where he assured me I should easily procure boats to convey it on to Oporto. On the faith of his representations, we therefore started, as soon as I could obtain sufficient transport for its conveyance, an operation of no small difficulty; and after a very tedious day's march, from the almost impassable state of the roads, we made our first halt at Pinhel, a poor and dirty village.

An incident occurred here partaking so much of the romantic, that I still remember the effect it produced, even on the unsentimental feelings of men little accustomed to those scenes of love that engross the lighter hearted inhabitants of a softer clime.

After seeing my party housed as well as could be expected in so miserable a place, I entered a small cottage where an old woman was seated, telling her beads with all the superstitious reverence of her creed. A lovely little boy of about two years old knelt by her side, in whose dark eyes and mantling complexion, the Spanish blood shone forth in rich luxuriance. My appearance evidently alarmed the aged woman, for making an effort to rise, she called out loudly "Henrica—Henrica," when a back door quickly opened, and one of the prettiest young women I ever beheld, entered, apparently lost in wonder at the unexpected sight of a stranger.

As soon as she was informed that I was an English officer, and required hospitality, she advanced towards me, and helping to disencumber me from my cloak, placed a seat for me near a *brassero* of lighted embers, whilst with an irresistible grace and modesty of manner, she proposed to prepare something for my supper; and in a short time I found myself seated at a clean spread little table, enjoying the coarse fare that the cottage afforded.

As my eyes rested with admiration on Henrica's beauty, I could not but observe the total absence of coquetry, that her manner displayed. She neither sought nor avoided my gaze; but once, when this homage to her charms assumed the expression of asking for a return, she proudly, but at the same time with feminine delicacy, gave me a glance of unfeigned displeasure, and quitted the little apartment. I would have given worlds to have been able to assure her of my good behaviour for the future, and my eye turned impatiently toward the door, but she did not return.

In her absence, I endeavoured to make myself as agreeable as I could to the elderly dame, and succeeded so well, that I was encouraged to ask if the lovely boy on her knee—at the same time slipping into his little hand a *crusado novo*—was her grandson? She answered that he was, and that Henrica was his mother. The intelligence made my heart beat. It would be very difficult, perhaps, to define why; but I well remember that my heart did beat.

"Where then is her husband?" was my next question.

The old woman paused; a shade of sorrow passed over her wrinkled brow, and a tear fell upon the head of the child as she leaned forward to kiss its innocent cheek, murmuring as she did so, "he is the offspring of un-wedded love."

My heart smote me for my curiosity, and I could have given a curse to the betrayer of Henrica's innocence, when the old woman, won by my kindness to the little fellow, slowly related to me the following circumstances concerning his birth.

"We are not Portuguese, Senhor, but Spaniards, from the fertile plains of Zamora. My husband was a rich cultivator of olives, and we were blessed with two sweet children. Francesco, peace to his soul"—here the old woman devoutly made the sign of the cross; "and Henrica whom you have just seen, Senhor. Until three years ago, no cloud had darkened our happy days, nor did we ever dream that we should be forced from the peaceful abode of our fathers to seek protection and safety in a strange land—for such is this to us. Foreigners came, and brought war and desolation with them. Our homes were plundered, and murder and rapine usurped the place of peace and love. Oh God! it was a fearful night when the stranger violated the home in which our children were born, and sent us wanderers on the earth; and yet even that would have been welcomed if it could have averted the misery our hearts had still to bear. But oh! that I should live to tell the tale, when the young and beautiful are laid low in the grave.

"On that fearful night, my husband was murdered—yes, murdered," she added, in a low voice, "in defending the hearth of his fathers; and Francesco, my brave Francesco, purchased with his life's blood his sister's honour."

The poor old woman paused, overcome with the recollection. With a tremulous voice she then proceeded.

"We escaped from the bloody scene, but not unprotected, for there was one who had loved Henrica from the time they had played as children together. Antonio Cabrera, accompanied us in our flight, and our misfortunes only bound him closer to us. The sequel, Senhor, will not astonish any one who has loved as they did. Trusting to the honour of her lover to make her his wife, as soon as it was possible, Henrica's love placed no obstacle to his happiness, and she became his, alas! without the sanction of the church. It was but very shortly afterwards that in traversing a mountainous district, in the hope of finding some spot sheltered from the outrages of the invaders, we encountered a party of French dragoons who had lost their route. Terror deprived me of my senses as they approached, for, Senhor, the sight of them brought fresh to my remembrance the image of my murdered boy. They required a guide, and deaf to the cries and entreaties of Henrica, they forced her lover away from us.

"Oh! it was sad to see her for many a long day after that cruel separation, how she dragged along her weary limbs from place in place in the hope of tracing him, and all in vain. At length we crossed the frontier, and found this little cottage deserted by its inhabitants. Here we established ourselves, and here also Henrica confided to me her situation. She gave birth to this dear child, and although her love for Antonio is too deeply rooted ever to admit of happiness being an inmate of her breast, I yet perceive that she has lately acquired a tranquillity of mind that I attribute to hope having once more taken possession of it."

As the old woman concluded her touching narrative, Henrica re-entered the apartment, and I could easily see by the abashed and crimsoned cheek with which she took her seat at a distance from me, that she had overheard enough to be conscious of the subject of her mother's discourse.

Sweet Henrica! no wedded dame, fresh from the importance of a special license and a Bishop's blessing, could have been regarded with a truer feeling of respect and devotion than you were by me at that moment!

After some general remarks on the state of the country, and other indifferent topics, Henrica rose to conduct me to my chamber, and bidding me sleep well, in the sweetest voice imaginable, left me to the protection of the "Blessed Virgin."

I rose before daybreak on the following morning, as it was necessary to proceed early on our wearisome route. The given point of rendezvous for my party was at the extremity of the long straggling village where we slept, and as the windings and turnings demanded some knowledge of the locality, Henrica insisted upon accompanying me so far on the road.

Taking her pretty boy by the hand, she hung over her arm a basket, in which were grapes, chestnuts, and bread made of Indian corn, which she had kindly prepared for my refreshment on the march, in return for the golden *moidore* I had presented to her child. As we walked slowly along, each hovel and cottage sent forth its inmates of the night, who had shared the rude fare and hospitality of the Portuguese villagers.

At length we were all assembled, with the exception of my servant, a Spaniard, whom I had left at a stable in the village in charge of my horse. He had entered my service at Almeida, in the garb of a Spanish muleteer, and never was there a handsomer or better specimen of that race of peasantry than he afforded. I had found him zealous in his duty, and strictly honest, with all the romantic sprinkling, and clever originality, peculiar to the nature of a genuine Spaniard of that class.

Henrica had transferred her basket to my arm, and was preparing to bid me farewell, when my horse and servant appeared in sight. As she was turning to depart, she suddenly stopped, as if transfixed to the spot. A shriek escaped from her lips, and holding up her child to the Spanish muleteer, who rushed towards her, she sank senseless in his arms.

Need I add that it was Antonio, or that he was left behind to revive her into joyful consciousness? To tell the tale of his escape, and to be introduced to his pretty son and heir? All this I have no doubt took place in due time, but we were bound on less agreeable duties, and our wearisome march recommenced.

CHAPTER 5

The Trouble with Carts

The rain was pouring down upon us in torrents, for the rainy season had set in, and the slow progress of the ox-wains that conveyed the ammunition was rendered still more tedious by the accidents that were perpetually occurring to them. Sometimes a refractory pair of the horned beasts would, as if by mutual consent, come to a dead stand still, nor recover their energies until the application of the goad taught them the necessity of obedience.

Upon approaching what had been described as a rivulet, over which we were to pass, we found that, from the continued heavy rains, it had swelled to the size of a river. To effect a passage, we attached cords to the horns of the cattle, and so hauled them with their burdens across the stream as best we could. Three of the wains, nevertheless, went swimming down the current, and no efforts of ours could save either the oxen or the cargoes. It was dark when we arrived at the opposite bank, so that we had nothing for it but to bivouack on the wet ground, amidst the groans and ejaculations of the Portuguese drivers, with cold and hunger for our companions.

I have often wondered that the whole party did not receive an unexpected and unwelcome supply of light and heat that night, for under every car of powder was to be seen the Portuguese driver seated with his cigar, whence the sparks fell in all directions around us. No inducement or threat could prevail with them to forego, even for one night, a luxury that might have produced fatal consequences to all.

By daybreak we resumed our dreary march, stiff with cold, and our drenched garments clinging to our benumbed limbs. The rain was still heavily pouring down, and the difficulties of the road increased at every step, often descending several feet perpendicularly, or blocked up by huge masses of broken rock, and frequently overhanging deep precipices, where one false step would have been destruction. Notwithstanding these almost insurmountable difficulties, we still crawled on full of hope that before the close of day we should be revelling in the comforts which we had been led to believe awaited us at Arueda.

How were we doomed to be disappointed! after a long and harassing march, we found that this land of promise, which we had approached by a winding descent of more than a league in length, had no pretension even to a name beyond what the ruins of an old building, and a few empty sheds might claim for it.

The despair of the Portuguese drivers is not to be described on finding they were still to be exposed to the inclemency of the weather. Leaning on their oxen, they contemplated in mute dismay, on one side the gigantic hill—the descent of which had given them an earnest of the difficulties to be encountered in ascending it on their return—and on the other, the roaring torrent of the Douro, which in its impetuous course seemed to threaten with destruction the temerity that would brave its power. The *"Santa Marias"* of some were answered by the more emphatic " *Carajos"* of the others, but even these died away before the necessities of the moment; and unyoking the oxen to afford them the shelter of the trees, the drivers spread their large cloaks in the empty sheds, and soon in sleep forgot their disappointment.

My party had not the same cause for anxiety and complaint as these poor men, who were taken from their homes for our service, and who risked in the loss of their oxen the only means of support for themselves and families.

The following morning, however, presented a curious scene. There stood the wains, securely packed, looking as though the earth had brought them forth, for no vestige remained of the means whereby they had been conveyed to that lonely spot. We could only conjecture that the rumours which every where assailed us, of the proximity of the French, had determined the Portuguese on sacrificing the wains carrying the ammunition to ensure the preservation of themselves and oxen. What was now to be done? My first care was to place the ammunition under shelter, and having ascertained that there was not a single boat to be had at Arueda, I thought it advisable to go over to the little town of San João de Pesquiera, to see if the *Juis de Fora* could afford me any assistance in removing it to Oporto.

On my arrival there, after a walk of three leagues—my Portuguese servant having decamped with my horse, as well as my slender stock of baggage—I found that the 79th regiment, and some other detachments under the command of Brigadier General Cameron had just entered the town on their way to Lisbon. They were in a wet, dirty, and most disorderly condition. I called immediately on the General, and made known to him the perplexing position in which I was placed. He demanded "in the name of the devil" what had brought the ammunition to that part of the world; and what I expected he could do with it? The enemy, he said, was at hand, and therefore if I could not immediately procure boats for its conveyance to Oporto, the only thing to be done was to destroy the whole of it.

General Cameron and most of his officers occupied a spacious quinta, belonging to Don Juan Paez, a relation of the King, and Captain-General of the Brazils. To this nobleman I was subsequently indebted for much kindness; and in the present instance, he invited me to join the party that had already assembled at his dinner-table. Near to the head of the table sat General Cameron, whose large and brawny outline of face and figure, contrasted strongly with the sallow, diminutive, yet gentlemanly appearance of his host; who, in total ignorance of our language, sat in mute contemplation of manners so different from his own. The sumptuousness of the repast gave a striking example of the vicissitudes of campaigning life. No luxury was wanting. In various forms the perfumed garlic and rancid oil assailed the senses, and wonder mingled with delight at the unexpected appearance of bottled Scotch ale, in addition to the potent and delicious wines of Lamego and Colares. Fully did the guests do honour to the feast, appearing to anticipate the wants of the future, as well as to supply those of the present; and many a coarse joke, and boisterous laugh bore witness to the strength of the "barley bree." To this may, perhaps, be attributed a jocose assertion made to our quiet host through the medium of a spruce little officer, who possessed a sufficient smattering of Portuguese to act as interpreter.

"Tell the wee Portuguese," said the General, "that half the men in my regiment are my ain bairns, and all called *Camerons.*"

Don Juan quietly measured with his eye the huge proportions of his guest, probably from the circumstance of the word *Cameron,* pronounced as it was by the interpreter, meaning in the Portuguese language *shrimp,* which epithet he justly wondered to find applied to the offspring of so monstrous a man.

The following morning was one of great disorder and confusion. By daybreak the sound of the drum called the men from their quarters, and from the appearance of the half-drenched, miserable looking troops that were seen issuing irregularly from the town, the inhabitants would have had some difficulty in prognosticating the valorous achievements that so shortly afterwards were to signalize their arms. I well remember a circumstance that took place here. One of the stragglers of the party, by birth a German, deliberately shot himself with his musket, considering death preferable to the hardships he was enduring. The last few stragglers had disappeared, and I was left alone to follow the orders I had received from the General, to destroy the ammunition in my charge, as no conveyance to Oporto could be obtained for it.

On my way back to Arueda, I considered the possibility of being able to preserve to the army this valuable convoy of ammunition, which had been disposed of in so summary a manner by General Cameron. The spot we occupied at Arueda was off the enemy's line of march, and this circumstance seemed to sanction the inclination I felt to take upon myself the responsibility of saving it; more especially as the power of destroying it at the last extremity would still remain. I decided, therefore, upon waiting at Arueda with my little party of artillery gunners, until the fall of the Douro should afford me a chance of conveyance, by boats, to Oporto.

Chapter 6

The Pursuit of Boats

During the three weeks that my stay lasted at Arueda, many were the adventures that I encountered in my several excursions in pursuit of boats. The peasantry having become aware of the vast quantity of ammunition in their vicinity, were clamorous to be supplied; and, from the resistance that had been offered to them on such occasions by the gunners, a vindictive feeling manifested towards us, that displayed itself on various occasions.

As I was once returning from an expedition that had detained me until the last shades of evening were giving way to the darkness of night, my road led me through a deep ravine, where, just as I had proceeded about midway, a shrill whistle was given, and quickly followed by a second. At the same moment, I saw, by the indistinct light, a group of armed peasants start from their concealment, and advance rapidly towards me. I ran with all speed to escape the result of an encounter with such unequal odds, when, in crossing a vineyard, leading from the ravine I had quitted, my feet became entangled in the long tendrils of the vines, and I fell to the ground.

My pursuers, whose heels were less light than my own, here discharged a carbine to retard my further progress, and in another second I heard the whiz of a bullet in the opposite direction. Never did I feel greater satisfaction than in finding it proceeded from the well-aimed piece of our gallant old Sergeant Cowie, whose regard for me partook of the nature of that of a nurse for her charge: it was often displayed with the same officious watchfulness, which, however, I had no inclination to find fault with on the present occasion. Becoming uneasy at my prolonged absence, and the lateness of the hour, he had sallied forth in search of me, and happened to come up just at the right moment. The peasants, concluding that he was supported by others of his party, took to flight, carrying off with them a wounded comrade, who bore testimony to the good marksmanship of my old guardian.

There was a corporal in my party of the name of Daglish, by birth an Irishman, and a sad wicked dog, though a great favourite with every one. He had a turn for gallantry—guitaring—singing, and all the lighter accomplishments;—in short, he had studied what the French call *l'art de plaire,* and withal had a stout heart, and a stout arm in the hour of need. This man was constantly getting into some scrape, in the pursuance, not of his duties, but of his pleasures; and so many were the shots fired at him by suspicious husbands, and jealous lovers, that it was reported by his comrades, that a charmed bullet alone could put an end to his career.

On the day following the little incident above related, I met a Portuguese on his road to inform me that some boats were to be had in a village, a considerable distance off, on the opposite bank of the river, and he offered to accompany me as guide to the spot. The feelings of the peasantry were not sufficiently friendly to allow of my trusting implicitly to their good faith, and as Daglish was, of all others, the best adapted to meet any unexpected difficulty, I selected him to go with me. We crossed the Douro in a little boat; a passage that was attended with some danger, on account of the rapidity of the current, nor did we omit to moor our bark carefully to a tree on reaching the opposite side.

After a long walk through a very romantic, wild country, and passing several villages which, though having a picturesque appearance from afar, were miserably poor and dirty, as a nearer view destroyed the illusion that distance had created, we arrived at the habitation of our guide. An elderly woman came out to greet her husband and ourselves, with much kindness of manner, and her daughter, a sweet pretty girl of fifteen, placed a *caldo de gallinha,* olives, and some excellent wine of *Peso de Regoa* before me, while Daglish seemed equally well provided for, if one could judge from his peals of laughter, as he sat surrounded by the peasants, who had assembled to take a look at him.

Having ascertained that the boats I came to inspect, might, at a short notice, be rendered serviceable, I gave myself up for the rest of the evening to the enjoyment of the little fête, which the villagers were preparing for us—or rather, I should say, for Daglish, for he had already, à *force de coup d'œils,* ingratiated himself with the fairer portion of the inhabitants. When the last rays of the setting sun had disappeared behind the mountains, the evening's merriment commenced. A young Portuguese struck with a masterly hand the chords of the guitar, and to his well-marked bolero and fandango, the graceful couples of both sexes bent their forms in the passionate and graceful attitudes of these truly national dances. The slow and soft measure of the waltz succeeded in its turn; and I encircled in my arms the sylph-like form of Isabella, my host's pretty daughter.

The sounds ceased; wine went freely round, and no small degree of astonishment was excited by the copious libations indulged in by Daglish. At length, more brisk and joyous than was even his wont, he started on his legs, and to his own whistling performed the sailor's hornpipe, with exertions and contortions that made the room resound with shrieks of laughter. Some degree of order was at last restored, and, as at a London rout, the company gradually dropped off. Our friend, Daglish, also disappeared, and I was left alone with Isabella and her mother.

It would have been most unnatural to have so soon forgotten the pretty head that had found a resting-place on my shoulder, during the mazes of the waltz;—and in truth, the recollection of it had taken from my eyes all desire to close them in sleep that night, I longed to rob from it a few hours to add to the day, and seeing a guitar, I placed it in the hands of the fair Isabella, in the hope of detaining her a few minutes longer in my sight. With an arch smile she warbled in her native tongue some stanzas that I have rendered imperfect justice to in the following translation.

> *The night-flowers are opening*
> *Their charms to the breeze;*
> *The moonbeams are dancing,*
> *Midst foliage of trees.*
> *Tis the hour for the lover,*
> *To steal the fond sigh,*
> *When Cynthia's soft cover*
> *Whispers, "No danger nigh."*

The fire-flies are sporting,
In amorous play
And young hearts are beating
To passion's wild lay.
Cupid hovers around,
Reveal'd in a sigh,
Or conceal'd in the sound
Of "No danger nigh"

Hark! a storm has replaced
The calm aspect of Heaven,
As if wrath now menaced,
Where love only had striven.
In vain shall soft echo
Repeat the last sigh.
Or implore love to go
With, "Now danger is nigh!"

As Isabella finished the last words she laid down the instrument, and kissing her hand to me with a most provoking expression, not altogether free from coquetry, tripped lightly from the room. The old mother then rose, and conducted me to my sleeping chamber, where a mat was spread for my repose. I threw myself on it without undressing, as our departure was fixed for a very early hour on the following morning.

Scarcely had the scene of the past evening began to blend with the shadowy dreaminess that precedes sleep, when I was disturbed by a tremendous uproar. I started up—nearer and nearer it approached. A thundering "God d—the villains!" from the well-known voice of Daglish, left me in no doubt as to the identity of the principal actor in the affray. I flew to my sword, and throwing up the window—it was not very high from the ground—out I jumped, to the no small joy of Daglish, who was fighting and swearing in the midst of a throng of peasants, armed with every thing they could lay hold of in the hurry of the moment.

As soon as I appeared, they attacked me also and a desperate fight took place between us. We wounded several of them in our own defence; and the rest were beginning to give way, when a reinforcing party came up with fire-arms, and sent a shot through the arm of poor Daglish—that stopped his hurrahs! Another bullet sharply grazing my side, we began to think that *sauve qui peut* would be our best defence against such odds.

Off we started as fast as our heels could take us to the spot where our boat lay, and succeeded in un-mooring it, and shoving off, just in time to escape from our assailants. But our danger was not to end here. The river was rolling with frightful rapidity, and our boat dashed down the current at a rate that makes me giddy to think of. Suddenly we came to an eddy, or whirlpool, and our boat, spinning round and round, shot head foremost with tremendous velocity into the depths below. As good luck would have it, the long branches of the trees that skirt the banks of the Douro extended to a considerable distance, and we had also the good luck to catch hold of them in rising to the surface after our cold plunge.

"Pray, Daglish," said I, when we had got safe back to our quarters, "what the devil was the cause of all this uproar?"

"Och, please your honour," responded Daglish, endeavouring to assume a modest look, "Does your honour ax the rason?—Why, 'twas nothing at all, at all, but a woman fell in love with me, and you see her husband didn't like it."

To so natural an objection I had no remark to offer, but I did not refrain from reading a lecture to Master Daglish on the necessity of controlling his affections.

For several succeeding days, I apprehended that some disagreeable circumstances would result from the affray caused by the corporal's adventure: but we heard no more of our village friends, and by degrees the recollection of them, even of the pretty Isabella, began to fade away. The men, however, had remarked that the natives were seldom to be seen in the neighbourhood, and we instinctively felt that their feelings were none the kinder for what had happened. So things remained for some time. The river gave no signs of decrease, and the weary days were passed chiefly in scouring the surrounding country in search of boats, or sometimes in a visit to the hospitable mansion of Don Juan Paez at San João de Pesquiera.

I had ridden over to dine with him one day, having obtained the use of a mule during my stay, when he mentioned that some of my countrymen were billeted at the house of one of his friends, and proposed that I should call upon them. At the period of which I speak, there were many stragglers belonging to the different detachments who had remained in the rear from various causes, and were pushing on as best they could to join their comrades. It has universally been the case, that national honour and humanity have been deeply tarnished by the class of stragglers that are almost always to be found at the tag-end of an army. Relieved from the responsibility and discipline attached to each individual in an organized force, their route is marked, with few exceptions, by violence and rapine. The arms they bear for the service of their country are turned against the peaceful inhabitants of the districts they pass through, and bloodshed but too often follows the commission of plunder.

The scene at which I was a spectator, on the evening in question, presented on the one side a degrading picture of the effects of liquor on minds already ripe for evil; and on the other, a fine trait in the character of a Portuguese youth, which I have pleasure in recording. As I entered the house where "my countrymen" were assembled, a most uproarious noise led me to the scene of action, which I found to be the kitchen. A medical officer of the party was vainly endeavouring to separate two combatants, who, with drawn swords, stood beside a heap of broken chairs and tables. One of them, a debauched looking, drunken young man, with an inflamed and coarse countenance, offered a strong contrast to the smooth olive complexion of his still younger Portuguese antagonist. I believe my entrance did more to put an end to the broil than the eloquence of Doctor Forbes, the gentleman above alluded to, who, being himself perfectly sober, and the only one who was so, related to me with all the indignation of a right-thinking mind, the origin of the dispute.

For two days and nights successively, these unworthy representatives of England's sons had been in a riotous state of intoxication, and upon this occasion had repaired to the kitchen to add to their already beastly state by mulling a few more bottles of the strong wine of the country. The fire was out, and with no other thought than the gratification of their own gluttonous desires, these reckless fellows deliberately hacked up, with their swords, whatever articles of furniture lay within their reach as fuel to the fire they had succeeded in re-kindling. In the middle of this scene of destruction, the young man of the house walked in, and gazing with uncontrollable anger upon the group marked out the most active among the rioters.

"We have given you," he said, "our best fare, and even complied with all your unreasonable demands; but rather than see your sword insult my father's hospitality, I would feel it plunged to the hilt in my own heart. Defend yourself!"

The young Portuguese had suited the action to the word, and as I entered, his sword was upraised in defence of the honour of the hearth that had given so kind a reception to men so wholly unable to appreciate it.

The moon was just rising behind the distant mountains when I mounted my mule to return to Arueda. After riding for many miles without hearing or meeting with any object to attract my attention, I tuned into a little wood that offered a shorter cut to the road beyond, but suddenly checked my animal at the sound of feet tramping with something very like well drilled precision on the road I had just quitted. As I paused, considering whether to retrace my steps or to proceed, a lively strike up of "*The British Grenadiers*," from a voice that I would have sworn to among a thousand, as the offspring of my friend Daglish's lungs, settled the debate in double quick time, and retracing the short distance, I found myself, on emerging from the wood, directly in front of four stout gunners, headed by the dashing corporal, who, with arm in sling, looked ripe and ready for adventure.

There was a tragic-comic mysteriousness in his face, that caused me immediately to say: "What Daglish! what the devil is the matter?"

"Lord bless your honour, why that's the very thing I don't know; but, between ourselves," and here Daglish gave a most knowing wink, "I think it's the women that's done it."

"The women done what?" I exclaimed, trying to suppress a laugh at the comical glance he gave me. "Daglish, you think of nothing but the women, I'm sorry to say."

Here Daglish assumed an air of offended dignity, and in his meekest voice replied:

"Your honour don't seem to understand the thing at all—at all. It's the women that can think of nothing but me, please your honour."

My risible faculties could no longer withstand this convincing proof of his humility, and after a hearty laugh, in which the gunners vainly endeavoured to refrain from joining, I desired Daglish to explain to me the cause of his appearance so unexpectedly on the high road. It appeared that very soon after I had quitted Arueda on that day, the suspicions of the sentinels on duty were excited In several individuals, at different periods, approaching the Magazine with an audacity they had never previously displayed. The circumstance was doubly remarkable from the fact before stated, of the manner in which the peasants had latterly avoided us; and the sergeant in consequence had thought it his duty to double the sentinels, and to send out whatever men he could spare reconnoitre the immediate neighbourhood. A few parties were observed in the distance, but evidently not desirous of coming in collision with our scouts. As evening drew on, they entirely disappeared, and the little force was concentrated by the sergeant within the precincts of their own quarters.

The sun had long declined, and the waning light was just merging into the duskiness that precedes the rising of the moon, when a figure was seen gliding along the wall leading to the shed where the ammunition was stored. The sentinels challenged once—no reply; twice—the same dead silence. Before the third challenge could be given, the stout arm of Daglish had grasped the intruder, and dragged him with no gentle force to the light of the broad lanthorn that hung suspended from a high post at a safe distance from the ammunition. As the light fell on the countenance of a Portuguese youth, the manly-hearted Daglish relaxed the iron grip he had taken of the boy's slender arm, although whatever suspicions the events of the day had created, were now strengthened into certainty, that some work of vengeance was contemplated and connected with the stealthy intrusion of the youngster into the very centre of our quarters.

Our sojourn in Portugal had been sufficiently long to enable the soldiers to make themselves understood by the natives, and Daglish fully succeeded in representing to his trembling prisoner, that he should swing in the place of the lanthorn over their heads, if treachery had brought him there. The boy, with the rapidity of language peculiar to the southerners, asserted that he was the brother of Isabella; that a plan was to be put into execution on the following night to fire the Magazine, and destroy the whole of the English party;

that Isabella had heard the object of the repeated conferences at her father's house; and, binding him to secrecy, had made him swear to apprise the "*Ingleses*" of their danger in time to avert it.

In relating to me the above account, Daglish added that he was well-disposed to believe the truth of the boy's story; but with the prudence of an old soldier, he had taken the precaution of locking him up until my arrival, and of bringing off an escort to protect me on my way back to Arueda.

It was getting late as we descended the ravine leading to the sequestered and lonely spot that held our little party. My curiosity and interest were equally awakened, and having ascertained that no new event had occurred to excite apprehension, I repaired to the miserable out-house that contained the young brother of Isabella. It was with a beating heart that I unlocked the door of his prison, for how was it possible to feel otherwise than deeply touched at the idea of Isabella having, with all the tender humanity of woman, sent a messenger to warn us of impending danger.

As I entered, a shriek of joy burst from the slender figure that stood pressed against the mud-wall, and as it threw off the large cloak and bounded towards me, it required but that short space to tell me that the sweet face I beheld, bathed in tears and suffused with blushes, was no other than that of the fair Isabella herself.

With clasped hands that required no interpreter to express their meaning, she besought me not to lose one moment in releasing her. She had risked, she said, her life that night to save us. And oh! there was something dearer to her than the life that she had risked. Another hour, and that was forfeited, for she had asked and obtained permission to visit some aged relatives, and the time had already passed that should have seen her under their roof. She looked so innocent and beautiful, that I trembled at the very thought of her fair fame suffering for our sakes, and with an eagerness far exceeding her own, I drew around her the broad-cloak she had thrown off—which had so successfully concealed from Daglish her female attire—and passed her arm through mine, to lead her from the spot. At that very moment the tall figure of the corporal appeared at the door. With some dexterity I contrived to blow out the candle I held in my hand, and calling out with a voice far less firm than I could have wished: "The boy is our friend, Daglish, and I will see him safe home." I walked off with my fair companion at a rapid pace, until we arrived at a cross road, leading to the village where her relatives resided. During our walk, Isabella described, with touching simplicity, the exasperated feelings of her countrymen resulting from the village scene in which Daglish had acted so prominent a part; she unfolded the whole of the fiendish scheme that vengeance alone could have hatched, and which was to have been perpetrated on the ensuing night. The peasants, she said, were to surprise the sentinels on duty, and before the alarm could be given, the explosion of the magazine was to have silenced us all for ever.

Compassion, she added, but here methought I felt a gentle pressure of the arm she leant upon, had prompted her to save us, and a visit to the village on the opposite bank of the river, had furnished her with a pretext to do so. Her brother's cloak to shield her from the cold, when crossing the water, was but a natural precaution, and thus equipped, the duskiness of the evening had concealed the rest.

After pouring forth my ardent acknowledgements of gratitude lo the noble-minded girl, I ventured to ask if there would be no anxiety felt in consequence of her late arrival?

"Fear not," she said with an arch laugh, "I have given you so good a specimen to-night of woman's subtlety, that you have little cause to suspect me of being unable to extricate myself from so slight a difficulty as the one before me. But here," she said, and her voice trembled, "we must part; you must not go a step further, for it would be fatal to us both." As she pronounced the last words, in a tone of subdued tenderness, she took from her neck a little medallion of the 'Blessed Virgin,' suspended by a narrow black velvet ribbon, and bidding me wear it on my heart *en recuerde de Isabella,* she turned quickly from me and disappeared.

There are perhaps many who can understand the feelings that tendered it impossible for me to retrace the road that I had just taken in company with Isabella. The night was as light as day, and I wandered on, regardless of time or distance, until fatigue, and the moon's retiring light, brought back my mind to the dull realities of life.

A little chapel stood on the road side. In Catholic countries they are numerous, and left open for the religious indulgence of pious travellers. I entered, and finding that it was dedicated to the 'Virgin,' some superstitious feeling, connected no doubt, with the medallion on my heart, prompted me to lay down to sleep on the hallowed ground, without any fear of those advances that caused St. Kevin so much uneasiness.

By dawn of the following day, I found my way back to Arueda, and calling the men together, we not only adopted precautionary measures against any attack that might be made upon us by the peasants; but caused our knowledge of the plot to be circulated throughout the neighbourhood.

In the security of my heart, I deemed it next to impossible that Daglish could have guessed at the sex of his prisoner of the preceding evening; but he was such a thoroughly shrewd fellow, that to sound the depths of his acuteness, I said to him on the next day:

"Well, Daglish, now that we are saved—thanks to the Portuguese boy—from being blown up; I hope you will learn a useful lesson from it, never to meddle with the women again."

"Och, plase your honour," retorted the sharp-sighted and ready-witted Irishman, "I never will get into another scrape with the women, unless they promise to turn 'boys' to help me out of it."

Chapter 7

Disaster at Oporto

The time had at length arrived when the fall of the Douro seemed to have rendered its navigation practicable, and I therefore directed the loading of the ammunition on board of three large boats, peculiar to the country, and usually employed for the transport of wine to Oporto. Their owners belonged to the class of peasantry that had already caused us so much annoyance, and not only were they still personally inimical to us; but the intense desire they manifested to possess the ammunition, obliged us to be ever on the watch to guard against surprise.

Each boat was manned by a crew of fifteen Portuguese, and having divided my own men into three parties of equal force, we darted down the river with a velocity that soon banished Arueda, and its surrounding scenery, like magic from our sight. As thus we rushed on through the boisterous waters of the Douro, it was impossible for the mind not to recur to the frightful loss of life that had taken place but a short week before on that same river. I had seen the ill-fated party as they embarked, and a more disgusting sight than they presented, I never remember to have beheld. Above eighty men, women, and children, who had been left in the rear of the army from sickness and other causes were making their way to Oporto. The countenances of the men indicated that they belonged to the worst class of stragglers that disgrace an army; debauchery and drunkenness were to be read in the sunken or inflamed eyes of some, whose wasted limbs spoke of premature decay, while the women seemed to have lost every attribute of their sex but the name.

With every variety of clothing, and want of clothing, these

beings showed, at least, a congeniality of taste in one respect. The well filled canteen of *acquadente* was an ever constant companion, strapped across the shoulder to ensure its safety, and showing good cause for the livid lips to which it was unceasingly applied. The curses and grumbling of the men were blended with the noisy, and still more awful imprecations of the women, as they bundled themselves and wailing infants into the boat that a few minutes afterwards was destined to hurry them, thus unprepared, into eternity. Upon hearing the melancholy event, I remembered with much pity a very fine young man, a surgeon, who unfortunately shared their fate; the tattered state of his dress, and pallid countenance showed how much he had suffered from want of necessaries, and the fatigue attendant on long and harassing marches—but to return to ourselves.

The rapidity with which we shot down the river prevented us from perceiving, still more from frustrating, the evil intentions of the crew. A bend of the river concealed a creek, well known to themselves, as adapted to their purpose, and with astonishing velocity our boat darted towards it, and we found ourselves fast aground.

The master and several of the crew leapt on shore, and we saw a reinforcing party advancing, the object evidently being to seize the ammunition. There was not a moment to be lost. After a desperate scuffle, each soldier—I had six on board—seized his man, and we managed to push off far enough from the banks, to prevent any addition to the number of our adversaries. A moment's reflection told me that the services of a part, at least, of the crew were, absolutely necessary to our safety, for it required a certain number of experienced hands to guide the long fan-tail, or rudder, that alone prevented the vessel from being thrown by the rapids on the shoals and rocks, that render the Douro so difficult of navigation. I thought it, therefore, wiser to enter into a parley with the master, and selecting an envoy from among the prisoners, I made him swim to shore with my conditions; they were peremptory and decisive. I pledged myself, if he did not return to his duty, to land my men and blow up his vessel.

The rough manner in which part of his crew had been handled, gave him no reason to doubt the performance of my threat, and as the loss of the vessel would have been to him a more serious evil than the possession of the ammunition would have been a benefit, even had it been wrested from us, he consented to complete his engagement, and we again shot down the turbulent river to Oporto.

My arrival at Oporto took place only a few days before its capture by the French army under Soult; and it is impossible to give a just idea of the state in which we found the city. Anarchy, disorder, and confusion, were its inmates; the streets were crowded with a rabble Portuguese soldiery, wasting alike their courage and powder in noisy bravado, and random shots, that frequently took fatal effect among the defenceless populace. In such a heterogeneous mixture, no one was in safety, and the shameful excesses that were then committed, formed a fitting prelude to the atrocities and horrors, that in a few days afterwards, were to overwhelm the devoted city of Oporto. Every soldier imagined himself an officer, and every officer a General, and with the exception of the Bishop—who still retained a tinge of that influence which the Catholic Church holds over even the most unruly of her children—all authority was disregarded, save, when it suited the opinions or feelings of the party.

At the earnest request of this dignitary of the Church, who had been nominated Regent of the kingdom, I issued two hundred thousand rounds of small-arm ammunition to the Portuguese troops, a great proportion of the latter being armed with British muskets; and the remainder of my troublesome charge, which had caused me so much anxiety, and so many perplexing and harassing hours, was at length embarked for Lisbon, just in time to save it from the French, who had commenced their attack upon the lines, before the transport that conveyed this valuable and important supply to the British army was yet out of sight.

The same wild and inconsistent enthusiasm that had caused the Portuguese troops to assassinate their Commander-in-Chief, General Freire, on the bare suspicion of his treachery, led to their nominating Baron von Eben, a German officer in the British service, as his successor. From every side, the peasants flocked in with their fowling pieces to join the troops under his command for the defence of Oporto. And in order to give time for strengthening the fortifications, Baron von Eben led forth his followers from the city with a view of occupying the enemy.

The impossibility of obtaining any advantage by such a movement over the French army, commanded by Soult in person, was so apparent, that the attempt can only be attributed to Baron von Eben's eagerness to justify the choice of the Portuguese; whereas, had he concentrated his men within the lines of the city, there might have been some slight chance of presenting an effective opposition to the enemy.

As it was, the Portuguese had no sooner taken up their position On a rising piece of ground, commanding the high road to Braga, than the French appeared in sight, and vigorously charging the main body, threw them into such complete consternation, that they either threw down their arms, or took to flight. Some few, indeed, rallied by their officers, stood their ground long enough to suffer from the cowardice of their comrades; but the contest was too unequal, and *sauve qui peut* concluded this unsuccessful and ill-imagined movement. It was with difficulty that Baron von Eben, and a few of his routed followers found shelter, within the lines that he had so injudiciously left, and the excited fury that sprung from that rencontre with the enemy, laid the foundation for the murderous scene that was so soon to be enacted at Oporto.

Some French stragglers had been laid hold of by the Portuguese, and byway of slaking their vengeance at a defeat, partly attributable to their own pusillanimity, these unfortunate men were dragged to the principal street, the Rua Novo, and there barbarously put to death—being crucified with their heads downwards, besides other mutilations of the most horrible description.

When three days afterwards, the French army forced the lines of Oporto, not only did the spectacle of their murdered countrymen present itself on their entrance, but as if to arouse to the utmost, the evil passions of the invading force, those soldiers, who had scarcely awaited the approach of the enemy on the field of battle, now fired from the tops of the houses, as they passed beneath, adding at every shot to the flames of fury that soon burst forth only to be quenched in rivers of human blood.

As the French troops rushed down the Rua Novo, their swords dyed in the blood of its defenceless inhabitants, thousands sought for escape by the bridge of boats, that formed a communication over the Douro with the village and Convent of Villa Novo.

So unexpectedly had the enemy poured into the city, that no hope of escape remained but the uncertain one of finding, on the opposite side of the river, a temporary refuge; and a mass of unprotected beings—men, women, and children, were to be seen flying, on the wings of terror, to the bridge.

What pen can trace the atrocities that were perpetrated in every quarter of the city at this awful moment. As each house became, in its turn, the scene of murder and violation, so did each scene exceed the last in horror; and, as if the hope of prolonging the work of destruction mingled even with the savage desires of the hour, a body of the enemy's cavalry galloped off to intercept the fugitives who were making for the bridge, while a murderous fire from several pieces of artillery opened on them in the same direction.

As the French dragoons pressed towards the bridge that afforded the last hope to the unfortunate inhabitants, there ensued a scene of horror exceeding perhaps any that has sullied the annals of war.

With pitiless ferocity, the blood-thirsty soldiers cut down every one, sparing neither age nor sex. Numbers of defenceless victims were thus destroyed, and as if to increase the intensity of suffering, the two first boats, supporting the bridge, sunk under the pressure of the weight, and masses of human beings were precipitated into the raging torrent beneath. Pursuers and pursued were to be seen clinging to one another with frantic eagerness in the last death-struggle, as the rapid current bore them from the scene of strife to the quietness of death.

Before this last occurrence, I had been fortunate enough to gain the opposite shore, nor should I have had the opportunity of describing—as an eye-witness—the fearful carnage of that day, if a circumstance had not happened that unavoidably detained me.

I had quitted the lines in company with Baron von Eben, his aide-de-camp, and my servant, a gunner in the artillery, but we had scarcely reached the head of the Rua Novo, in which street were Baron von Eben's quarters, than he remembered having left behind him a valuable jewel, the gift of one of our Princesses. It may be remembered that this officer was in a very remarkable manner favoured by the royal family of England. To recover the treasure, the Baron returned to his quarters, attended by his aide-de-camp, who was destined to be sacrificed for the bauble, for, almost immediately afterwards, the leading column of the French army came pouring in, and the poor fellow was cut down, waiting for his General's reappearance. The latter escaped by jumping out of a back window that looked on a narrow lane, and succeeded amidst the general confusion in joining the fugitives on the bridge.

My own progress thereto had been none of the smoothest. Many of the Portuguese had become emissaries and spies in favour of the enemy, and were almost as active in the cause of destruction as the French.

Having waited the reappearance of the Baron as long as prudence warranted, I thought it might be as well to move in the direction of the bridge. The crowd was densely thick, and as my servant pressed closely at my heels, that we might better stem the current that hurried us along, some Portuguese miscreants surrounded us suddenly, and an elevated stiletto over my head soon acquainted me with the hostility of their intentions. I clenched the arm that would have struck the fatal blow, but at the same moment, the cowardly villain, bending suddenly down, seized my finger between his teeth, nor quitted his hold, until he had nearly severed it from my hand. The agony I endured would have maddened me into an act of summary vengeance, but I was forestalled by my active gunner felling the dastard to the earth with the butt-end of his carbine.

At this crisis, the pressure of the crowd increased as the intelligence of the enemy's approach became more certain, and thus we were hurried on, almost irresistibly to the bridge, that once crossed, was fated to be an impassable gulf to the destroyers.

Upon gaining the summit of the eminence, on which stood the Convent of Villa Novo, the whole of the scene, as it lay stretched below, might have been taken for a panorama, but for the fearful sound that fell upon the ear. Even at that distance the shrieks of the suffering women were plainly heard, while the sobs and groans of the house-less wanderers around us, made more terrible this agonizing picture of the evils of war.

The whole country, as we advanced towards Albergaria—a small village on the road to Coimbra—presented one continuous scene of disorder and confusion; all confidence was destroyed between man and man, and friends and foes were alike jumbled together in one heterogeneous mass. A few hours, however, produced the natural effect of dispersing the poor outcasts, who had each some temporary shelter to seek in their forlorn condition; and some who like myself were bound to Lisbon, made Albergaria their resting place for the night.

On my arrival at this little village, in company with a Portuguese General who had joined me on the road, I heard a voice, that I thought familiar to my ear, and looking up to a window from whence the voice proceeded, I saw the well-known face of Sir Victor Arentschild, Colonel of the German artillery.

Those who have been acquainted with that gallant soldier will not require a pen and ink description of him; but to those who knew him not, I will describe him as he then appeared. A fine tall man, of true German exterior, with a fair face, and noble countenance. A very long neck, which was on this occasion, stretched out of the window to the utmost extent, and blue eyes, extremely dilated, as he wildly called for a friend who would be responsible for his character. We found that Sir Victor and his servant had been stopped by the Portuguese on suspicion of their being French spies, and were temporarily locked up to be hanged at a convenient opportunity.

When fairly out of danger of the halter, through the interference of the Portuguese General, who had known him at Oporto, Sir V. Arentschild related to us the circumstance of his detention, concluding with:

"By Gott, my servant is die true philosopher; he say to me, 'Sar, we shall have die cold bed to-night. When a man talk of die cold bed, and say nothing of die step to dat cold bed, which is die halter, then a man is by Gott die true philosopher.'"

Leaving Albergaria after a night's rest, I pursued my way on foot to Coimbra, which was already full to overflowing with the wretched fugitives from Oporto. The *estralagems* affording accommodation of a miserable description, were open only to those who had the means of paying for it, and the denuded victims of war's oppression were forced to seek the shelter of some empty sheds, in which they huddled together in wretched despondency. The night was dark and cold, and must have appeared interminable to the poor creatures, judging by the sighs and lamentations that escaped from them. Towards morning a confused bustle and repeated exclamations of "*quittadina,*" "*star doudo,*" blended with the expressive "*o la!*" so often used by the Portuguese, caused me to rise from my mat, on which I had passed the night; and, following in the wake of curiosity to ascertain the cause, my eyes rested on a fearful spectacle.

Two females, whose respective ages led to the conclusion of their being mother and daughter, were standing in the centre of a numerous group of the fugitives. It was evident that they also belonged to this latter class, and equally so that they had escaped too late, for it was impossible not to feel, at the first glance directed to their hapless appearance, that death to them would have been mercy. The materials of their dress were of that costly texture that denotes the class of the affluent; but every vestige of its original form had been destroyed; it hung in tatters on the naked and exposed shoulders, while stains of blood, thickly coagulated on the remaining scanty garments, bore fearful evidence to the reeking slaughter that had surrounded the unfortunates. The countenance of the elder female wore an expression of resigned, but utter helplessness, that went straight to the heart of every one who knew the insufficiency of innocence and weakness to oppose the perpetration of those base and lawless actions that characterised the French army in the Peninsula. Yet, even this face of settled suffering was a relief to the eye that had dwelt upon the wreck beside her.

Over this unfortunate young being, the mother leaned with earnest anguish, repeating at measured intervals "*Minha filha! o la! minha filha.!* A few moments sufficed to show that the young girl's last moments were rapidly approaching; the frenzy which for the last few hours had mercifully brought oblivion of the past, was, from the effect of weakness, gradually giving place to the feeble consciousness that precedes the last struggle of existence. During her removal to the *estralagem,* the extent, no! not the extent, but a portion of the brutality this poor young creature had experienced became perceptible, and a thrill of horror ran through the assembled throng. The cupidity of monsters in human form had torn from her ears the jewels that ornamented them, carrying away from each a portion of the flesh, and the blood flowed in streams, clotting up the dishevelled hair that still hung in beautiful luxuriance over her violated person.

Two fingers were severed from the left hand; and the swollen appearance of the others evinced that the temptation of jewelled rings had led to the commission of this diabolical mutilation.

The suffering girl was laid upon the matted floor I had quitted, surrounded by a motley group of human beings, who although ruined and house-less, had at least the melancholy satisfaction of comparing their position with that of the hapless creature before them. In a low whisper to the anxious parent who appeared to have lost, in her child's sorrows, all memory of her own, the presence of a "*clerigo*" was demanded. A venerable man approached, and kneeling by the side of the dying girl poured out those words of comfort that lead from the turbulence of this world to the peace beyond it; a bright and sunny smile played, for a moment, on the countenance of this child of misfortune, and pressing the crucifix to her heart, she ejaculated with energetic effort the words, "*que felicidade, alegri—gloria;*" while they lingered on her lips, the soul fled.

The tree lay where it fell. That same night the insensible clay was consigned to consecrated ground by the aged priest who had attended her last moments. And on the following morning the unhappy mother pursued her route alone.

Chapter 8

Fire on the Powder Ship

On my arrival at Lisbon I found my two friends, Lieutenants H—y and F—r, with whom I had sailed from England, and by good fortune we were all billeted in the same quinta on the beautiful banks of the Tagus. Our patron had two very pretty daughters with the languishing dark eye, and soft mantling complexion peculiar to the Portuguese women in their first youth; but how to make two fair ladies suffice to the ardent aspirations of three lovers was a problem more difficult to solve than any I have yet found in Euclid. It was in vain for the poor padre to prohibit his pretty daughters from a sight of us. At night when all was still, and the silvery moon threw her soft shadows on the earth, we would steal beneath the latticed windows of our young beauties, and strive to out-rival each other by the vehemence and passion of our gestures. This could not last; whether our friend H—y discovered that the glances thrown at him were only random shots, or whether he had started fresh game elsewhere, I know not; but he deserted our nocturnal rambles, and left the field clear to the pursuit of F—r and myself.

One night, or rather morning, I was startled from a sound sleep by a violent rapping at the door of my room. "Let me in for God's sake," said a voice that could not easily be mistaken, and in another moment H—y stood before me in a very strange plight indeed—in such a one as I imagine Don Juan might have found himself, after his lucky escape from the search of Donna Julia's Lord and Master.

"Why H—y," I said, "what the devil is the matter—where are your garments?" He looked wonderfully like Joseph flying from

Potiphar, only no one could have suspected the handsome and gallant H—y of shirking danger, whether in the service of the Goddess of Beauty, or the God of War.

As soon as his joyous laugh had subsided, he related his adventure: "he had been dining out, and was returning, as he assured me, soberly home, when a lady, charmingly modest in her appearance, gently brushed against his arm with her silk mantilla as she passed him. H—y followed the mantilla with suitable alacrity, and observed two very fine eyes peeping round merely to see if he had understood the signal given him. The old duenna seemed to grow more sluggish in her movements as her mistress's pace quickened, which H—y perceiving, he slipped a few *crusado novos* into her hand, and so gained the outposts in a twinkling.

"The pretty mantilla suddenly turned into a house, and H—y entered also. His fair acquaintance gave him a very nice supper, took great care of him, and at length suggested that a little repose would be desirable.

"With this repose he was comfortably indulging himself, when he was alarmed by the approach of a most unwelcome intruder in the shape of the lady's husband, and the necessity of his absenting himself became so urgent that without stopping to dress he leaped out of the window into the garden."

These adventures served to while away the time, while we remained impatiently awaiting the signal that was to bring us in collision with an enemy who had treated the sacred name of liberty as a word of derision, and substituted in her place the curse of foreign invasion and despotic tyranny.

The movements of the French army at this juncture of the war were sufficiently formidable to justify the precautions that were taken to insure the safety of our troops in the event of the enemy penetrating into Lisbon.

Sir John Craddock was in command, and by his directions, every necessary preparation was made for the immediate embarkation of the men, if requisite, and the military stores were ordered to be distributed on board the several transports that lay in the Tagus. The shipping of these stores was consigned to my charge, and gunners, as well as sailors from the different vessels, were placed under my command, by Colonel Robe of the artillery.

A large party of these men were employed in transshipping the stores of a vessel heavily laden with powder—it being considered unsafe to allow so large a quantity to remain concentrated in the proximity of the surrounding shipping—I had just retired to the cabin, on business connected with my duty, and was engaged in writing reports and directions for the different transports, when a sailor rushing past me attempted to precipitate himself through the stern window into the water. I seized him by the leg, and hauled him back to account for the action: terror was depicted on the fellow's countenance, as he exclaimed, "Fire! the ship is on fire."

I sprang to the deck, and there found sufficient cause to justify the alarm that had been created. Volumes of smoke were seen issuing from the after hatchway, totally obscuring the opposite side of the vessel. A panic, amounting to frenzy, seized the working party and crew, and every boat within grasp was put in requisition to bear them from the scene of danger. Many had sprung over the gangway and bows to escape the explosion they considered inevitable; and some met with a watery grave in this moment of general alarm. The vessel was thus almost instantaneously deserted by all on board with the exception of two sailors—one of them the same who first gave the alarm, and who, as it afterwards appeared, was the originator of the accident.

These men willingly consented to unite their efforts with mine to extinguish the flames that were now beginning to mingle with the dark masses of smoke that burst forth from the bread-room, or *lazaret,* as it is called in merchant-vessels. Having penetrated to the spot from whence the flames issued, I found that the bulkhead was on fire. This divided the *lazaret* from the magazine, containing three hundred barrels of fine grain powder, and fifteen hundred thousand rounds of ball cartridges.

The smoke was at times so overpowering, that I was forced back to recover from its effects. At other moments, I succeeded in throwing over the devouring element the buckets of water, which the alacrity of my assistants supplied. After some time thus passed in anxious suspense, the fire gradually became less and less vivid, the smoke wreathed into lighter and lighter columns, and finally we had the satisfaction of receiving the reward of our exertions in the total extinction of the fire.

When I could find time to look around me, I saw that the vessel had not only been deserted by those on board of her, but by every vessel within range. The anchored transports, that previously surrounded her, had slipped their cables, and drifted down the river with the tide, and the first token given of returning animation was the appearance of a boat nearly an hour afterwards from the flag-ship, Admiral Berkeley, to inquire into the nature and origin of the accident.[1]

---

1 .Upon inquiring into the origin of the fire, it was found that the steward had gone into the *lazaret,* through the cabin hatch, to procure provisions for the ship's company; and having struck a light had left it sticking between the hoops and staves of a cask, where it set fire to the bread-bags and other stores, extending to the bulk-head of the powder magazine.

CHAPTER 9

The Murder of Prisoners

At this period, I bade farewell to Lisbon, in pursuance of orders from Woolwich, and through the kindness of Admiral Berkeley obtained a passage to England on board the *Africain*—Captain Raggett—a very fine frigate, in charge of a convoy of four transports and some other vessels. The weather was so stormy, that we were driven to take shelter in the bay of Vigo. The town of Vigo had recently been taken from the French by the Spaniards, with whom co-operated three British frigates; the *Lively*, *Active*, and *Endymion*, under the command of Commodore Crauford; and the enemy, still holding a position on the adjacent hills, the marines had been put on shore to garrison the castle that commanded the approaches to the town.

The transports had suffered so severely from the heavy gales, that the *Africain* was detained in harbour until their damage was made good, during which time I took up my quarters on shore, and availed myself of the hospitality of the marines at the castle. The empty and desolate rooms of this edifice had been changed into habitable and almost comfortable quarters. Union jacks and cots from the ships had lent their aid to effect this purpose. The former had been used most dexterously in the erection of partitions between the eating and sleeping departments, and the good-fellowship of the inmates enhanced the value of their good arrangements.

At the taking of Vigo, three French officers, fifty soldiers, and five women had been made prisoners. The former were permitted to go at large on parole, and being all three nice fellows, in their way, had become daily guests at the mess-table of the marines. One of them was a particularly fine young man, and a favourite with everybody. Another was a most amusing Gascon, and his attempts to translate into English his marvellous exploits would keep the whole party in a roar of laughter; the third was very melancholy, and seldom spoke. We afterwards heard that his gallantry in the field had recently obtained for him the grade of *sous-officer,* and that the conscription had torn him from a young bride, which accounted sufficiently for his taciturnity.

One morning it was rumoured that the Spanish authorities had applied to Captain Crauford for the custody of the prisoners, in order to remove them to an opposite point of the bay; and the rumour gaining ground, the Gascon called at the castle to see Lieutenant Griffiths of the marines—who spoke French well—to request him to intercede with Captain Crauford against granting a request that would place the lives of the prisoners at the mercy of the sanguinary Spaniards. Griffiths executed his mission, but received an unfavourable answer from Captain Crauford, who felt he had no power to withhold their custody from the authorities, more especially as he had only co-operated with the Spaniards in taking Vigo; and consequently could not consider the prisoners as his own. This answer damped the spirit of the whole party, and on sitting down that day to dinner, there was not one of us who did not feel the inexplicable, and indefinable *mal-aise* that precedes an evil that we fear, and are powerless to avert.

The Gascon vainly endeavoured to force the joke that died away on his lips. The deep sigh from our unusually silent guest told the tale of his thoughts being far from the table at which he sat a prisoner; and if any cheerfulness was mixed with the subdued feeling of the party, it was infused by the young Frenchman, to whom we were all so partial, and who tried to inspire his companions with a confidence that he did not himself feel. The dinner had scarcely been removed, when a bustle in the outer court of the castle was succeeded by the entrance of an orderly into the room where we were seated; his intrusion was too soon accounted for. A file of Spanish soldiers awaited to receive the prisoners. We rose simultaneously, and closed round the young Frenchmen, whose disturbed looks betrayed their consciousness of the danger that threatened them. The moment was one of deep pain; to keep them against orders was an impossibility, to part with them wrung the kind hearts that had received them as comrades; but the necessity was imperative, and with sad forebodings as to their future fate, we conducted our friendly foes to the trap prepared for them by a less generous enemy.

The savage countenances of the escort were not calculated to reassure us, and instinctively we followed in the rear, to avert, at least the insults that a merciless soldiery might inflict on their way to where these poor fellows were to be embarked. A large felucca lay close to the shore, in which already had been placed the other prisoners—including the five women who had been captured—and with a malicious and indecent haste, the remaining three victims were hurried from the landing place on board.

"*Adieu, mes amis*" fell sadly from the lips of the hitherto joyous Gascon, as he extended his hand towards us. A savage looking Spaniard struck down the raised hand, and we turned away, filled with a thousand fears that the brutal act was only the precursor of greater violence.

That same night, the castanets and guitar were sounding blithely at the Governor's house in Vigo. A gay *tertullia* had brought together, not only the native residents, but every British youngster, who could get leave of absence from his ship or quarters. The same marine officers, who had witnessed the embarkation of the French prisoners were now convulsed with joyous laughter at the ineffectual endeavours of a fair *espanolita* to pronounce the words of our national anthem. A light-hearted middy had once been guilty of the treasonable offence of teaching her 'God *shave* the King,' and no after instruction could chase from her tongue those first precepts. The lofty rooms resounded with mirth and gladness, the little fans were actively working their way into the hearts of our uninitiated tars. Bright eyes beamed upon bright eyes, when a movement, sudden and general, agitated the assembly like the fall of a burning meteor into the bosom of a placid lake. Triumphant glances sped from the stern eyes of the hidalgos, shouts of exultation rang from the gentle sex, and one universal burst of frantic enthusiasm flashed through a circle that but a moment before looked spell-bound by love and song. But why do the young British officers stand aloof, silent and dejected from the rest of the throng, each seeking in his comrade's eye a confirmation of the horrible truth that sickens his mind, and leaves disgust and abhorrence in the place of admiration and happiness?

They stand aloof because the triumphant glances of the hidalgos tell of fifty-three French prisoners having been shot in cold blood on the opposite shore of the bay;—they stand aloof because the shouts of exultation from the gentle sex tell of a fact, that their manly English hearts can scarcely yet believe—that five defenceless French women were on the same evening tied together, and consigned to the raging waves, by Spanish men!

The convoy being in a state to put to sea, we set sail with a fair wind, and after a moderate proportion of pitching and tossing, across the Bay of Biscay, the "*Africain*" dropped her anchor at Spithead. In another hour, I was on my way to Woolwich, where I found an appointment waiting for me in the expedition preparing for the coast of Holland.

Chapter 10
To the Scheldt

It was in July, 1809, that the finest armament ever sent by England from her shores was assembled between the North and South Fore-lands off the coast of Kent. Upwards of one hundred pennants were to be seen lightly streaming in the breeze; and transports—the number of which presented on the ocean the appearance of a distant forest—were bearing from their native land the flower of her youth and chivalry.

This gallant force formed the ill-fated expedition destined for the Scheldt; and had its results been at all commensurate with the gigantic scale of its preparations, England would not have had to deplore the loss of so many of her sons in vain.

It was thus on the morning of the 28th of July, that we left the British shores, the coast being lined with spectators to witness the splendid spectacle, and on the evening of the same day we entered the Scheldt, and anchored off the Island of Walcheren.

The transports containing the division of the army under the command of Sir Eyre Coote, were removed to the Roompot Channel, and on the evening of the 31st, the troops were landed on the island about three miles from Ter Vere, under cover of two mortar brigs, and six gun boats, directed by Lord Amelius Beauclerc. The landing was effected without opposition, our gun boats having silenced the enemy's fire from the little fortress of Der Haak, and the brigade that had been put on shore, under the command of General Fraser, bivouacked that night among the sand-hills.

I had disembarked with Colonel d'Arcy of the Engineers, in order to take charge of the *matériel* that had been sent on shore for the erection of a battery against the fortress of Ter Vere. About midnight, we were roused by a brisk cannonade in our front, and the men were immediately under arms. The cause of the disturbance was, however, soon explained. Colonel Pack, in command of the pickets, observed that the garrison of Ter Vere had thrown patrols outside the town; this circumstance suggested to him the possibility of stealing, under cover of the sand-hills, to the gates, which he naturally concluded would be left open to re-admit the patrols, and by this means to surprise the garrison. Acting upon the idea, the gallant Colonel advanced with his regiment, the 71st, and reached the outer drawbridge in safety; but at this point, the sentinel on duty gave the alarm, the inner drawbridge was rapidly drawn up, and a heavy fire opening on the adventurous party, they were obliged to retreat in double quick time back to the sand-hills. This unsuccessful but bold attempt cost the regiment forty-five men, among whom was the surgeon, who had his head lopped off by a cannon ball.

On the following day, the fortress was bombarded by a flotilla of guns and mortar-boats; and Congreve rockets were thrown in from the dyke. Our boats suffered severely, but that they had the best of it, was shown by the surrender of the fortress on the second day.

In the meantime, Middleburg, the capital of the island, had sent in terms of capitulation, and fifteen thousand of our troops had advanced against Flushing. The enemy, who offered but little resistance, was driven within its walls; the town was invested, and preparations immediately commenced for its siege.

The fall of Ter Vere had allowed the Ordnance transports to enter the Veer Gat for the disembarkation of the heavy artillery and engineer stores required for the erection of the batteries; and Captain Cockburn of the navy—an officer who was ever ready to forward the interests of the service—having offered to clear the transports of all they contained, operations were accordingly commenced. The beach of Ter Vere was of small dimensions, and by the second day, it was literally covered mast high, with guns, carriages, artillery and engineer stores of every description, in one vast heterogeneous mountain; the lighter articles, required in the first instance for batteries, lay at bottom, the heavier at top. In short, it would have puzzled any man to have discovered how human hands could have performed such a feat as was here displayed, bearing, however, satisfactory evidence that Captain

C— had performed, à *la lettre,* the duty he undertook of clearing the transports. Numerous boats were still plying to and fro, adding, at each trip, to the colossal mass.

Having been with Colonel d'Arcy to establish the Engineer Park at West Zooberg, I returned to Ter Vere to make arrangements for bringing up the stores required to erect the batteries, and just at the moment that my wondering eyes fell upon this heap of disorder, the chief officer of the Ordnance, whose duty had been interfered with by the too zealous assistance of the navy, came up to the beach, in bitter wrath.

"Who has done this," thundered out the Artillery Commissary, "without my orders, and interfered with my arrangements?"

Lord A. Beauclerc humbly showed that Captain Cockburn was the guilty party; but the wrath of the representative of the Honourable Board of Ordnance was not to be so appeased.

After venting his spleen to the no small amusement of some naval youngsters in attendance, he gave orders to separate, and convey the stores, according to his arrangements, which difficulty falling upon me, I was ably and good humouredly assisted in it by Lord A. Beauclerc himself.

Some of the larger transports lay off at a distance of about three miles, and in order to prevent an increase of the confusion on shore, I determined to proceed on board them to cause such proportions as would be required for service to be transshipped into small craft, and brought up to the landing place.

The transshipment was to take place by daybreak the following morning, and the necessity for giving immediate directions being imperative, I pushed off in a ship's boat on one of the darkest and most tempestuous nights I ever remember.

We had scarcely cleared the canal of Ter Vere, before I discovered that the men had been making too free with the Schiedam of the country; but it was too late to return, for wind and tide were both against us. On we went, rapidly carried by the force of a strong current, and unconscious of the course we were pursuing, except when an occasional flash of vivid lightning illumined the surrounding darkness, and showed us some large ship lying at anchor that we must almost have touched in our hurried course. At the moment when uncertainty as to our safety began to give place to more serious alarm, all feelings of anxiety, as far as I was individually concerned, were suddenly put an end to by a violent blow on my breast which knocked me clean out of the boat.

Having thus unexpectedly parted company with my boat and crew in the midst of the wide waters, it is necessary to say what became of me.

I found myself upon a see-saw between heaven and earth; or as sailors would call it, betwixt wind and water. At one moment, I mounted high in the air, while the wind howled, and heavy peals of thunder rolled angrily over my head; the next moment saw me plunged into the roaring abyss of waves beneath, struggling in all the dread torments of a drowning man.

In these alternate positions, I remained some time clinging to an unknown monster with all the strength of despair, when a flash of lightning discovered to me, as I was again soaring to the skies, the bows of a large ship, immediately over my head, and the object to whose caprices I was thus subjected. This was no other than the cable of the said ship, which had caught me across the breast, as we unconsciously passed beneath it, and to which I had mechanically clung.

The imminence of the danger gave me fresh energies to avert it. I suffered a few more plunges, clinging more firmly than ever, and taking care at each soaring to climb nearer and nearer to the ship; by which means, the higher I climbed up the cable, the less deep became my immersions in the water; until at length, reaching with my hands the bows, I sprung upon her deck.

A light guided me to the cabin, where I found the captain snugly ensconced in his berth. On seeing a spectral object with dripping hair and garments, he became as terrified as I had been, though from a different cause, and staring in my face, called loudly to the cabin boy. In the meantime I quietly seated myself until two men made their appearance; and when they asked me with wondering aspect where I came from, it was evident they suspected that my answer would not savour of this world; for as no boat had come alongside their ship that night, my visit could only appear supernatural.

I related my adventure, exchanged the salt water that had taken possession of my inside for a glass of grog, and being provided with dry clothes and a berth, I remained until daybreak, when a boat was manned for me to proceed on my duty.

The Engineer Park at West Zooberg was placed under my direction, and I was charged with the details of getting up the Ordnance stores for the prosecution of the siege of Flushing; this laborious duty was increased by the bad state of the roads off the *chaussée*. The twenty-four pounders, being drawn by country horses unaccustomed to such heavy draft, often stuck fast for hours; and on two occasions a heavy gun was overturned into the deep broad ditch skirting the road side.

During these operations, a party of sailors, commanded by Captain Richardson, made themselves conspicuously useful, and contributed not a little to the liveliness of the proceedings. The same day would see them cutting fascines for the batteries; dragging a heavy piece of ordnance out of a deep rut; rigging a gib to fish up a twenty-four pounder out of the ditch; and if the outposts were engaged with those of the enemy, a dozen of these chaps would scamper off to partake of the fun. Upon one occasion, a sortie was made by the garrison, and shortly afterwards two of our sailors brought in a French rifleman dangling between them on a pike. An artillery officer demanded the cause of this inhuman spectacle.

"Please your honour," said Jack, "the fellow didn't fight fair."

"Not fight fair!" repeated the officer; "what, do you mean?"

"Why, I mean your honour, that he didn't fight fair; he popped at us from behind the hills and then hid himself; and then popped at us again, and that wasn't fair play—so we killed him, and spitted him up, as an example to others."

The several departments of the right wing of the army, selected for the reduction of Walcheren, were more than fully organized. I say more, from the circumstance of there having been placed in each department, a number of elderly gentlemen of superior rank in the service, whose military experience extended little beyond that afforded by the minutiae of field days, and sham fights at home.

At certain periods of the day these officers, splendidly attired, with bran-span new epaulettes, and snow-white feathers, attended by aide-de camp and adjutant, in similar *bonne tenue,* would show themselves in the centre of all the laborious work that was going on so well without them—and then new orders would counteract preceding ones, as if for the sole purpose of displaying superior knowledge, and individual importance.

Often have I heard, during my superintendence over the operations of our zealous and hard-working gunners, one of these intelligent fellows call out to some jolly tar who was hard at work like himself:

"I say, Jack, here come the long feathers to undo our day's work."

The engineer department was the only one deficient in officers, considering the extensive operations they were called on to perform; and although the extreme zeal and gallantry displayed by these few made up for the deficiency of numbers, it entailed on the whole of the corps duties almost too arduous for the human frame to bear. As I was going one night from the Engineer Park, to one of the batteries in quest of the commanding officer, Colonel d'Arcy—well known by the appellation of "old blue breeches" from the celestial hue of his nether garment—I met the object of my search preceded by a sapper bearing a dark lanthorn. After twice accosting him, and receiving no answer, I ventured on a closer inspection of his person, and found that he was fast asleep. The fatigue he had undergone had lulled his senses into forgetfulness, while his body still retained the walking action into which he had placed it; and this somnambulism was to the lullaby of whistling shells, and roaring artillery from the enemy's batteries.

At length, after eleven day's incessant toil, fifty-two pieces of heavy Ordnance were in readiness to send forth their coaxers for admittance to the town of Flushing, and at noon, on the 13th of August, our batteries opened their fire, assisted towards the evening by a battery of six guns manned by the sailors.

During that night, numerous flights of rockets were thrown from the sand-hills, under the immediate superintendence of Colonel Congreve, who has stood sponsor to this useful branch of flying artillery; but whether that officer was unacquainted with the properties of these children of his adoption, or whether he had arrived too newly from the perfumed atmosphere of Carlton House to relish too close a proximity to the coarser smell of shot and powder, I know not; but certain it is that the first flight of these aerial sharp shooters fell in the midst of our own pickets, and did much mischief.

The bombardment during the night presented a magnificent spectacle. Our shells, fired from the batteries at an elevation of forty-five degrees, crossed, in beautiful curves of streaming light, those from the mortar brigs, while the long fiery tails of the rockets, as they sped through the dark air like strange meteors, and the darting fire and roar of the twenty-four pounders from the batteries, all contributed to the awful sublimity, though desecration, of that hour assigned by nature for the rest of man.

On the following day, the engines of destruction against Flushing were increased by seven line of battle ships, led by Sir Richard Strachan, bringing their broadsides to bear in gallant style upon the sea defences. Much painful anxiety was felt on shore at perceiving that two of these fine ships—one of them bearing the Admiral's flag—had taken the ground. The well directed fire, however, of the others, covered and averted the mischief that might have been sustained by this untoward accident, and at length the flowing of the tide relieved them from their crippled position.

At four o'clock, p.m. a flag of truce from the garrison produced a cessation of hostilities, but the terms of capitulation proposed being rejected, hostilities recommenced with still greater vigour on our side.

Towards midnight the town of Flushing appeared one scene of conflagration, and the fire from the ramparts, that had blazed away so unceasingly, began gradually to slacken until two o'clock in the morning of the 15th when a second flag of truce announced the surrender of the garrison.

From that moment a change came over the scene, that may be likened to the sudden lull of mighty waters, which in their tumultuous bosom had only just engulphed many a gallant bark; or, to the rapid transition from the thunder-loaded clouds of Heaven, to the smiling serenity of a summer sky; or, in short, to anything that will give a just idea of peace—darkness—stillness—replacing strife of war—conflagration—and the discordant sounds of man's ingenious devices for the destruction of his fellow men.

The surrender of Flushing took place earlier than had been anticipated, for although the town and its inhabitants had greatly suffered, no practicable breach had been made, the defences were still capable of holding out; and General Monet, with a garrison of five thousand men, might and ought to have given the besiegers much greater trouble than he did, even had he felt reluctant to risk the last extremity of an assault.

The surrender was strongly protested against by the officer second in command, and that Buonaparte shared those feelings was proved by a court-martial being ordered to investigate the General's conduct on charges of cowardice and treason.

Unable to undergo the ordeal, from being sent a prisoner to England, he was condemned *par contumace.*

At noon, on the 15th, Lord Chatham, who had roused himself from his slumbers some hours earlier than usual to enjoy the honours and glory due to the Commander-in-chief of a victorious army, appeared with a numerous staff at the batteries of West Zooberg.

Surrounded by the principal officers of the artillery and engineer corps, his Lordship, with much condescension, surveyed, with his telescope the operations that had been performed during his repose in snug quarters at Middleburg, where vulgar sounds of shot and shell had not intruded on his ear; and having expressed to General Macleod, and Colonel d'Arcy his approbation at the manner in which *his* plans had been carried out by their respective corps, Lord Chatham again withdrew with his military cortège.

With the possession of the little island of Walcheren, ended the achievements of an army of forty thousand men, backed by a fleet of ninety-seven ships of war, exclusive of gun-boats, &c. and it would have been well if—as soon as the wisdom of our Commander had discovered all further operations against the enemy to be impracticable—he could have profited by a previous example recorded in the old song; and like the renowned warrior therein immortalized: "With all his men marched out to fight, and then marched back again." But the worse was yet to come.

A fever, peculiar to the island, during the autumnal months, burst forth in August among the troops with unexampled malignancy. The nature of this disease was such as scarcely ever to admit of perfect recovery, either consigning its victims to a premature grave, or throwing over the energies of life a withering blight. At one time, the deaths averaged a hundred daily, and to this terrible state of human suffering was to be added want of hospitals for the sick, and the total deprivation of those comforts such a situation demanded.

Among the many who were thus cut off in the pride and vigour of manhood, I know of none who excited more universal regret than Major B— of the — regiment; and as much perhaps from the circumstances attending his death, as from the affection which his gallant bearing had won from all who knew him. Poor B— was a thorough soldier, and a man of the tenderest and kindest feelings, he united prudence to bravery, gentleness to strict discipline; and in the mess-room, as in the barrack-room, was universally beloved.

Over the youngsters of his regiment, he had acquired an influence almost paternal, and when his look turned with severity upon the young delinquent, it gave certain proof that more than the exuberance of youth had caused the offence. At a time when all vied with each other in the display of valour, B—'s gallantry shone conspicuously.

Upon one occasion, the flank companies of the regiment, headed by himself, having repulsed a sortie made by the French, and being in hot pursuit of them, were suddenly stopped in their career by one of the wide and deep ditches that intersect so frequently the roads in that country, B— in the ardour of his spirit, leaped over it with astonishing agility and power; but his men, less accomplished in gymnastics, were unable to follow their leader, who, unable to leap back again, in consequence of the height of the opposite bank, stood alone on hostile ground. The enemy quickly perceived, and took advantage of his position; and our soldiers fearing to fire lest their Major should be the victim, it ended by poor B— being marched a prisoner into the town of Flushing.

After its surrender, I heard that he was seized with the fever, and I hastened to visit him at his quarters. It should here be mentioned that B— was a married man, and tenderly attached to his wife; yet his affection for her did not for a moment interfere with the duty he owed to his country, nor did she, to whom his feelings were ever sacred, place any obstacle to their separation. Silently breathing a prayer for his safety to the God who slays, or spares, according to his will, on the battle field as within the precincts of the domestic hearth—she prepared to accompany him to the spot of embarkation, and with a breaking heart, but tearless eye, witnessed the splendid departure of our troops from England. She watched, until it was no longer perceptible, the white sail that bore away him who threw a halo of brightness over her existence, then, turning away in silent agony, returned alone to the cheerless apartment, which only the preceding hour was gladdened by his presence. Oh! there is no pang like that which tears the heart at seeing one depart, in whom we have concentrated all hopes of earthly happiness. No ray of sunshine gilds the parting hour, and sad experience daily tells that the gloom is often too faithfully ominous of the evils of absence. When affection is of that deeply rooted cast, that from every part of the universe it turns, with the truth of the load-stone, to the object of its attraction, then it is, when the heart sickens and withers under the torture of a protracted separation, that the depth of love's purity is fathomed. But when lighter feelings profane love's shrine, and assume not only his name, but appearance also, the injured Deity unmasks the counterfeit through the medium of absence.

Upon entering Major B——s apartment I found him very ill, and with great difficulty endeavouring to trace a few lines to prepare his wife for their earthly separation. In vain I bantered him on the gloomy tendency of his mind. "I shall never see her more," was his only reply, and placing in my hands the letter he had concluded, he requested me to forward it to England by the packet that was to sail on the morrow. For many days the poor fellow lay hovering between life and death; at times giving no hope of recovery, and at others, so borne up by the buoyancy of his spirits, that he seemed to defy the power of the dreadful malady that was preying on his vitals.

Upon the evening of the seventh day, a great change had taken place for the worse, and I had determined upon taking my station by his bedside for the night, as he had shown symptoms of delirium. I dismissed the attendants, and the stillness of the hour was alone broken by the hard and laborious breathings of the sick man.

An unusual bustle below caused me to rise from my arm-chair to inquire the cause; but before I could reach the door of the chamber, it quickly opened, and a female figure threw herself on the bed where the poor fellow lay. The suddenness of the movement caused a momentary blaze in the lamp of life, that was soon to be extinguished for ever, and perhaps accelerated the fatal event.

A ray of consciousness lit up for a moment his countenance, and as if the return of reason was also the signal of the soul's departure, his eyes met with the fondest expression his wife's agonized adieu, and closed upon the world's cares for ever.

Would that truth permitted me here to devote one bright

page to the constancy of woman's love, or even I would have been content—considering the rare, meteorological nature of this sublime moral quality—to have been able to record some steadiness of purpose in Mrs. B——, in unison with the loss of such a husband, and with the tender anxiety that prompted her to brave the perils of a voyage to receive his dying breath. Would that I could indulge myself in paying this tribute to woman's constancy; but truth forbids it. After a display of bitter anguish, which I now believe wrung the stout hearts around her, more than it lacerated her own, she proposed returning to England with her little boy, the living image of his father.

Among her fellow-passengers was an Irish Captain of the —— regiment, who wooed and won the fair widow with many wonderful tales of past deeds. I know not whether they were such as Othello related to his lady-love; but the results were the same. Mrs. B—— like a second Desdemona, loved him for 'the past,' which she thought promised fair for 'the future,' and on my return to England, at the close of the year, the first news I heard was that she was about to surrender to the Hibernian Captain her liberty and revered position as the widow of the gallant Major B——.

CHAPTER 11

Pestiferous Walcheren

On the 14th of September, Lord Chatham, with a great part of the troops under his command, sailed for England, it being found necessary to abandon all idea of pushing up the Scheldt for the purpose of destroying the dockyards and arsenals of Antwerp and Terneuse. The troops that remained were deemed essential to retain possession of the Island of Walcheren, for the purpose both of blockading the Scheldt, and enabling our merchants to enter British goods into Holland, and also to deprive the French of the means of equipping a naval force so near to our own shores. It was this part of the army that suffered so severely from the raging pestilence of the fever.

It may easily be supposed that various remedies were adopted in the hope of checking the intensity of this baneful disease. To the soldiers an extra ration of spirits was administered daily, which added to what they were able to procure at a very cheap rate, left them pretty frequently with the fever that drunkenness inflicts. The officers, in their turn, were nothing loath to ply themselves with precautionary measures, that suited so well the hard-living days of that period. Some of them anticipated the Homoeopathic system, by sipping small quantities at a time of the powerful Schiedam, till the total aggregate left them much in the same condition as those who finished a pint bottle before dinner, on principle.

Colonel C— commanding the 85th regiment, engaged a servant from the ranks on the day after landing, and being a humorous, though very drunken dog, he entered into a serious contract with the man, that he was only to get drunk on the days that he, himself, was not so. The soldier agreed to the arrangement, and entered

Colonel C——'s service, where he remained three months. At the end of that time, he one morning entered his master's room, and tendered his resignation.

"Why do you wish to leave me, John," inquired the Colonel, "I am very well satisfied with you?"

"I am sorry I can't say the same, Sir," answered John bluntly, "but when I entered your service, you engaged that I might get drunk whenever you were not so; and hang me, if in three months, I have had my turn once."

There was one of the superior officers of the garrison, Colonel M——, who had an unconquerable aversion to Schiedam, both for himself and others; and so sharp was his look out among the youngsters, and so severe his reprimands, that a petty warfare sprung up between this sedate gentleman, and the young fellows who would occasionally have their larks in the little dull streets of Flushing.

The discovery was soon made, that a fat Dutch *Vrow* had found the place in Colonel M——'s affections, that he had refused to Schiedam; and thereupon it was determined that he should receive demonstrative proof that the object of his nocturnal absences was no longer unknown.

Each succeeding night saw a dead dog or cat tied up to the knocker of the Lady Dulcinea's abode; and as each escape produced greater boldness, less precaution was at last used.

It was the turn of a very young officer to perform the feat, that had gone some nights without discovery. The dangling kitten was placed in a becoming posture to receive the nightly visitor, when Colonel M——, sword in hand, rushed from the corner of an adjoining street. It was an unequal chase, for the Colonel's legs were of so unmeasurable a length, that his stride would have made three of most men's; but fear lends wings, ay, and wits too. The young officer bethought himself in his flight of turning into the little inn, where lived a young creature who had looked sweetly on him, and up the stairs he rushed into her chamber. The girl, with true female instinct, felt there was danger, and pulling a cap of her old granny's well over his face, she slipped over his uniform a *chemise-de-nuit*, thrust him into bed, and laid down by his side. At the same moment, Colonel M—— burst into the room, with sword in one hand, and lanthorn in the other, literally frantic with choler. Under the bed, into the closets he looked, roaring out at each step that he had seen with his own eyes the fellow enter that room.

As if awakened from a deep sleep by the hubbub, the girl jumped out of bed, and attacking the Colonel with all the vigour of a female tongue, at the violation he had dared to offer to the sanctity of her apartment, she succeeded in frightening him so completely, that he was only too glad to back out, apologizing at every step for his intrusion.

As the intentions of the Government seemed undecided, as to the expediency of retaining or abandoning so fatal a possession as Walcheren had proved, no serious measures were adopted to strengthen or improve the defences and fortifications until the middle of September, when the peasantry of the country, aided by one hundred civil engineers, brought out at an immense expense from England, were put in requisition for that purpose.

From that period, the operations of repairing the defences and raising others were carried on so vigorously, that from dawn of day till after night-fall, the working parties were kept at their respective posts; while, at the same time, the assignment to myself—as Commissary of Ordnance—of thirty seven transports, laden with valuable engineer stores, bore evidence that the evacuation of the island was not contemplated by the authorities at home.

Sudden was "the change that came o'er the spirit of their dream."

In the midst of all these warlike preparations that had continued unabated until the middle of November, an express arrived from Government with orders to evacuate Walcheren, but previously to destroy the whole of the works that had been completed at such an enormous sacrifice, both of money and of life.

Of the profligate expenditure of the former, some idea may be formed from the fact of the valuable contents of the thirty-seven transports having been thrown into the canal, to admit of the embarkation of the troops on board them; and the reckless sacrifice of the latter is shown by the fever having carried off nearly one-half of those who died in performing what their survivors were called upon to destroy.

It must be admitted that never were orders more zealously executed than those for destroying the naval basin, the piers of the Hood gates; in short, every defence that could avail as a *point d'appui* to the French. And on the very night of our embarkation, as the flames from the burning arsenal and dockyard threw their lurid reflection on the muddy waters of the Scheldt, there was not an individual who did not hail the *feu de joie* that seemed to celebrate his deliverance from the pestiferous Island of Walcheren.

Thus terminated an expedition, which however grand in its conception, totally failed owing to the stupid ignorance of those entrusted with its execution. And in addition to the loss, without price, of so many of her gallant troops—nearly one half of which, according to the return made to the House of Commons, were either victims to the fever, or suffering from its effects—England had to bear the loss of twenty millions of her public treasure.

It was at the hour of midnight, on the 23d of December, that I left the shores of Walcheren in the last boat that conveyed our troops to the transports in waiting to receive them; this circumstance was owing to my being the only one out of eight officers of the Field Train that constant exposure to the blighting influence of the climate had left to perform the duties of the department.

I had been occupied until a late hour with a party of gunners and artificers in the destruction of the arsenal, and this last duty probably brought me the evil that I had hitherto escaped from.

On the succeeding day, I was seized with the fever in its most malignant form, and was soon reduced from health and strength to the aid of crutches to support my enfeebled limbs. The last remnant of the troops disembarked on English ground on the first day of the new year, and those who had recovered from the effects of the fever, received orders to join the army in Spain under the command of Lord Wellington.

It was some time before my strength rallied sufficiently to enable me to embark for the Peninsula. Change of air, however, worked its usual effects in my favour, and having been specially appointed by the Master-General of the Ordnance, Lord Mulgrave, as Military Commissary in charge of the Field Train department of Royal Artillery, I soon was enabled to join the troops under the command of General Graham, for the defence of Cadiz.

Chapter 12
To Iberia

It was a few days after my arrival at Cadiz, that the little fort of Mattagorda fell to the enemy, but not until its garrison, under their brave commanding officer, Captain Maclain, had made a lengthened and gallant defence. The death of Major Lefevre of the Engineers, which took place here, was remarkable as an example of the waywardness and caprice with which fortune is sometimes pleased to bring about the most important events by the agency of a mere trifle. This officer had instructions from the General, to send orders to the Commandant of the Fort, to withdraw the garrison whenever he considered it no longer tenable; and Lefevre considered it right to deliver these orders in person, on account of the mission being a dangerous one to execute.

There remaining no hope of retaining possession of the fortress, the garrison, in pursuance of instructions, was withdrawn. Major Lefevre and the Commandant being the last to descend the ladder, conducting to the boats in waiting—under cover of the fort—to take off the troops.

A point of etiquette here suddenly arose between these gallant officers as to which should be the last to quit the scene of danger. The commanding officer, drawing back, politely offered the precedence to the Major, who, equally polite, was anxious to concede it to the Commandant of the Fort. As thus they stood, irresolute, a thirty-two pound shot, in violation of all rules of good breeding, struck off the Major's head, and so the question was, decided.

The survivor now considered the field of honour his own. He was deceived; for one of Eve's fair daughters—and of what are they not capable, when incited by that passion which Gall and Spurzheim have named acquisitiveness—that passion in the sex so strong, that whether it is developed in plundering hearts, or plundering purses, makes us alike the sufferers—one of these gentle spirits had followed our survivor's steps, and thus not only robbed him of the glory he had coveted of being the last at the post of danger, but had managed also to extract the watch and seals from the fob of the poor victim to etiquette.[1]

Among the many traits of gallantry that distinguished the defence of Mattagorda, may be remarked the following. During the progress of the siege, Lord Macduff used frequently to visit the fortress to infuse cheerfulness among the besieged, and to carry to them those comforts denied to their position. On one of these occasions, the enemy had just opened a tremendous fire from a new battery, and at the same critical juncture, a cannon ball laid low the flag, which, but a moment previously, waved proudly over the walls of the fort.

Our ships, lying in the bay, watched with intense anxiety the downfall of the colours, that portended, as they surmised, the surrender of the fortress. With equal anxiety, thousands of spectators assembled on the ramparts and towers of Cadiz, straining their eyes to catch the fatal confirmation of their fears. When, amid clouds of smoke, occasioned by a murderous fire from the enemy, the standard of England appeared, hoisted and supported by many gallant fellows. Among them was Lord Macduff, who received a severe wound while proving how dear to the British soldier is the standard under which he mingles glory with his country's name.

With such scenes, inseparable from war, were blended the magic visions that Cadiz then presented, forming so varied and exciting an *ensemble,* as never can be surpassed.

What pen can do justice to Cadiz in the minds of those who saw that Queen of cities at the period alluded to? Who has forgotten the brilliant scene of the Almeida, where all of rank, and beauty, and valour were at once assembled? Where beauty, in her most seducing form appeared, and excited the brave to the performance of those deeds of valour she knew so well how to reward. Where the danger that hovered around seemed only to render the fleeting

---

1. I do not pretend to identify this female with "the heroine of Mattagorda," whose destitute old age has recently excited so much of public notice and sympathy; but, to the truth of the above circumstance, I can bear evidence, inasmuch as ten pounds were paid for the ransom of Lefevre's watch and seals by the Paymaster of the Artillery.

moments of enjoyment more intense, by forging the links that bind the defenceless to the defender.

Are there any, who, having since inhaled the atmosphere of St. James', have ceased to remember the gay Bechecha's assemblies, where the castanets and silver-toned guitar accompanied the light and graceful forms of the Andalusian women in their voluptuous and unrivalled dance? Sometimes the hissing rush of a death winged messenger from the enemy would, for a moment, stop the dance. The cheek of beauty would turn pale, or glow more richly; the low ejaculations of *carramba* would mingle with a prayer to the blessed Virgin for protection, and the lovely dancer would again resume the soft waltz, as if forgetful of the past and present danger.

In scenes like these, we beguiled the moments stolen from more serious pursuits; nor did we forget to exercise ourselves in the more robust and manly recreations that characterise us at home. Many were the dogs that had to mourn their proximity to our officers; a chief amusement being to hunt them in lieu of fox and hare; and the worthless cur was to be seen winding through the redoubts that crowned the heights of the Isla de Leon, and followed at full speed by the lovers of the chase, within the very outposts of the enemy, who wondered not a little at the "view holloa" that rung from the lungs of General Graham himself.

In the meanwhile, the enemy daily afforded us ruder play; and each day brought some hostile demonstration which laid low many a buoyant spirit, that had revelled in the scenes of Cadiz.

One evening that I was sitting after dinner with two Marine Artillery officers, Lieutenants Worth and Buckland, in one of the towers that seemed as if erected for the better contemplation of the beautiful bay, we perceived an occasional shot from the enemy's fort of Catalani, directed upon some of our gun-boats; and almost immediately afterwards, my companions recognized the private signal they had established, when on shore, flying at the mast head of their ship. The next moment saw them in their boat, pushing off to their sea-quarters, and on the following morning I heard with a grief that was shared by all who knew them, that as one of these promising young officers was reconnoitering the position through his telescope, he was cut in two by a cannon ball, which at the same moment took off the head of his gallant companion.

Upwards of twelve months passed away in this protracted warfare, when a combined plan of attack upon the enemy's lines, was formed between the Spaniards and ourselves.

Cadiz was now about to be nearly deserted by those who had contributed so much to her amusement as well as safety; and the few who were to be left had duties to perform—of a different nature certainly, but not less arduous than those of their fellow-soldiers—in the consolation they were expected to administer to the deserted but fascinating *espanolitas,* who had again to seek new objects for future tears.

The preparations being completed for the embarkation of the British and Spanish troops—the former amounting to four thousand men, and the latter to eight thousand—we sailed from Cadiz on the 21st of February; but the arrangements made for the transport of the Spaniards were so defective, that not only were they detained in the bay for thirty-six hours after our departure, but were so closely packed during that long period, in country feluccas, and other small craft, that scarcely a sufficiency of room was allotted for each man to stretch his limbs.

The agent to the Artillery division of transports landed at Tarifa, and on returning to his ship, made signs to the Commodore-Captain Brace—to the effect that the guns and horses might be disembarked with safety; nevertheless, the transports were suffered to proceed onwards, and were anchored that night off Algesiras, where the troops were put on shore.

On the following day, they were marched towards Tarifa, by a mountainous track impassable to Artillery, and consequently it became necessary to transship the whole of that branch of the service and ammunition destined for Tarifa, into feluccas that were better adapted to stem the rapid current that ran from thence into the bay of Algesiras.

This operation fell exclusively under my direction, as Military Commissary to the army and although the navy co-operated most zealously in the laborious transshipment, the sole responsibility rested on myself, of classing the requisite calibres of ammunition for each gun, so that in the event of one of the feluccas being lost, there might be nothing wanting to the efficiency of the remainder.

The unavoidable delay that was thus occasioned, detained our troops at Tarifa until the 28th instant.

Chapter 13

The Spanish in Arms

At this period all Spain was up in arms, and every heart responded to the cry of liberty. The peasantry looked upon exterminating the French from Spanish soil with the same religious zeal that burnt in the hearts of the early Crusaders, and the inscription their banner bore "*vincer o morir pro patria et pro Ferdinando Septima;*" was not a vain bravado, but the expression of a deep laid sense of hatred and vengeance. Nor were the peasantry of Spain alone inspired to free their country from the foreign yoke. Although a formidable party had weakened the strength, and neutralized the patriotism of the class of nobles, there were a chosen few, who joined hand in hand and heart to heart with the people, against the common foe.

In the province of Andalusia, the national war assumed an appearance of regular combination, that did not exist to the same extent elsewhere. Active and enterprising leaders rose up to organize the inhabitants of the mountain and the valley, and direct their efforts to advantage, while the dreaded Guerilla bands added their strength to the main force.

Of these mountain warriors, it may not be uninteresting to give an account of three days close comradeship with them, during the period of General Graham's halt at Tarifa, awaiting the arrival of the feluccas with the artillery from Algesiras.

Don Merino, a Spanish officer, with whom I had been intimate at Cadiz, received orders from General La Pena, to communicate with the Guerilla chiefs of the mountains of Ronda, to ascertain their strength, positions, and means of co-operation against the enemy. I obtained leave to accompany him, and we started on our mountain expedition, immediately after the arrival of the troops at Tarifa. The town of Ronda, although garrisoned by the French, was literally in a state of siege: ten thousand armed *serranos,* or mountain peasants, occupied the surrounding hills, while within the town, treachery and murder lurked in every heart against the *gavachos* as the French in ridicule were called. Each inhabitant of Spain was an individual enemy to the invaders, bringing, as in a private quarrel, the concentrated feelings of hatred and revenge to strengthen the power of his arm.

The French army suffered incredibly from this mountain warfare, which was carried on by a mysterious agency that increased its terrors. The same code of thoughts and actions pervaded, as it were, simultaneously the whole body of the mountaineers. Signals only known to themselves, and which, if seen, would have been passed by unperceived by any—save those to whom they were intelligible—brought them together from distant parts, or gave notice of some special expedition, demanding immediate attention. The sick, the stragglers, the convoys of provisions, the messengers, were all equally the prey of the mountaineers.

The rocky defiles, the narrowest passes, were to them as the web to the subtle spider; there they would watch, but not without a fore-knowledge of the enemy's approach, nor without an almost certainty of glutted vengeance; and from thence carrying off to their strongholds their luckless victims, would put them to death by cruel tortures and slow mutilations, too horrible to record. This system of harassing warfare had been one of the greatest scourges to the French army, and I was very glad of the opportunity to become acquainted, in a friendly way, with men who were seldom known in any other light, but that of roving marauders, or, at best, as cruel and barbarous defenders of a lawless freedom.

It was evening when we left Tarifa for the mountain regions of la Ronda; my companions entertaining me on the way with marvellous stories of the prowess of the great Guerilla chief we were about to meet by appointment at a *cortejo,* or isolated farm house, two leagues from Moron.

An Andalusian sky rose like a purple dome, spangled with silver stars, over our heads. We had left the plains and vallies far behind, and our mules had borne us up the steep and rugged declivities of many a wearisome hill, when Don Merino proposed a halt. It was at a curious spot of nature's own creation. Several mountains of almost equal height rose in majestic grandeur, forming an amphitheatre of proportions as regular, as if the eye of man had scanned the measurement, and his hand directed the execution of it. A placid lake lay at their feet, reflecting the star-lit sky.

Dismounting from his mule, Don Merino advanced towards an aperture in one of the mountains, with an apparent knowledge of the locality, that awoke suspicions in my mind, which after circumstances tended to confirm; and taking from his belt a whistle, that sounded wild and strangely in that solitary spot, and silent hour, he awaited the result at the entrance of the aperture— nor long, for the last echo had scarcely died upon the ear, when every mountain seemed to have brought forth a host of armed men; and we stood encircled on every side by the warriors of the hills, both mounted and on foot.

The genuine Guerillas differed materially in appearance from the Serranos; the latter were not under the command of one chief, as were the Guerillas, but acted each on his own responsibility. At one moment cultivating his land; at the next, flying to the signal that called him to the mountain strife. Ever ready on the hills to wreak his vengeance on the French—ever watchful on the plain over his paternal property. Their dress also was different. The Guerilla in his short jacket of russet brown, and leather leggings of the same dark colour, was wanting in the jaunty smartness that characterized the Serrano. The latter was almost invariably clad in velveteen of olive green, profusely ornamented with silver buttons, and laced with ribbons of many hues. A tight white stocking encased his well-shaped leg, over which *bottinos* of curiously wrought leather, completed its symmetrical appearance; and a small *sombrero*, shaded by its plume, and saucily stuck on one side, gave the last finishing stroke to a Serrano's toilet.

The Guerilla always wore a belt of thick leather, amply furnished with murderous weapons, which were generally the trophies of success—their own arms being discarded, and replaced by the more highly finished ones of the French officers they killed.

Nothing could have presented a more inspiring scene than this bold mountain pass; the haunts of men as wild and free as the pure air they breathed.

Surrounded by these mountaineers, Don Merino seemed transferred to his own element, and briefly explained to them his mission to their chief, Don Murillo Davila.[1]

The spot that had been named for the rendezvous was still two leagues farther, and twenty chosen men were ordered to escort and guide us through the perplexing mazes and cragged defiles of these mountainous regions; but, before we started, I had an opportunity of experiencing the frank hospitality of the mountaineers. One of the Guerillas, under whose command the troop was left, in the absence of the chief, stepped forward with a courteous ease that well became his manly appearance, and invited us to partake of the rude fare preparing for his comrades. We gladly assented, and the Guerillas, separating from the rest, and headed by their leader, filed through the aperture of the mountain, motioning us to follow.

Their number amounted to forty-eight; twenty-two were mounted, and twenty-six on foot. Yet, notwithstanding the smallness of this force, I heard that the individual valour, and formidable success of this picked band, had rendered it a terror and a scourge to the enemy.

Passing through a subterranean passage, about ten feet in length, we emerged, on the other side of the mountain, upon an extensive open space, covered with beautiful verdure—a fitting banqueting hall for the guests who were expected. Over a charcoal fire, a kid, swimming in olive oil, was undergoing the process of cooking, under the auspices of an old, haggard, wrinkled crone.

Garlic, salted cod-fish, brown bread, *borrachos* or skins of wine, lay scattered about. A guitar here, a monk's cowl there; a file of formidable *trabucos*[2] within easy reach. Sundry articles of female attire for the purpose of disguise. Stilettos, blunderbuss's, hatchets, and axes, completed the picture of this impenetrable Guerilla lair.

No sooner had the troop defiled from the dark passage into the pure soft light shed by the stars above, than all discipline seemed at an end, and with discipline, all traces of the savage barbarity that marked their lives. To have beheld them on that green carpet of nature's workmanship, so blithesome, so light and happy looking, one might have imagined that dark passage to have divided the world of innocence from the world of sin. Some joined in chorus to the chords of the gui-

---

1. A Guerilla chief, second only in reputation to the far-famed Empecinado.
2. Carbines.

tar; others snatched up the castanets, and danced in admirable style, the Bolero or Fandango; while one Diego, a merry rascal, amused himself by teasing the old dried-up representative of womanhood.

At length the kid was pronounced *quieta;* and on the grass, in the primitive style of those days, "when forks were not in use," we sat down to the repast. The *borracho* of wine made its way merrily round the group, notwithstanding the usual abstemiousness of the Spaniards, and the manner in which it was administered by one to another, was very comical. In each skin, a small pipe was inserted, through which, by a neighbour's dexterity, the potent *vinho da Xeres* was squirted down the throat of him whose turn it was to drink. I took the liberty of protesting against such a system of infusion, but not before having received the assurance of Master Diego being a practical joker, inasmuch as, to the no small delight of his comrades, he transferred the pipe from the place of its destination, to the vacancy between my chin and leathern stock. After this achievement, large cups made of horn, were introduced, and when all were filled as bumpers to the brim, I rose to propose for a toast, *"L'Espagna et los Guerillos."*

At the same moment playfulness and fun ceased; the stern compressed look, the dark and flashing eye, the rapid fall of every man's hand to his armed belt, spoke of that war "to the knife," that had become religious fervour in the Spaniard's heart.

The hills re-echoed the enthusiastic shouts, and it was amidst an uproarious outbreak of *"Viva la Espana y la libertad. Mueran los Franceses,"* that the Guerillas, selected for our escort, led the way through the dark passage of the mountain to the world without.

The night, now far advanced, was serene and lovely, and a late moon cast its pale light over the picturesque scenery around us. In the distance, the snowy summits of Sierra Nevada, the boast of Grenada, were clearly visible, while between us lay the verdant vallies and fertile plains of Andalusia, rich in vines and olives, beautifully contrasted by rocky mountains, on whose topmost pinnacles stood mouldering castles and ancient battlements, once the strongholds of the Moors and Romans. Many of these were temporarily fortified by the French, as points of retreat and defence against the attacks of the mountaineers, or at other times, to protect the passage of their provisions and ammunition across the mountains.

Our party proceeded in silence over the difficult ground; sometimes our path wound over dizzy precipices, and sometimes through the rugged bed of a winter torrent. More than once the drawling cadence of a muleteer's song sounded in the distance, or a solitary herdsman passed near enough to exchange the customary salutation, "*Dios guarde à usted,*" as he wended on the way that led to his flock.

We had journeyed on about one league, when a horseman was seen ascending a narrow path of the mountain. The escort suddenly halted, and drawing up on the brow of the hill with military precision, awaited the approach of him, their practised eye had recognized as their redoubted chief, Don Murillo Davila.

Advancing with frank courteousness towards my companion and myself, this chief of the Guerillas informed us, to my no small astonishment, that he had already been made acquainted with our visit to his mountain recess, and consequently had tarried for us at the *ciajo*, even longer than the projects for the night could well admit of.

"There," said he, pointing to a distant tower, that seemed to repose its dark head upon the azure sky, "there, in those walls lurk the enemies of Spain, Amigos." He pointed again to the distant object.

With flashing eyes the Guerillas raised their carbines to the tower; it was a reply not to be misread, and Davila, moving into the centre of his followers, proceeded to give, in slow and measured words, his orders for the attack.

The thirst for blood was now aroused, and on the dark and savage countenances of these blood-stained men, it would have been impossible to have traced one passing ray of that light joyousness I had witnessed.

The joker Diego, looked even more savage than the rest, and to an injunction laid upon him by his chief, growled out the Spanish proverb, *"En el hacer de una muerte,"*[3] with an unction of purpose that placed his zeal in the cause of destruction beyond suspicion.

The party filed off two by two in the direction of the tower, and the chief, after following it with his eyes, until the dark shadows mingled with the rocks, beckoned us to follow him to the valley beneath. Without the interchange of a single word, we descended a steep path, overhanging a village, that lay at the foot of the mountains.

---

3. In the doing of a death.

As we approached the haunts of men, our guide became more watchful; drawing from his saddle bow, a ponderous blunderbuss, he examined with minute attention the priming, and returned it to its place. The carbine that was slung over his shoulder, underwent a similar inspection, and a glance at the *cuchillo,* that was stuck in his leathern belt, satisfied the Guerilla that the annihilation of human life lay in each weapon that he bore.

A path to the right diverged from the one we were following, and our guide, still leading the way in silence, pursued it until we came in sight of a rich meadow of pasture land, watered by a running stream. Here we halted, and Davila, dismounting from the beautiful Andalusian horse he rode, desired us to tether our mules to one of the olive trees that skirted the verdant plain; then turning to the noble animal that stood by his side, he said, "Francisco, I must speak with thee."[4]

The docile creature so apostrophized lowered his ear to the level of his master's mouth, apparently listening with profound attention to the slow, distinct words that the Guerilla whispered in his ear; and that he not only heard, but understood, was placed beyond a doubt by his walking slowly and cautiously to a part of the meadow, where the luxurious grass reached a height unknown in our more torpid temperature; there stretching himself at full length, he lay completely concealed from sight.

With encouraging and coaxing words, the Guerilla chief commended his obedience, and "*Adio Francisco!*" having been duly responded to by a *sotto voce* neigh, the Guerilla led the way on foot to the village before us. We had scarcely advanced on the open road, the distance of five yards, when a horrible spectacle presented itself. The mutilated body of a Frenchman lay pale and ghastly in the moon's light; his bloody clothes lay strewed around, and the dust

---

4. The Andalusian horse differs little from the Arabian. His large clear eye is capable of expressing either anger or affection, as the circumstance demands, and the manner in which he holds familiar intercourse with his master, would appear incredible to those, whose only opportunity of measuring the faculties of those noble animals is derived from a casual glance into the stables allotted to them.

The Spaniard, like the Arab, domesticates with his horse—treats him as a friend—caresses—remonstrates; but never chastises him. The little children roll with him on the grass, their language and ideas seem to become his own, and instances innumerable might be recorded, when he has exercised a combination of thought that appears miraculous, for the preservation of his master's life.

that our feet pressed was caked into hard substance by the gory dye. Davila bent with savage exultation over the prostrate body, and then kicking it with his boot, muttered, "*Perro Frances, ni sequieras serves de abano para tierra española.*"[5]

A few yards farther lay the remains of a French officer's uniform. The epaulette had been torn from the shoulder, and the spoliation of the buttons and braiding that once had decorated it, was characteristic of the finery-loving Serranos, by whose hands the unfortunate man had most probably fallen.

Our guide advanced towards the door of the first house we had seen since we quitted Tarifa. Scarcely had a cautious knock been given, before the door opened, and we followed the Guerilla into the interior of a room occupied by a party well worthy of a place in Spanish reminiscences. Two women of remarkable stature, and robust limbs were preparing food for a group of men that were easily to be recognized as Contrabandistas—a race that inhabited the mountainous districts, included under the name of Sierra de Ronda. The inhabitants of these parts were almost all smugglers, and even in time of peace had never been submissive to the laws of the Government. Assembling in bodies, under the command of some chosen chief, they eluded all attempts to subdue them; often resisted the regular troops sent against them, and, with astonishing dexterity, managed to carry off, in spite of the revenue officers, rich stuffs and other prohibited articles, that found a ready sale in the neighbouring towns and villages.

Their wives were usually women of immense strength; coarse and bold in their appearance, and often displaying their hatred to the French, and love of independence by wearing on their *basquinos* printed portraits of their King, and of those among their Generals, who had been most conspicuous against the invaders. The dark and sunburnt countenances of the Contrabandistas turned with the rapidity of the lightning's flash to the entrance of the Guerilla chief; who preceded Don Merino and myself into the crowded apartment.

Four or five young peasants sat smoking their cigars in indolent luxuriance round a *braziero,* their hair was fantastically confined in silken fillets, streamers of gaudy ribbons waved from their gay shoulder knots;

---

5. Dog of a Frenchman! thou art not worthy to manure the soil of Spain.

and but for the sparkling eye, that gave some index of manly spirit, the whole appearance of these young Andalusians would have been as effeminate as that of the smugglers lusty dames was masculine.

In a distant part of the room sat a man, almost concealed by the folds of his *capa*. On his head was a *sombrero* of extraordinary dimensions, at which the younger inmates of the room cast many a sly look, not unmixed with apprehensive awe. A lovely young woman, whose soft cheek had been pressed by the Guerilla's lips, on our entrance, with more than ordinary tenderness, completed the party.

Contempt and distrust marked the expression of Davila's face, as he picked his way through the many legs that impeded his progress across the room, to where the individual with the large *sombrero* was sitting; the latter rose as he approached, and extending his hand, exclaimed in a tone of greater surprise than pleasure, "*Murillo* Davila!"

The proffered hand was allowed to drop un-pressed to its owner's side, and the Guerilla chief even stepped back, as if to avoid a nearer contact with the person before him. The insulted Spaniard hastily placed his rejected hand upon the *cuchillo* that glittered in his girdle. Davila, with equal rapidity, half drew forth his own, but instantly replacing it:

"Cura,"[6] he said, "we shall meet again in a more fitting place; until then keep your *cuchillo* for the enemies of Spain. It is already stained enough with the blood of Spaniards. Death to the French can be the only bond of union between Davila, the Guerilla chief, and Cura, the leader of the Contrabandistas."

Scowling looks of vengeance flashed from the eyes of the smugglers upon our party, at the conclusion of these last words, and starting up with a vehemence that can only be understood by those who have seen the Spaniards under the excitement of inflamed passions, the whole room was in an uproar. I had heard that it was rare for any number of these mountaineers to be assembled together without broils taking place, that invariably terminated in bloodshed. And so it would have been in this instance, but for the rapid and effectual intervention of the women. Before the smug-

---

6. The lawless and blood-thirsty Cura was a native of Valencia, and for a considerable time was the leader of the Contrabandistas in the mountains of Ronda. The influence he acquired as a stranger among them, was owing partly to the superiority of his education, and partly to the mystery that was attached to his real origin and station in society. He was known only by the name of "The stranger with the wide bonnet."

glers had time to draw their knives, the two women extended their brawny arms in a *cordon sanitaire* around the would-be combatants; and partly by menaces, and partly by coaxing, aided and abetted probably by an auxiliary force in the shape of a smoking olla, succeeded in restoring tranquillity, if not harmony, to the party.

So numerous had been the events of the night, that time had waned away unheeded, and I should have found it difficult to decide whether the leader of the Contrabandistas, and his band were engaged in a late supper, or an early breakfast, when a distant trumpet sounded the reveillé. Davila and my companion, Don Merino, were in low and earnest conference, when this official announcement from the enemy's camp of the dawn of day burst upon our ear. Almost immediately afterwards, the shepherds horn from the neighbouring mountains was heard rousing up the mountaineers, and upon this last signal, the Guerilla chief summoned us to prepare for departure. Upon a musty sheet of old parchment, extracted from the antiquated hoards of the parish priest, Davila had rudely traced for the information of General La Pena, the positions to be maintained by the different bands under his command; the stations of the French in the neighbourhood of La Ronda, and other intelligence of the enemy's movements, derived from intercepted messengers, and various other means, that none but the Guerillas could employ.

Before three days had expired, he pledged himself to be near the Spanish army, and Don Merino having thus succeeded in his mission, was scarcely less anxious than myself to rejoin the allied forces at Tarifa; but other adventures were still in store for us.

Another affectionate caress was bestowed on the pretty Spanish woman as the Guerilla led the way to the door by which we had entered; and as it closed upon us, Don Merino whispered to me that three months had scarcely passed away, since the soft-eyed Andalusian had plighted heart and faith to the stern Guerilla chief.

The shepherd's horn was still sounding from the distant hills, as we retraced the road of the preceding night, leading to the meadow, in which our beasts were tethered. In the same spot lay the murdered Frenchman; two large eagles were dispatching the poor remains with horrible avidity, and the eyes, and prominent parts of the face were already devoured. It was a relief unspeakable to turn from the melancholy spectacle to the fresh verdure of the meadow beyond; for it was not possible, even in those days when the frequent sight of human suffering deadened the poignancy of feeling, to do otherwise than heave a sigh at the contrast nature afforded.

On one side, the brilliant rising of a southern sun, darting his first rays over a landscape that even at an early season of the year bloomed rich in vegetation, and of hopeful promise of the future; the freshness of the morning breeze, the first warbling of the birds, the rippling of the mountain stream, this was nature in her garb of loveliness that no evil power could deface, much less destroy. On the other side, Man—for whose enjoyment the fair scene was made—lay in putrefying corruption, tainting the sweet air, like sin corroding the purity of the soul.

From these reflections, I was roused by the sonorous and deep-toned voice of the Guerilla, at the entrance of the meadow. The well-known sound roused up the head of the delighted Francisco above the long blades of grass, where he had passed the night; but still the docile creature maintained his post until called; then, no joy could equal his; bounding like a dog to his master's side, he laid his head upon his shoulder, covered his face with caresses, and proudly placing himself in a position for his chief to mount, seemed to invite him to confide in his trusty guidance to their mountain home.

I cannot record the same zealous alacrity on the part of our mules. These creatures seemed to feel no inclination to enjoy our company, and a most amusing chase ensued, that displayed a degree of resistance unequalled, I believe, even in the annals of mulish obstinacy. The iron-set features of the Guerilla chief relaxed into something very like a smile, as Don Merino and myself, being ignorant of the cognomens of our beasts—which by the bye is considered by Spanish mules an unpardonable offence—employed every name in the calendar of Saints to induce them to return to their allegiance. It was of no avail, and might so have continued, had not the same capricious spirit operating in an inverse direction, caused the animals to place themselves, by mutual consent, once more at our disposal.

Having mounted, we left the valley with its olive trees and green meadows, for the naked rocks and barren mountains that towered above us, higher than the eye could reach. The rays of the sun were gradually dispelling the mists that still hung upon the hill tops, and as their summits opened to view, we saw them clothed with thousands of armed Serranos, who had poured forth from concealment at the sound of the signal horn. Some movement was evidently in contemplation, for the inhabitants of the towns—discernible by their dress—had joined their neighbours of the mountains; and the addition of an innumerable host of women and children, showed that the French were in possession of the towns and villages from whence they had fled. Cowled monks were also among them, haranguing the multitude with declamatory violence; and parish priests in long black gowns, shouldered their carbines, and pointed to the distant spires of the desecrated churches of their homes.

The Guerilla chief glanced round at the moving hills with visible satisfaction; but still his eye strained to a distant point, as if from there, and there alone, he could either receive knowledge of the cause, or some information that would render such a force valuable. A dark cloud seemed for a moment to sweep over the azure sky that bounded the ridge of a distant mountain. "*Allà.* Yonder—there they are," burst from his lips.

Francisco needed not the spur to share his master's feelings. On, on, he rushed, climbing like a cat over jutting rocks, and yawning fissures, making good his way, in a direct line, to the rencontre of the advancing troop.

Francisco was a patriot, not so our mules; and but for the knowledge shown by Don Merino—which still puzzled me—of the mazy mountain paths, we should have tarried just long enough to have been picked up by the French in their ascent to the mountains. But, this is anticipating events, which ought to be given from the spot of ground, from whence the topographical knowledge of my companion allowed both himself and me to survey them in comparative safety.

It was about two hours after we had quitted the village in the plain, that a body of French hussars were seen ascending a ravine, skirted on each side by steep declivities, that bound the sight within a narrow confine, from the wide range of mountain scenery beyond. A detachment of infantry brought up the rear, its centre closing round a convoy that might have been provisions, ammunition, or wounded comrades. A considerable number of tirailleurs were thrown out in the advance, but the Serranos, besides being too subtle to present themselves as targets to the practised rifles of the French, were careful to conceal their numbers, until the enemy was fairly within their power.

With noiseless stealth, the mountaineers retreated from the brows of the hills they occupied, to others that commanded the pass through which the French must of necessity defile; and having stationed themselves in groups behind jutting rocks, and whatever masses of mountain verdure afforded cover, they remained awaiting in silence the approach of the foe.

In the meantime, the women from the village of Teba—where Don Merino and myself were posted—and which stands on the tip-top pinnacle of a rugged mountain, issued from their eagle's nest, to take a share in the attack. Dressed in their picturesque costume of blue and red, and armed with household implements, though some of them bore carbines, they placed themselves at different points, as a reserve force in case of need, and this with an air of fierce determination that made them by no means contemptible enemies to encounter.

While these movements were in progress, a troop of horsemen that we soon recognised to be Davila's band of Guerillas, wound in single file over a distant ridge of dark hills, shortly afterwards re-appearing on the opposite side, in the same order, descending a rugged precipice.

It was obvious that the Guerilla chief's intention was to intercept the enemy's retreat in the rear, and by this movement, to cut off all chance of escape.

Unconscious of the ambuscade thus formed, the French hussars led the way until within five hundred yards of the Serranos' outposts. The first shot fired was from one of their own tirailleurs, who, seeing the *sombrero* of a mountaineer peeping from behind a fragment of rock, let fly his piece to intimidate whatever stragglers might be on the alert. At this signal, the attack began, and the Spaniards, still concealed by the unequal ground of the hills they covered, poured down a storm of bullets on the enemy beneath them.

In vain the hussars tried to push their horses up the steep acclivities on either side. Each desperate attempt was foiled by the continuous volley of the assailants from above, who, emboldened by their own comparative security, came down at length from the heights, to seek a nearer and a surer aim. With loud and exulting shouts they leaped from rock to rock, keeping up with the hussars, as the latter urged on their horses through the defile in hopes of reaching the plain, well knowing that the Serranos were as unequal to sustain a charge of cavalry on level ground, as they felt themselves to be unprepared for the irregular but harassing movements of this mountain warfare.

In the meantime, the convoy and its escort had found a temporary shelter under a sloping hill; and a party of skirmishers taking advantage of the position, returned the assailant's fire with a warmth, that told effectually upon the most daring of the Serranos, who had ventured within range. The hussars urged on their panting horses over the unequal ground, and gained the plain; but not without exposure to a dropping fire from the heights, and when at length the plain was gained, a wild throng of mountaineers rushed to the rencontre with an impetuosity that was often displayed at the first onset by the Spaniards, but which died in the open field almost as soon as born.

The hussars, by a well imagined feint, appeared to turn, as if in consternation at the strength of their opponents. The movement brought down a scampering reinforcement from the hills, in which the women, and even children joined. The hussars here suddenly wheeled round, and charging with energy the disordered multitude, made a fearful slaughter of the panic-struck mountaineers, who dispersed in every direction, closely followed by their incensed enemies. In the ardour of the chase, the French forgot that unity is strength, and as they separated in pursuit of the Serranos, the latter again rallied on the magic soil of their own mountain tops, and turned their re-loaded carbines on the hussars. Men and horses fell on the ascent to those hills, that now again stood crowned with their own people; and now came the women's turn to assist in the work of vengeance by inventing tortures for the hapless beings that death had not placed beyond their reach.

At this crisis, a tremendous volley of yells and discordant shouts, mingled with groans and cries, issued from the defile through which the French had passed, and almost at the same moment, the rear-guard, with a convoy of sick and disabled soldiers, burst from the sortie, flying on the wings of the wind, before Davila's ruthless band of Guerillas. Humanity shuddered at the scene that followed; the defenceless sick were butchered with a cruelty that exceeds all power of description, but which can be well understood by those, who, at a later period, witnessed a repetition of such acts, during the civil war in Spain. As ants are seen to bear off to their retreats the victim that numbers only have subdued, so did the women strain every nerve to drag up the hills such wretched individuals, as were, from wounds and loss of blood, incapable of resistance. When at a convenient distance from the scene of carnage, these fiends bound their prisoners on faggots, and setting fire to the piles, left them in hopeless agony to a slow and horrible death. Others were stripped of their limbs, one by one, till nothing remained but the mutilated trunk, for which some additional torture was prepared.

While these horrors were enacting on the hills, the Guerillas had finished the work of massacre on the plain. Not one man remained of those surrounded by the Guerilla band; and although a few of the hussars managed to cut their way through the Serranos, and to effect an escape, it was doubtful that they avoided the danger that lurked at every step on their progress through the mountains.

With hands still reeking from the bloody scene, the Guerilla chief, attended by some few of his followers, joined Don Merino and myself at the little village of Teba. A crowd of female peasants pressed upon his footsteps, loaded with the spoils of the day, for in the short time that had intervened since the combat, every article of clothing had been stripped from the dead; and boots, epaulettes, military caps, &c, were brought into the village to expose as trophies outside the walls of the houses. The genuine savageness of a Spaniard's nature was never more fully displayed than by my companion, Don Merino, during the progress of the day's events. He had enjoyed the slaughter—from the convenient distance where he had placed himself—as keenly as the German sportsman relishes a battu; nor is this last diversion, by the bye, an inapt simile of the massacre we had been spectators of. A massacre most horrible, it is true, but as I afterwards heard from Davila, only a just retaliation for the atrocities perpetrated two days before on the defenceless inhabitants of Grazalema.

We were becoming very anxious to return to the head-quarters of the army, but Davila's information of the enemy's movements on the line we must traverse, was not to be accounted of light import, and we submitted to his decision of tarrying under the protection of the Guerillas until the dawn of the following day. Again we re-entered the wild scene of the previous night's conviviality—again we listened to the wild strains of mirth from men on whom the stains of murder were scarcely wiped away—again the *borracho* went its rounds; and toasts, and songs, and boisterous jests at length concluded this memorable day on the mountains of La Ronda.

We bivouacked in our cloaks on the green sward, under a soft Andalusian sky, and when the first bright streaks of dawn appeared on the grey horizon, we quitted the mountain-home of Davila, the Guerilla chief, to rejoin the army at Tarifa.

Chapter 14

Barossa

On the 28th of February we commenced our march to Barossa, having previously been joined by the Spanish force under General La Pena; and on the second day's march we fell in with an outpost of the enemy, on the heights of Vegar; they had two guns in position, and made an effort at defence, but we soon dislodged them, and bivouacked that night on the plain below.

An adventure here befell me, which would have retained a place in my memory, even had I not found it recorded it in my journal.

The night had been bitterly cold, and early on the following morning, I imprudently strolled beyond the Spanish outposts, in the direction of an old building, partly from curiosity, and partly in the hope that it might be inhabited by those, who could give me something better for my breakfast than my haversack supplied. As I approached the dwelling, by a sloping ground that concealed me from our men, I was startled by the sound of a bullet, that whizzed close to my head; and, looking up, saw a man in the act of aiming at me. My first impulse was to rush upon him, and to this movement, which un-steadied his aim, I was indebted for my life, at the same moment, several others started from their concealment, and, believing myself to have fallen into the hands of the French, I tried to regain, by the fleetness of my heels, our own outposts; but my assailants having cut off the road, I had nothing for it but to fly to the building, where I was so closely pursued, that I had barely time to save my life by surrendering.

It was then I discovered that my adversaries were Spanish Guerillas, whose merciless and ferocious habits, I had recently become too well acquainted with to feel otherwise than very uncomfortable at the approximation of a huge battle-axe to my head, by one of the wildest-looking of the party. They affected in doubt my assertion of being an *"officiere Inglese,"* but after a conference among themselves, at last consented to march me before them to a Spanish picket, having previously disencumbered me of my watch, money, and sword. As luck would have it, I was taken before General Gagio, one of my old Cadiz friends, who led me to his bivouack, caused every thing taken from me to be restored, and after partaking of his excellent breakfast, I got safe back to my party.

It was on the 5th of March, at about 9 o'clock, on a fine clear morning, that we entered the plain of Barossa. The troops had been upon the march upwards of seventeen hours; an unnecessary infliction of fatigue, that can only be accounted for by the circumstance of General La Pena having assumed the chief command of the allied army.

The Spanish force consisted of twelve well-appointed battalions of infantry; twenty-four pieces of artillery fully horsed, and amply provided with ammunition; and about six hundred cavalry, commanded by General Whittingham—an English officer in the Spanish service.—Lord Macduff had also a command, as a Major General of Infantry.

The British troops—having been joined by the 28th regiment, from Gibraltar—mustered about four thousand five hundred strong. These consisted of the 95th rifles, commanded by Colonels Barnard and Norcote, the 87th, 67th, and 47th regiments. The 28th, under Colonel Belson; two companies of the 20th (Portuguese) under Colonel Bush; a battalion formed of the light companies of the several regiments under the command of Colonel Brown of the 28th; three brigades of artillery commanded by Major Duncan; and one hundred and seventy of the 2nd German hussars under Major Busche.

Brown's battalion was ordered to take post upon the *Cerro di puerco*, a commanding height overlooking the plain of Barossa. In the rear of this position lay the sea, at the distance of about half a mile. In front, the plain, of about a mile and a half in extent, partly bounded by a forest. To the right, the road to Conil, by which we had entered the plain, and to the left, a thick pine-wood, from the extremity of which the sea-beach ran down nearly to the bridge, that had been thrown by the Spaniards, over the *Rio Sancti Pietri*. The Germans had halted in the rear of Brown's battalion; and the party, under my command, in charge of the reserve ammunition, took up a similar position.

In the meanwhile, La Pena had led off his troops, through the pine-wood, towards the *Sancti Pietri,* and having ordered General Graham to follow with his division, the allied forces filed off through the wood, leaving Brown's battalion, the German hussars, and the reserve ammunition, in the respective positions I have described.

It had been rumoured that an attack was to be made the following morning on Chiclana, and the enemy's works in front of Cadiz; but the idea of the French leaving their stronghold to attack so formidable a force as the allied army then presented, had never been contemplated, consequently the men were allowed to stretch themselves at ease on the slopes of the hill.

The morning was particularly still, and not a sound issued from the plain, after the last tramp of the soldiers had died upon the ear. The scene was one never to be forgotten, and only to be faithfully described by one, who like myself, was an eye-witness of the whole.

We had been twenty hours under arms, and upwards of seventeen on the march, during which time, no man had tasted food beyond the dry biscuit that his haversack contained, nor had one drop of brandy, from his canteen, revived exhausted nature on the wearisome route. It may, therefore, be easily imagined that no sooner was permission given to the men to rest, than they availed themselves of it by throwing themselves in every direction on the green sward; and, the hussars dismounting for the same purpose, loosened the girths of their horses, that they might also share in the rest permitted to themselves.

As if by the touch of a magician's wand, slumber seemed at once to seal the eyes of the weary objects that lay around; and a profound repose pervaded alike both animate and inanimate nature.

It was then that a horseman, followed by a single orderly, galloped up from the pine-wood, through which the allied forces had disappeared to view, and calling upon Colonel Brown to bring off his men, without the loss of a moment, to the protection of the wood, was thus the first to announce the immediate approach of the enemy. That horseman was General Whittingham.

Every eye started from repose to strain itself in the direction of the coming foe; and not in vain, for, issuing from the forest was distinctly visible a body of cavalry, advancing towards the right of Brown's position, followed by two columns of infantry.

The Germans vaulted into their saddles; and Colonel Brown, feeling the impossibility of keeping his ground, against such unequal odds, was rapidly leading off his men, when he perceived that the French cavalry had wheeled round, and was vigorously advancing upon his right flank. Without a moment's loss of time, he threw his little battalion into square, and calmly riding round it, called out, in a voice that rung in the ears, and reached the hearts of all that heard it.

"Be steady, my boys, reserve your fire till they are within ten paces, and they will never penetrate you."[1]

At this moment, the gallant Germans, headed by Major Busche, swept past an angle of the British Square, and the next moment charged right through the French squadron. So impetuous was the movement, that before the French could recover the shock, the Germans had reined in their horses, wheeled round, and again broken through the enemy's disordered line. The overthrow was now complete; the French dragoons were dispersed in every direction, and some of them hotly pursued by the victorious Germans, passed within only a few yards of our square.

The triumph, however, was but short; for the French infantry had moved forward in two columns, one of which had pushed on to the heights we had just quitted, while the other had obliqued towards the centre of the pine wood. The former now opened a fire from three pieces of artillery, that made murderous havoc in our square; and although we had gained the edge of the wood, it was with the loss of more than one-third of the gallant flankers.

At this crisis, General Graham was seen emerging from the wood with his staff, closely followed by the Guards, and the 87th regiment. These, as they disengaged themselves, in single file, from among

---

1. In this moment of stern and anxious, yet uncompromising resolution, an incident occurred, so ludicrous, that just as the sublime and ridiculous often meet from opposite points, so in this instance the faces that still radiated with the inspiring call of their leader, related into a loud laugh at the untoward interruption he received. The words above recorded, had scarcely left the lips of Colonel Brown, when a tall hard-featured Irishman, stepping close up to him, exclaimed in the broadest accent of the Emerald Isle: "Colonel, I say, what shall I do with Commissary O'Meara's baggage?" "Take it to H——ll," was the answer.

the trees, formed into line, though subjected to a dropping fire from the skirmishers that preceded a column of the enemy rapidly advancing on the left.

Colonel Brown's voice again rang through the air.

"Hurrah flankers: here comes Graham and the Guards. I will insure you all now, for half a dollar, by God."

The Rifles and Portuguese companies running to the right in skirmishing order, commenced the action on our side, while, at the same time, the 87th formed into line, having on its left, some companies of the Guards. During this formation, the artillery commanded by Major Duncan had been brought up, and taking a position in our centre, unlimbered within two hundred and fifty yards of the enemy. Never were guns better served, and the gaps in the enemy's ranks showed the precision with which the spherical shells were thrown. It was at this moment that General Graham called out "Give them the steel, my boys."

The 87th, under the gallant Colonel Gough, advanced directly in front of the enemy's column, and, though exposed to a heavy fire, reserved its volley until within fifty paces. With an hurrah that mingled with the roar of the artillery, the gallant fellows then rushed on to the charge, and a most sanguinary conflict ensued. The column thus charged was composed of two battalions of the 8th regiment, mustering one thousand six hundred men; their loss was incredible, for out of that number, only two hundred left the field.

The Colonel and nearly all the officers fell, and the struggle for the Imperial eagle proved how gallantly it was defended.

A very young officer of the 87th, Ensign Keogh, was the first who boldly attempted its seizure. Poor fellow! He fell pierced with wounds in the attempt. A tall, and very powerful man, Quartermaster Grady, cut down with his own hand two grenadiers, who defended it with great bravery; and as a third grenadier fell mortally wounded in his attempt to save it, the Eagle was wrested from his dying grasp by Sergeant Masterman, who retained it as a trophy gained by the valour of the 87th, on the field of Barossa.

Thus six hundred British bayonets proved an over match for one thousand six hundred of the enemy.

The British troops were divided into two columns, one commanded by Colonel Wheatley, and the other by General Dilkes.

The latter, attacking Rufin's division that had taken up the position from which Brown's battalion had retired, intrepidly ascended the slopes, under a murderous fire of artillery and musketry; and gaining the summit, drove the enemy in gallant style, at the point of the bayonet, headlong into the plain below.

In the meanwhile, Wheatley's column was not less successful, on the left in front of the wood. The panic, occasioned by the brilliant charge of the 87th, was followed up by the gallantry of the guards and the 47th regiment; and Laval's division being totally discomfited, was driven helter-skelter to the wood, which also afforded shelter to the whole of Rufin's division, as it came scampering down from the heights, leaving its General in our hands. Our men chased them to the outskirts of the wood, but there the pursuit ended, for we were in no condition to hazard, for an uncertain advantage, the laurels of the day.

One hour and a half had barely sped since nine thousand bold men, headed by a Marshal of France, had emerged from the forest, in all "the pomp and circumstance of glorious war." In that short space, one-third of their numbers lay stretched upon the plain. The emblem of their glory, the Imperial Eagle, was wrested from them, six pieces of artillery remained in our hands, and the wood now closed on the fugitive remnant of an army, which, on that morning, more than doubled in numbers, the little famished, exhausted band, that stood victors on the field of Barossa.

The last of the fugitives had sought refuge in the wood, when two battalions of the Spaniards made their appearance on the scene of action and such was the disgust and excitement, produced by their presence, when all was over, that notwithstanding the worn out state of our men, they would willingly have stood up, to drive these fellows back to the hiding place of themselves and comrades.

Had the fourteen thousand Spaniards, under the command of General la Pena, who were resting inactive within little more than a mile from the battle field, but faintly imitated the valour of their British allies, we should not have had to deplore the loss of twelve hundred gallant soldiers, nor would the French have resumed—as they did on the following day—their hostile position before Cadiz.

Cowardice, or treachery—perhaps an equal proportion of both—must ever be coupled with the name of General la Pena.

After a halt of some hours on the field of battle, General Graham withdrew the troops to the Sancti Pietri, and early on the following morning, we re-entered the lines of Isla de Leon.

Once again restored to the tranquillity of my old quarters in the Calla de la Carne, the events of the preceding fortnight found ample time for criticism which was denied in the excitement of the period they were in progress.

In commencing from the embarkation of the British troops from Cadiz, a series of blunders and bad arrangements followed one after another in such rapid succession, that one finds it difficult to contemplate them without expressing opinions that at this distant time are better withheld. It may, however, be allowable to mark out faults without alluding to the individuals by whom they were committed, and therefore in commencing from the embarkation of the troops from Cadiz, the first error to note down will be the glaring one of perpetrating an embarkation of nearly the whole of the British garrison, and a numerous body of Spaniards, in open daylight, under the very eyes of the enemy, concealing no part of the movement, and therefore allowing a more than sufficiency of time for whatever operations, offensive or defensive, that the enemy might think proper to adopt.

The next error consisted in allowing the fleet to pass the shores of Tarifa, when all the artillery and horses might have been safely landed there. This is a fact to which I can bear testimony for having myself disembarked in a boat with Captain McCullock, the principal agent of transports, who made the signal that he could land the artillery and horses. The fleet, notwithstanding, passed the port, and brought up that night off Algesiras. This was a serious evil, it exposed the men to extra marches, and caused the detention, of nearly a week, of the troops at Tarifa, waiting for the arrival of the guns and ammunition.

Again: what disasters might have been produced by the error of placing British troops under the command of an unknown Spanish General, whose conduct, on the day of battle, not only proved him to be a rank coward, but also gave rise to well-founded suspicions that his wish was to sacrifice the brave troops that had been so rashly entrusted to his command. Hence came the terrible march of twenty hours preceding the day of battle which brought them in contact with an enemy, superior in number, unimpaired by fatigue, and united under a skilful leader. Is it too much to say that none but British soldiers could have fought their way through the trammels and difficulties with which error had surrounded them?

The battle of Barossa was a regular stand-up fight, without premeditation, combination, or tactical manoeuvring. The brave Graham was taken unawares; had no time for consideration, and simply relied on his conviction that each man would do his best. This expectation was responded to nobly, and although no solid results attended the battle of Barossa, it will ever take its place as an action, in which the energies and courage of the British troops shone conspicuously.

It was not long after the battle of Barossa that a malignant fever, well known by the name of "the black vomit," burst forth in the garrison of Cadiz. Like a fearful scourge, it spread its devastating influence around, sweeping from the land of the living almost every object it attacked.

As day by day numbers were thus consigned to the grave, it was strange to witness the indifference displayed by the survivors, who, in their turn, were perhaps doomed to be laid low within a few short hours. And yet so it was. The sound of guitar and castanet from the gay circles, in which our young officers shone the gayest of the gay, often mingled with the creaking of the cart wheels that were employed in carrying to their last home some who had recently mixed with the same gay throng; but, no thought of to-morrow seemed to disturb the enjoyment of today; and neither surprise nor concern attended the announcement of each succeeding victim to the ravaging pestilence.

Captain Shenley's company of artillery were dreadful sufferers by this fatal disease; and when, at last, he himself was carried off, there was perhaps more sympathy shown on the occasion, than for any other officer in the garrison, who had preceded him. Poor Shenley was a right joyous fellow, but his qualities of good comradeship are best given by the epitaph he selected for himself:

Here lies a jolly dog
Who lived every day of his life.

He was always the last to quit the convivial board, and the first man on parade in the morning, giving, as he used to say, a good example in all ways to the rising generation.

The circumstances of his death were very afflicting. The delirium of lever was upon him when his wife and children arrived from Woolwich, and although he survived two days, no lucid interval granted them the consolation of knowing that he was conscious of their presence.

One exception must be made to the indifference that was apparently shown to the tenure of life during the raging of the fever, in favour of our Chaplain, Mr. Heyward, whose original and quaint humour must ever find a place in every reminiscence of Cadiz.

Anxious to be at his post by the bedside of the dying, he was equally un-anxious to make one of the number; and the extraordinary measures and precautions he took to avoid contagion, caused many a joke among the soldiers.

"Which way does the wind blow?" were his first words on entering a sick ward, having been admonished by the surgeon to keep on the windward side of the patient. In following this advice, there was, however, some difficulty; for as the beds of the sick lay in different directions, the same breeze that placed poor Heyward in safety on one side, wafted the contagious air over to him from the other; and so there he used to twist and twirl like a weather-cock in a hurricane, facing the four cardinal points in turn, without the power of commanding his own stability. No doubt his disinclination to quit this world arose from the great enjoyment he felt in it. Nor must it be denied that he also contributed largely, by his agreeable ways, to the enjoyment of others; his *bons mots* were always to the point, and if, as sometimes happened, a soldier's toast was proposed in his presence, or joyous song, with less of romance than truth in its composition, the Doctor, as we used to call him, would only say, "Gentlemen, I am more than usually deaf to-night."

I remember on one Sabbath morning, our good Chaplain had gone through the service before the General appeared; the latter having been detained beyond the usual hour by some cause or another. A message was in consequence delivered by the *aide-de-camp*, requesting, on the part of the General, that the sermon, which was nearly concluded, might be recommenced.

The Chaplain of course obeyed the mandate, but after it was all over, the younger officers began quizzing him most unmercifully on the additional labours he had undergone, and one of them said, "Now acknowledge, Doctor, that you thought it a terrible bore."

"Indeed, Sir," replied the Chaplain, with his peculiar quiet unruffled manner, "you quite mistake my thoughts; few Divines have enjoyed, like myself, the gratification of having their sermon encored."

The fever was beginning to lose its intensity, and the daily decreasing number of deaths gave still greater confidence to those who had hitherto escaped; when I was seized with the sudden and well-known symptoms, in riding home from the fortress of Portales, which poor Brett, of the artillery—afterwards killed at Seville—so gallantly defended.

The first sensation was so similar in its effects to those of a *coup de soleil,* that for some minutes I believed myself indebted to a broiling sun for the whiz into which my brain was spun, but a very short period settled that question, and many days elapsed before my senses were sufficiently returned to understand that change of air was the remedy that had been found the most efficacious, when circumstances permitted it to be used.

I was, therefore, put on board ship, and sent off to Lisbon, where I was billeted in the "*Quartier Buenos Ayres,*" at the house of a young and beautiful Marchese; but the fatigue of the voyage had been too much for my exhausted state, and immediately on landing, I suffered a relapse, that placed my life in imminent danger. It was some days before I recovered from the delirium of this paroxysm of fever; and the first object that presented itself to my weak and wandering senses, was the Marchese bending over me with a tender expression of pity in her angel-like countenance, that I can never forget.

For weeks she was my gentle nurse, and when at length my natural strength of constitution gave hopes of returning health, she would diversify the amusements of the day, until I marvelled in find it so soon past. Her sweet voice would harmonize with the soft accompaniment of the guitar, and deeds of valour, and tales of love, would, from her lips, waft me from the dull reality of existence to the sunny region of romance.

One evening, the couch on which I still reclined, was placed by the side of an open window leading to a terrace where the delicious perfumes of the citron and orange-flower were fanned by the sultry breeze. As my fair nurse approached to place in my breast the rose she had just gathered, a chain she wore, to which a medallion was suspended, became entangled round my arm, and fell to the ground. It opened in the fall, and I started at seeing tile noble and expressive features of my friend, Colonel Don Antonio Xavier, who had shown to me at Oporto the kindness of a brother.

In one moment the illusion that fancy had flung around me was destroyed; nor could an eternity of time have restored me to the feelings that were past—never to return.

I saw the beautiful Marchese but once afterwards, and that was, when in a few days my health permitted me to resume my duties at Cadiz, I requested an interview to express my gratitude for the kind attentions of my hostess.

On my return from Lisbon to Cadiz, I found that a change had come over the state of that fortress. The city was no longer kept in a state of feverish excitement and alarm by the dropping shells from the enemy's batteries. Fort Pontales had ceased to dart its booming shot against the batteries of the Trocadero; and Isla de Leon alone bore evidence of the proximity of the foe. The blockade was there most vigorously maintained, and the extremities of the Puente du Zuazo were occupied, as before, by French and Spanish guards. The Isla de Leon contained upwards of fourteen thousand troops, including the British; and, aided by the fleet in the bay, they had the power of harassing, at different points, Victor's army, which from frequent draughts, in aid of other movements, was reduced to a weakness that admitted only of its acting on the defensive.

The Cadiz beauties still crowded on the Almeida, and their fluttering fans were telegraphic as of old; the little feet had lost nothing of their mincing tread, and the splendid uniforms of the Spanish officers had even gained in splendour from the habit of competition; but the spirit of former days seemed to have flown. With the absence of danger had disappeared also the enchantment that springs from danger. Woman's eye no longer implored the protecting arm of man, and his self-importance had diminished proportionately. It is even possible that time had afforded too rigid a test to many a passing fancy, that had owed its origin to a momentary and perishable excitement, as it had also shrouded in gloom, many a heart, in which love and duty had vainly tried to accommodate matters.

There are few who may not recollect the exquisitely formed

and graceful Donna V—a, the young and apparently happy wife of the Conde V—a, Colonel in the Spanish service, and one of the few aristocratic patriots of that army. It was only a few nights after the landing of the British troops at Cadiz, that I met, at a crowded tertullia, this fascinating specimen of Andalusian beauty. All were enchanted with her, but none so much so as Lieutenant W— of the —th regiment; and it was also remarked that the lovely little Senora yielded readily to the dangerous happiness of being admired.

The peril of a moth, within the magic influence of the flickering flame, is not more imminent than that of woman when led onwards by the allurement of admiration. The brink of the precipice is soon gained, and the dizzy brain precipitates to destruction the frail being, who has depended too presumptuously on her own powers of support. That proximity between the sexes is the lever by which is raised its cargo of attendant evils, is a truth that none who have studied human nature can deny; nor that to the same account might be placed the smuggling on board a vessel, bound for England, of the charming Comtessa by Lieutenant W— who had previously secured to himself a conveniently-timed leave of absence from his regiment. It is scarcely needful to add that the parties had eloped![2] Other events, of a similar nature, had taken place during my comparatively short absence from Cadiz, contributing to the change that had spread over the surface of society. The lightness of flirtation, and mere ball-room sentimentality had, in many female hearts, deepened into true and lasting attachments. Levity was superseded by seriousness, and the spell of mirth was broken, not to be re-invoked! To most of our young officers, the change was beneficial in causing them to turn from the rich banquet of voluptuousness that Cadiz offered, to a more anxious and sober review of the progress of our arms in Spain.

---

2. This lady was subsequently married in England to Lieutenant W—, who obtained in after years an appointment as store-keeper in a northern county. In 1828 he died, leaving a large family, wholly dependant on the slender pension to which his widow was entitled. Surrounded by the clouds of adversity, it would be too much to inquire if the sigh of regret never rose to her memory.

CHAPTER 15

The Defence of Tarifa

The preservation of Tarifa from the hands of the French was at this time an object of great importance, thereby to prevent the supplies that the Campina could afford to the blockading army, for the accomplishment of this purpose, a brigade of artillery, with the 47th and 87th regiments under Colonel Skerret, sailed from Cadiz for Tarifa, accompanied by two battalions of Spaniards and ten guns, under the command of General Copens. The siege and assault of Tarifa by General Laval, including the gallant and successful defence made by the garrison, formed the only event of decisive importance since the battle of Barossa, in which the British arms were engaged. It afforded a subject both of exultation and reflection; the latter, inasmuch as no proof more striking could have been afforded of the importance of a judicious selection of those individuals to whom are entrusted the fiat of conquest or defeat. As an example, the commanding officer of this expedition, although unimpeachable in the courageous bearing of a soldier,[1] was wanting in the bold decision, which, in military practice, must often take the lead of science, and established rules. The quality was wanting, as shown in the opinion given by this officer on the untenable condition of the town. He saw no farther than its mouldering walls, and imperfect fortifications, whereas, a perspicuous moral view would have discerned strength where weakness was perceptible, and the triumph of boldness, aided by valour, over a timid adherence to the rules of art. The preservation of the fortress was therefore mainly attributable to the Engineer officer, Captain Smith, who by a more skilful and enlarged view of the application of its resources, over-

---
1. Colonel Skerret fell in 1813, in the unsuccessful attack of Bergen-op-Zoom.

ruled objections that tended to its evacuation; nor did that officer fail to place, foremost among such resources, the well-tried powers, and dauntless bayonets of the 47th and 87th regiments.

Although many were the individuals who distinguished themselves in the defence of this time-worn, and hitherto neglected fortress, none earned a brighter repute than Lieutenant Edward Mitchell of the Royal Artillery, whose gallantry and skill were alike conspicuous.[2]

At this period, Cadiz was no longer the magic emporium of military aspirations. The Spaniards themselves were far from regarding us as invincible allies, and the Conferences of the Cortes, and the Councils of the Regency tended but to one object; that of transferring all responsibility and expenditure of arms, money, and blood to the British nation; and as in the opinion of the Spaniards, we had but slowly responded to this raised expectancy, a perceptible diminution had taken place in the enthusiasm, with which our first appearance had been greeted.

During the most active progress of the war at Cadiz, the British Government had sent out fleets of transports, laden with valuable cargoes of ammunition and stores necessary for the defence of the city, and the Isla de Leon. The demands for these supplies were made by myself as the Military Commissary of Ordnance—in conjunction with the commanding officers of artillery and engineers—and were consigned to my charge. Those transports laden with military stores, intended exclusively for the Spanish service, were consigned to the British Consul, made over by that functionary to the Government, and by Government consigned to the interior of a large unfinished cathedral. In a few months, the edifice was crowded with arms, accoutrements, and artillery stores of every description, while further supplies were arriving from time to time, to augment the accumulation. No communication was made to me by the authorities at home respecting the appropriation of these stores, and the Spaniards were meanwhile making requisitions on our depôts for whatever batteries were worked by them, at a time when gun carriages and perishable stores of every kind were blocking up the Mole, exposed to the weather, and to pillage.

When the Regency was asked to allow some of these idle stores

---

2. This lamented officer died on service, in Syria, 1837.

to be applied to the defence of the Isla de Leon, it refused, giving as a reason, that such stores were intended for a distinct and particular service. What that service was, never transpired, unless it was that of equipping a couple of old six-pounders, to accompany a battalion of Spaniards, embarked under the command of Colonel Roche, with all the pomp and circumstance of a military expedition for Alicant; and which guns were left upon the beach, as they were disembarked, without even having been mounted upon their carriages. The secret of this lavish supply of stores to the Spaniards may be said to have originated with the British officers, who were permitted to join the gaudy staffs of the Spanish Generals.

These gentlemen, many of them suddenly elevated from subaltern officers to the rank of Colonels, and even Generals, in the Spanish service, were, in many instances, suddenly impressed with a sense of their own importance, and by way of impressing it upon others, made applications to the British Government for military stores, without exactly being able to define the object for which they were required; neither could the Spanish Generals, who authorized the demands.

At a later period of the war, when pressing applications for stores were made by myself, and other competent and authorized officers, we were but indolently and partially supplied, while large depôts of every description were scattered about, in out of the way places, under the feeble protection of a Spanish guard; exposed to the depredations of the native peasantry, or to the seizure of the enemy.

Chapter 16
To England

During the period that Sir Richard Keates had the command of the fleet in the bay, I had lent him a horse to carry him on his occasional excursions to the redoubts at the Isla de Leon; for this good service, he used to say he would mount me on a marine horse across the bay of Biscay, and an opportunity now offered to test the sincerity of his promise.

The inactivity that prevailed in the garrison of Cadiz had induced many officers to apply for a short leave of absence, to recruit their health after the ravages of the fever. I was among the number, which reaching the ears of the Admiral, he sent to tell me he had ordered accommodation to be provided for me on board the *Bulwark*, seventy-four, then about to sail for England. This was a special favour, and I appreciated it as such, for the comforts of a man-of-war formed a strong contrast to the discomforts of a transport.

Among our passengers on board the *Bulwark*, was a staff-surgeon of the name of Nicolay, whose constitution had been so much undermined by the fever, that he was obliged to return to England. He was an amiable, and highly accomplished man, uniting to the robuster qualities so essential to his profession, a delicate and refined mind. He was a good linguist; a good musician; and his evening parties at Cadiz generally brought together the nicest and best fellows of the garrison.

We had not long embarked, when a manifest change for the worse took place in his health; but as he was naturally of a delicate appearance, we did not apprehend the presence of danger.

Men are at all times un-watchful nurses to their fellow-men, and not the less so, perhaps, when fresh from scenes associated with dangers and death. A woman's eye would doubtless have discerned, in the fevered glance, and hectic colour of the invalid, the progress of a disease, of which he was himself unconscious; but we saw it not. And on the sixth day of our passage, having, as usual, passed a great part of the fore-noon in the cabin, where he lay a silent sufferer, we sat down at three o'clock to dinner in the ward-room, with keen appetites and careless hearts, as sentinels against the admittance of sickness and sorrow. The cloth had just been removed, when the steward hastily entered; his look of consternation communicated itself to every countenance, and rising simultaneously, we hurried, guided by the name that had fallen from his lips, to the berth occupied by poor Nicolay. Alas all necessity for human aid was over; a few drops of blood slowly trickled from his pale lips; the eye was glazed and fixed; one effort as we approached—one fruitless effort to speak, and all was finished! We looked from the bed of death upon each other; surprise had scarcely yet made way for sorrow; but there were two young officers present, to whom this sudden calling away of a mutual friend was not void of profit. These young men, of impetuous and impatient spirits, as yet un-subdued by experience, had become, by the very similitude of their natures, fierce opponents to each other. The seeds of enmity were rankling in the breast of each, and the termination of the voyage was looked forward to as affording the *terra-firma* on which was to be settled, by the laws of honour, their pygmy feuds.

As the more indifferent portion of the party returned from the scene of death to the ward-room, it so chanced that the would-be combatants remained together gazing abstractedly on the placid countenance of their departed friend; one who had often vainly endeavoured to check the rising burst of animosity between them. Was it the recollection of such moments, which made the eyes that had glanced in fury on each other, turn with subdued pride, and mournful meekness, to seek a mutual pardon? So it was; and the fiery youngsters, who, but a few minutes before, would only have sought a look for the purpose of insult or defiance, now met with hand clasped in hand, and faces bedewed with tears over the inanimate corpse. There is yet one alive who can bear testimony to the truth and fervour of a friendship that took its root beneath the fostering hand of death.

There are few things more painful to witness than a death at sea; for, although philosophy may smile with cold contempt at the ritual of Christian burial, and religion look, with eye of faith, to that time when the sea shall give up its dead, still the weakness of man's heart shrinks from the consignment of a fellow-being to so vast a grave.

The evening gun had just proclaimed the moment when the sun's disc sinks in the far west, and the tranquil waves were yet tinged with his glorious farewell to the day that succeeded poor Nicolay's demise, when the boat-swain's whistle piped all hands to quarters. At the gang-way, on an inclined grating, bearing towards the water, lay the remains of our lamented fellow-passenger. A tightly sewn-up hammock—to the foot of which two thirty-two pound shots were attached—served the purpose both of shroud and coffin; and over all was spread the union-jack. The Captain and the officers, the crew and passengers, stood with heads uncovered, while the former, from the book of Common Prayer, read the beautiful Burial Service of the Church of England. Not a sound broke on the solemn stillness, save the rippling of the waves against the heavy sides of the vessel, and the lazy flapping of the sails against the masts. As the words, "We commit his body to the deep," fell from the Captain's lips, the grating inclined downwards, the gangway opened, and the body glided with a plunge, that thrilled through more hearts than one, into that perfect emblem of eternity—the fathomless ocean.

For a moment, the calm waters opened to receive the deposit, and as quickly closing, the ship sped gently on her course towards England, where an aged father and a fond wife were anxiously expecting the beloved son and husband we had just committed to the deep.

On landing at Portsmouth, we experienced the proud gratification of feeling, by our reception, how great was the interest manifested in England for the army of the Peninsula. Every little act of courtesy and kindness was proffered almost enthusiastically, and the very name of "a Peninsula officer," seemed a talisman, by which privileges were granted, and restrictions withdrawn.

Among the habits that had been induced, partly by the hardships of a campaigning life, and partly by association with the Spaniards, that of smoking had become so general, that it was almost as necessary as food or sleep. Colonel Birch, of the Engineers, was one to whom a cigar imparted so much of luxurious happiness, that, calculating by an inverse ratio his misery must have been great without it. This gallant officer was a passenger on board the Bulwark, on leave of absence to recover his health after the Cadiz lever, and the severities of the recent campaign. He was of a very studious cast, and would pace his cabin from morn till noon, and noon till night, with some favourite author in one hand, while the other ever and anon lifted to his mouth the odoriferous cheroot. To so genuine a lover of the intoxicating weed, it was of serious import to possess it of true and unadulterated race, and the Colonel had consequently brought over a rare box of super-excellent cigars to last out his short sojourn in England.

Although less of an amateur than my friend, I had brought the same quantity for my own immediate use; but aware that of all articles of a contraband nature, none were more strictly prohibited than cigars, I had taken the precaution to place the box in my portmanteau, in that negligent position, which seems to say, "I am not here for criminal concealment, and pray do not disturb me." On the morning of our landing, I recommended the Colonel to stow away his box of delights in some safe corner, but he scouted the very idea of flinching from the enemy, and nobly offered to prove, at the risk of losing his pets, that an open fight was better than stratagem.

Onwards marched the hero to the custom house, followed by his servant, bearing the precious freight. My portmanteau was already within the clutches of the inspector, and as my feelings were less interested in the result, I amused myself, like an indifferent spectator, in watching the issue of our respective plans. Over my cigar-box, I had placed an article of linen; the identical article was lifted up by the custom-house functionary, and the culprit stood revealed; but, with a dexterity and anxiety that seemed to respond to "Pray do not disturb me," the officer—and a slight smile curled his lip as he did it—threw back the friendly covering over the offender, closed the portmanteau, and presented me with the key.

Now came my companion's turn. Boldly facing the enemy, he proudly prefaced his harangue by taking some credit to himself for not attempting to defraud his Majesty's revenue. The officer's looks plainly said, "What a pity that your conscientiousness has gone to so unnecessary an extreme." In vain the poor Colonel asserted that the forbidden fruit was for his own individual enjoyment; in vain he descanted on the privations he should endure without it. To each remonstrance, the custom-house officer could only express the regret he honestly felt, at his duty having been forced upon him, when he was visibly anxious to forego it, in favour of a "Peninsula officer." Colonel Birch lost his cigars, and vowed ever afterwards that *honesty might be carried too far.*

I found Woolwich a complete bee-hive of activity and motion. The Arsenal contained a mass of artificers, engaged in constructing gun-carriages, ammunition cars, and all the numerous appurtenances connected with artillery service. The barrack field was crowded with squads of raw recruits, and beardless officers, strutting about with virgin swords dangling by their sides. One young artillery officer actually betook himself to campaigning in his own apartment, so that he might be better able to endure hardships when called upon to do so. Report says, that in addition to sleeping on the hard boards, with his portmanteau for a pillow, this aspiring son of Mars inflicted on himself the penalty of short allowances, and was even seen, by a Paul Pry in embryo, to light a faggot fire on Woolwich Heath, and toast a morsel of raw beef thereby, on the point of his sword. Be this as it may, it is certain that the fulminating principle of military ardour could not have chosen a more harmless escape-valve than this *playing at soldiers,* on the friendly soil of one's own hearth.

After a brief sojourn in England, which completely restored me to health, I received orders from the Commandant of the Field Train, General Sir Anthony Farrington, to join the head-quarters of the army in Portugal, and nothing could have been much more welcome than such a summons.

CHAPTER 17

Return to Portugal

It was in what sailors call dirty weather that I embarked at Portsmouth on board the *Cora* to return to Lisbon, in company with a fleet of transports carrying out detachments, horses and stores, for the army in the Peninsula. I had scarcely time to get my horses slung on board before she sailed, and my first movement was to make acquaintance with her accommodation and passengers.

The cabin was large and airy, divided in twain by a canvass bulk-head; the one side appropriated to General and Mrs. Hay, and their two daughters; and the other side to a more promiscuous and numerous assemblage, consisting of Colonel Coghlan, of the 61st regiment, a deputy Commissary General, three Artillery officers, one Engineer officer, and a singular character bearing the name of Captain Lancaster, who had been promoted from the Stock Exchange to the office of paymaster to a battalion of the King's German Legion in the Peninsula, and was on service for the first time. A staff surgeon, and an Hanoverian hospital mate, completed the animal menagerie to which I was about to offer an addition in my own person.

Having enumerated a party often, it may be supposed that some difficulty occurred in placing that number into the six berths—three above and three below—that our half cabin afforded; but where there is the will there is the way, and so in this case. The Deputy Commissary General slid into the graces of the mate by sliding into his pockets some dollars, for which consideration he obtained the mate's roost in the steerage. The recruit from the Stock Exchange procured a cot, that was slung in the cabin during the night and taken down in the morning, while to accommodate the remaining two, a couple of berths were knocked up by the carpenter over the heads of those, who filled the second tier of sleeping boxes. An exalted position that took among us the name of the one shilling gallery. Its occupants were one of the Artillery officers, and the Hanoverian hospital mate, a young fellow full of fun and frolic. So thus we were all disposed of.

The Paymaster from the 'shady side of Pall Mall,' had parted from his moorings with as many heavings as ever agitated a vessel outward bound. His wife and wife's sister accompanied him on board, and as the departing hero sat on deck between them, his arms fondly encircling the waist of each, turning from side to side, administering comfort and gentle consolation it was almost a pity to think that he was not *de facto* the fighting man his gay dress declared him, but far more likely to come back rich and fat at the end of his campaign, than to offer any bodily illustration of the miseries of war.

At length with tears and sobs, the trio separated. A little boat bore off to Portsmouth the widowed wife and her companion, but still the Captain remained on deck, agitating his silk handkerchief in repeated acknowledgements of the telegraphic signals that waved from the boat, until time and distance made each imperceptible to the other. The *Cora*, in the meantime, had spread her sails, and started on her way rejoicing.

Our fleet consisted of about twenty sail of transports, under convoy of a frigate and sloop of war. After clearing the Isle of Wight, we all bethought ourselves of examining the state of our sea stock, for each party having dropped on board as strangers to each other, no combination of gastronomic forces could be effected between us. Each had supplied himself with what was most in harmony with his palate on shore; but Colonel Coghlan and myself knew enough of the probabilities of a sea voyage to allow such knowledge to influence our choice of provisions, and therefore hams, potatoes, tea and sugar, and some dozens of good wine and porter, were the only accessories to the ships rations that we provided for ourselves.

The hospital mate, with true Hanoverian sagacity, had relied on the probable prostration of appetite that would follow our ship's first tossings. A circumstance that he rightly conjectured would afford him an easy introduction to the hampers of the sufferers, and consequently he had adopted 'nil' as his motto during the voyage. The Deputy Commissary had made the first step in his profession by catering for himself in the most delicate and luxurious manner, and the conjugal love and attention of Captain Lancaster's lady had found an escape valve in the fabrication of sundry pies and choice morsels for her warrior Lord.

Thus primed, the gallant *Cora* glided past the coasts of Hampshire and Dorsetshire meeting with little worthy of notice beyond the lights and shades that new characters exhibit, and the usual excitement of a start, falling by degrees to the mean temperature of settled resignation to the caprices of wind and waves.

General Hay's motive for visiting England was to bring back his wife and family to reside at Lisbon during the occupation of the Peninsula by our army; and it may here be observed that the system which prevailed among our officers, at that period, of sending for their families when on foreign service, was not only the cause of many evils, resulting from the unhinged and disorganized state of society under such circumstances, but it also imposed a heavy burden of anxiety and sorrow on the better and more devoted portion of the sex. How many could be named, who, at Lisbon, suffered torments from the effects of idle rumours and false reports, fabricated for local purposes only, and thus anticipated, over and over again, the bereavement that they were perhaps destined to be spared. Besides, the parties being necessarily separated from each other during active warfare, there remained not one beneficial purpose fulfilled, to poise against the many evils resulting from the practice. But to return to our ship companions.

The lady of the kind-hearted General Hay, was no less a Caledonian by birth than accent; with much of beauty and amiability to boast of, notwithstanding a certain degree of pride that might perhaps never have appeared, but for the *mélange* of odds and ends assembled on board our transport, and the events both grave and comical that drew it forth. The two daughters were nice unaffected girls, and a raw boned Scotch servant, the very personification of Meg Merrilies, completed the family group that a frail canvass alone divided from our live stock association.

To organize the latter into something approaching to a state of civilization, a code of regulations and laws were enacted, to Infringe which was to incur certain penalties, framed to unite the party in harmony during the voyage. The doctor undertook the office of purveyor to the mess, and the hospital mate was selected to preside over the cellarage.

The first dinner on board did much towards developing the characters and habits of each individual present; indeed there is no better test at any time than a dinner table to prove the habitual intercourse of a man, with what is denominated good society, and which, although it may not extend beyond the conventional laws of courteous observances, gives a decided external superiority over those, who have not been subjected to its influence.

Colonel Coghlan was our president, he possessed eminently the demeanour and courtesy of a polished gentleman, and these qualities extending their influence around the table, gave it, from the first moment, a tone which was not afterwards lost sight of. The first subject for sly merriment was searching for opportunities that would bring forth Captain Lancaster's predilection for substituting Vs for Ws, and Ws for Vs. "A glass of vine, Colonel," to the president, was accepted with a good humoured smile, and as the black bottles, not decanters, went merrily round, the anti-combative disposition of the citizen captain, was laid bare to the quick. Prefacing his questions with an invariable "pray Sir, inform me," the denizen of the Stock Exchange arrived step by step at the altitude, from whence to dart the queries that lay trembling to escape from their hiding place. "Pray Sir, inform me," addressing the Colonel, "where is a Paymaster expected to be when the regiment is engaged?"

"At his post, Sir," replied the Colonel drily.

"Then of course a Paymaster's post is with the money chest. Pray Sir, inform me if he has a body guard to protect it?"

"A Paymaster's duty, Sir," rejoined the Colonel, chuckling at the Captain's rising colour, "is to guard the money chest at his own body's risk, if necessary."

"Good God, you don't say so!" ejaculated the alarmed Paymaster, "I had no idea of that. Pray Sir, inform me if you ever heard of a Paymaster being wounded, or killed."

"Both, both, my good Sir, I assure you; it is a misfortune of frequent occurrence," rejoined the Colonel, while the titter round the table was gaining a very audible ascendancy. It was time to change the subject. The Captain filled his glass, and rising, addressed the president: "Sir I feel myself bound, as a military man, to call upon yourself and these *other gents* to fill a bumper to the health of the ladies who have honoured this transport with their presence, and I moreover propose that the toast be drunk with three times three."

The latter part of the toast was objected to by the president, on the score of the slight partition that divided the *gents* from the objects of their loyalty; but the toast itself was given in the stentorian voice of the Lancastrian Captain, and of course met with deep and true homage from us all.

Still warm with the enthusiasm produced by 'vine and voman,' the gallant Captain withdrew with others of the party to the deck. The evening was gloomy, and the wind had gradually heightened from fresh to what is called a stiff breeze. The fair *Cora* had already given certain indications of her intention to pass the night in a manner uncongenial to her guests, and her movements were becoming sufficiently agitated to cause the pacing of her deck to be a matter of no small difficulty to landsmen.

The ladies had formed a group with the General and Colonel Coghlan, and were chatting with easy freedom, when a sudden jerk threw them to some distance, reeling and catching at every object, animate and inanimate, within grasp. The same plunge that sent poor Mrs. Hay in *a. pas de glissade* towards the opposite side, where Captain Lancaster was vainly endeavouring to preserve a footing, brought at the next moment that worthy gent most innocently and unintentionally to her embrace. They stood in mute dismay, clasped in each other's arms. It was an opportunity not to be lost. "Dear lady," gasped the hero, "I had the happiness, as a military man, of proposing your health this day in a bumper."

"General Hay—General Hay!" screamed out the offended lady, still clinging to the object of her horror, who with no less fervour clung to her, as another and another roll of the vessel made the disentanglement less and less practicable.

Vainly did the General endeavour to effect the rescue of his wife. His own steps were equally uncertain; and it is impossible to say how long the indignant Mrs. Hay might have remained in the embrace of the military man, had not the Captain of the vessel delivered her from the perilous position, and conducted her to the cabin below.

From that moment open war was declared between the ladies and the Lancastrian Captain. Whenever the gaunt figure of the latter appeared in sight, the fair ones beat a hasty retreat. Was it in remembrance of the past, or in anticipation of the future? No one knew, but so it was.

In the meantime the fleet made but little progress down the channel; the weather was rough and boisterous, and it was not until the eighth day that we fairly entered the Atlantic. From that moment, we experienced a continuation of the most horrible weather. The wind had increased to a gale; the sea ran mountains high, and on the second day the fleet was so widely divided, that not a sail remained in sight.

The effects were visible on board the *Cora*; the sound of mirth was changed to the plaintive cries of "steward," "cabin boy," issuing from the berths in which the sea-sick passengers lay. All rules and regulations were now at an end; the one shilling gallery was never vacated. The hero's cot swung day and night alike, and often as the ship rolled deeper on her side, would strike against the canvass partition, endangering its fastenings, and the privacy of the ladies on the other side. In short, with the exception of an artillery officer and myself, who retained what the sailors call our sea legs, no one ventured to quit his berth.

The gale increased to a fearful height; not a stitch of canvass beyond a storm stay-sail could be set. The hatches were battened down; and every wind-sail—by which air was conveyed to the horses below—was torn away by the wind as soon as placed. The sea that broke furiously over the decks, had swept away the long-boat and one of the crew, and but for the judicious and well exercised knowledge of the Captain of the vessel, a Scotchman, we never should have weathered the violence of that storm.

It lasted four days, an anxious period, even to men inured and accustomed to an ocean life; but to landsmen, and above all to women, it required all the hidden resources of the mind to bear it well. And these resources of the mind had certainly not failed our ladies on board. After Mrs. Hay's first urgent entreaties that the

General should exercise his high authority, and "order the Captain to turn back until the weather calmed," no further remonstrance nor complaint was heard; and a serene silence reigned in the ladies' cabin, that was left for Captain Lancaster alone to disturb.

On the morning of the fifth day, the fury of the wind abated, to the great relief of every one on board. The Captain and crew were worn out with the incessant watchfulness that the peril of our situation demanded, and the passengers on whom this responsibility was not imposed, were equally wearied with the unceasing and distracting noise of the raging elements.

But although the gale had spent its violence, the waves were still strong and turbulent. Our vessel still pitched and tossed, although the lightness of her cargo enabled her at times, to bound over the uncertain waves in comparative smoothness. It was during one of the momentary lulls, that Captain Lancaster bethought of refreshing himself with clean linen, a luxury not wholly uncalled for, considering that he had been confined to his cot unable to move hand or foot, for the last four days.

With some exertion, the hero managed at last to sit bolt upright, and moreover to preserve his equilibrium a sufficient length of time to shoot over his head the clean shirt presented by his servant; arrested in its passage downwards, the clean article took up its position round the neck of its owner, whose endeavours were directed to the disencumbering himself of the discarded one. This last perplexity was no sooner achieved, than before it could be replaced by the new-comer, sling went the cot over to the larboard side, with a vehemence that left its incumbent no alternative but to seize the canvass bulkhead for support. The sudden jerk, and heavy weight were in themselves sufficient to cause the catastrophe that followed, but when to these was added another lurch of the vessel, more mischievous than the first, can it be wondered at that Captain Lancaster vaulted through the canvass like one of Ducrow's celebrated horsemen, and bringing down the whole of the partition in his flight, never stopped until he alighted, head foremost, on the berth in which Miss Hay reposed.

No tongue, nor pen, nor pencil, can do justice to the scene that followed. Almost stunned by the violence of the fall, the luckless wight still retained sufficient regard for his personal safety to hold fast on the side of the berth, notwithstanding the vigorous opposition of Janet, the Scotch maiden, who, rushing to the rescue of her young mistress, pulled first at one protruding leg, then at the other, then at both legs together, to force him from his grasp.

In the mean time, Mrs. Hay's alternate cries of "help General," "help Captain," diversified with "Janet, for God's sake, throw some covering over the man," brought assistance, and with assistance relief, both to the assaulter and assaulted. The former suffered himself to be led quietly back to his den, and the canvass partition nailed him out once more; but it was not so easy to subdue the wrath of the General's lady—she insisted on the poor *military man* being turned out of the ship, and it was only when her husband good humouredly assured her that there was no place but the open sea to put him in, with the improbable chance of a Jonah's escape, that she consented to allow him to remain on board. To preserve peace, the Captain of the vessel gave up his own berth, and so precluded the possibility of another vaulting feat into the presence of the ladies.

The weather had now become moderate, and although the poor *Cora* was in a hapless plight, her fore-top-mast gone, and most of her sails, the Captain, in a few days afterwards, anchored her safely in the Tagus off Belem. Long before that time the passengers were in complete readiness for disembarkation. Colonel Coghlan and myself accompanied General Hay and his family on shore, where his son, Captain Hay, of the Royals, was in waiting to carry them off to the apartments he had provided in the quarter Buenos Ayres. Colonel Coghlan took up his quarters at Lisbon, preparatory to going up the country to take the command of his regiment, the 61st, and I made the best of my way to the artillery quarter at Campo Clara. Every one had his whereabouts defined and provided, with the exception of the unfortunate Paymaster, Captain Lancaster, and to him we performed the last good service of recommending him to put up at Moore's Hotel, and forthwith to report his important arrival to Colonel Peacock, the Commandant of Lisbon.

Chapter 18
Scandals!

The cantonments of the British army at this period, after the disastrous retreat from Burgos, were in the vicinity of Almeida, near the Agueda, Lamego on the Douro, Upper Beira, and the Valley of Mondego. In these well chosen winter quarters, which provided the men with good shelter, and afforded facilities for the supply of provisions, the army underwent a regular system of re-organization, both as regarded its physical and moral condition. The severe privations the troops had undergone in their retreat from Burgos, had not only induced disease and sickness in their ranks, but a cankering feeling of discontentment and insubordination, more difficult—but still more necessary to subdue.

The Siege of Burgos had been undertaken with means so inadequate to ensure success, that it is impossible to speculate upon the causes that induced an experienced Commander to hazard his own reputation, and the lives of his soldiers on such fearful odds. Every military man possessing some experience in his profession, felt, though he would not utter it, that neither British valour, nor yet a General's name—unaided by the sinews of attack, artillery and ammunition—could triumph over the difficulties offered by the fortress of Burgos.

The result proved the correctness of the misgivings, and British valour, although strained to a pitch of the highest devotion, fell powerless before obstacles that needed shot and shell to lay them bare, before British bayonets could effect the rest. As if the whole arrangements of the campaign were doomed to mingle together in one vast error, the supplies of the Commissariat fell short, and being totally inadequate to the public wants, the army was, consequently, reduced nearly to a state of starvation.

In like manner the transport for the wounded was far too limited for their numbers, and many of these poor fellows terminated their sufferings in lingering agony on the road sides, to which they had crawled.

When men are placed in an extreme position of peril and suffering, it is requiring too much of them to bear up with patient resignation, without making an effort to ameliorate their condition, when the means of doing so presents itself. On the retreat from Burgos, the British soldiers were in a state bordering on starvation. Hunger, and bivouacs in the drenching rain, do more towards levelling *castes* than the fiercest democrat can effect, and during these sufferings discipline had gradually slackened from the higher ranks to the lower, until the latter, losing sight of all considerations, or rather sinking them in the one absorbing interest of self, committed depredations on their marches, in direct violation to the general orders of Lord Wellington. Hence arose the well-remembered sweeping censure, addressed to the British army by its Commander, a censure that has been as often attacked as defended, according to the spirit of the writer. Those most favourable to it have not scrupled to assert that Wellington was himself ignorant of the privations his army had endured, which, if true, must nevertheless expose him to the charge of having been over hasty in condemnation, without a sufficient inquiry into the offences alleged to have been committed. It is undeniable that the army considered the censure passed upon it as an act of great injustice, and there were many who were not backward in laying it to the account of spleen, at the termination of a campaign, which the stubborn bravery of British soldiers alone, saved from still more disastrous results.

Be this as it may, the moral feeling of the army required training, and the inactivity of a few months, aided by the favourable position of winter quarters, and a strong reinforcement of untainted recruits from home, tended in no small degree to the healthy restoration of the whole. On this new, or rather reformed basis, was reared that perfect machine alluded to by the Duke of Wellington at a later period.

While this organization of the army was progressing in cantonments, the streets of Lisbon were thronged with military detachments just arrived from England; others on the point of embarking; the sick, the wounded, and officers upon leave, whose tarnished jackets, soiled feathers, and weather beaten faces, spoke of long marches, nightly bivouacs, and all the other hardships they had lately had to sustain.

There are many who may remember the extraordinary appearance of a young officer, belonging to one of the light infantry German regiments—his fair and youthful face was to be seen at all hours of the day peeping out from the housings of his mule, as he lounged through the streets of Lisbon. On a nearer inspection, it was a startling discovery to make that both his legs were off close to the hip, and that it was only by this bolstering up, that the mutilated trunk preserved its balance.

The poor boy had undergone the dangerous operation of amputation of the two limbs after the siege of Badajos, and might possibly, with the assistance of his joyous spirits and somewhat unreflective character, have done well, but for the sympathy that his early misfortunes created. To every convivial party, the young German was invited, his servant on such occasions bringing him in his arms in a kind of cradle to table. The mess rooms in those days were not remarkable for abstemiousness—teetotalism was yet unborn, and the result of those meetings told on the shattered constitution of the youth—he died shortly afterwards at Lisbon.

It will easily be credited that in the heterogeneous and mixed society, pent up within the walls of Lisbon, there was much held back from the broad pure light of Heaven. In other words, when wives, widows, and maids, separated from their natural protectors, are assembled together in close proximity with men of unsettled habits and uncertain movements, there is less of restraint over the passions; less of the wholesome dread of opinion; less of the individual shrinking from responsibility, than operate upon members of a community, guarded by the influence of ordinary circumstances.

And so it was at Lisbon. A too near amalgamation of the sexes produced, in the first instance, a state of society, corrupt and immoral, which society was afterwards made use of as a cloak to individual cases of a still more flagrant character.

Among the many combining causes that demoralized the intercourse of the British officers with their fair countrywomen at Lisbon, may be named the influence of feverish wines upon the already excited imaginations of the weaker sex.

It seems almost a blasphemy to hint at the bare possibility of an influence so opposed to the general habits and principles of our countrywomen at home; but while stoutly adhering to the fact, it must also be admitted that much palliation existed in the heat of the climate; in the freedom with which the wines of Lamego and Colaris were introduced; and, above all, in the agitation which prevailed at that period, in the mind, causing it to seek a momentary lull from anxiety in the exhilaration that wine produced. It is, however, certain that no interval was ever more closely filled up with intrigues and flirtations than this time of repose, enjoyed by the British army in Portugal, and the fatal results that emanated from one of these derelictions, created feelings of excitement and horror that never can pass away from the memory.

Mr. R——, an officer in the Ordnance department, arrived at Lisbon, accompanied by a female relative—the sister of his wife, who was expected soon to follow. Notwithstanding that the grave has long closed upon the actors in this deep tragedy of real life, and that consequently no throb of wounded feeling—no fresh probing of an imperfectly closed wound, can follow the revival of a by-gone event, it is yet unnecessary to dilate upon the details beyond saying that the general attention of gossips was directed to the circumstance of a young, unmarried lady occupying the position in Mr. R——s establishment, which would have been more suitably filled by his wife. That an attachment existed between the parties was as evident as that the fatal sequel was produced, not from the continuation, but from the cessation of that attachment on the side of the lady.

Among the many officers who were daily visitors at Mr. R——'s, may be remembered the unhappy hero of this tragic tale. Captain S——r, was gay, thoughtless, handsome; and in his first acquaintance with the sister-in-law of Mr. R.— was probably void of offence, save in the too ardent expression of an admiration that was incompatible with his position as a married man.

It has been said that the first false step of woman in the path of frailty, hurls her head long over the precipice of perdition. It is difficult to determine upon the absolute truth of this assertion; but most certain it is, that women, so situated, are very frequently successful adepts in tempting the sons of Adam. Had poor S——r exerted within himself the moral courage of flying from the danger he was too weak to oppose, his evil genius would have been cheated of the fearful punishment that followed a surrender to the tempter's power.

But such was not to be. Each day saw S—r an eager and a welcome guest at the *quinta,* to which R— and his frail mistress had retired. The luxuriance of the climate; the surpassing loveliness of the scene around them; above all the fervency of their own young, but erring hearts, forged the chain that was to be snapped by violence and bloodshed. They loved, guiltily it is true, but with a faith and earnestness that might, in earlier years, have shed a halo over their existence.

Thus stood matters for a considerable time, in the meanwhile their ill-concealed passion had become the theme of every gossip's tongue; but the lynx-eyed jealousy of R— had not required the busy aid of others to explain the altered mien, the estranged look, that once had turned in fondness upon himself. More substantial proofs were yet required, and he resolved to watch for them. For that purpose, invitations to a banquet were issued from the *quinta* to a number of officers quartered in Lisbon. Among the invited guests was Captain S—r. After events proved that he was not deceived as to the apparent friendship of this outward demeanour; neither was the frail but unhappy being whom he loved. They both felt that the crisis was at hand; and thus entwined in the meshes of dread of discovery—impossibility of flight—remorse—and the countless evils of a position, that only their own hearts could feel the miseries of the wretched pair conceived the project, that was afterwards but too faithfully executed.

The conference between the lovers on the morning of the evening's festival was long and earnest. They separated, but not unseen; and the fire of jealousy burned only the more fiercely, for the fresh fuel that had been thrown upon it.

At the appointed hour of evening, when the fervent heat of a southern sun was just beginning to yield to a refreshing sea breeze, the invited guests assembled at the *quinta.* During the progress of the entertainment it was remarked that R— was pre-occupied, and apparently indifferent to all that was passing around him. Although a discerning observer might have marked the agitation of his eye as it glanced by turns, to the ashy paleness of the fair brow that graced the festive board, or the flushed and disturbed countenance of his favoured rival.

The dining-room opened with glass doors to a beautiful lawn, redolent with the rich perfumes of rare exotics; beyond it were citron and orange groves, leading by various paths to a summer-house, in which the young English girl had wept away the hours of many a summer's morn, since she had been transplanted from her native land to the licentious shores of Portugal.

The state of society at Lisbon was too lax to admit of the presence of one lady imposing much restraint upon the male party assembled at Mr. R——'s, and soon the wine flowed freely round, and tongues—careless of being listened to—united in one general din, the usual attendant upon conviviality.

Amidst the general festivity, the absence of the lady—which took place soon after the removal of the cloth—produced no observation; and yet there were two by whom it had not passed unmarked. With well-feigned indifference Mr. R—— appeared to turn all attention from the side of the table where his rival was seated, and to be wholly engrossed by the conversation of Captain Tyler, of the Artillery, who sat next to him.

The bait took; and in another moment a vacant chair showed the absence of Captain S——r. With a convulsive start, R—— rose from the table, and advancing to the open window leading to the lawn, lingered for a few seconds, as if to cool his fevered brow with the evening breeze. Another moment, and the loud report of a pistol was heard. "Great God! he has shot her!" was the first exclamation of the frenzied man.

A second report followed almost instantaneously the first, and the whole party, aroused to the sense of their host's position by the words that had escaped him, pressed upon his steps, in the direction of the summer-house, the scene of the morning's conference, and as R—— too keenly felt the most probable spot for the evening's assignation.

The lovers were indeed there, but murder and suicide were there also! The misguided pair lay weltering in their blood at a short distance from each other; and as the maddened R—— knelt in piteous agony by the side of the bleeding corpse of her, who had been so fatally dear to him, his self-accusations were dreadful witnesses to the unholy connexion that had existed between them, and which had forged the first link in the chain of guilt that now lay completed before him.

The whole attention of the party had been riveted on the heart-rending scene that followed, and R——'s vain attempt to revive into consciousness the murdered girl; and it was only when the inanimate body was about to be removed, that it was seen that the murderer's hand had failed to complete the crime of suicide. The ball had only torn away the scalp, producing a momentary insensibility; but returning reason brought with it all the horrors of the past and present, and rising unobserved, he rushed from the scene with all his remaining strength. The unhappy man reached the dressing-room of Mr. R—— before the alarm could be given, and had drawn a razor across his throat, before the weapon could be wrested from his grasp.

The mortal sufferings of this wretched individual were not terminated by this second attempt at self-destruction, as if an avenging hand stayed life for the greater expiation of so great a crime. Captain S——r was removed, in a shocking state, to the criminal prison at Lisbon; and as many difficulties arose in bringing an English subject to justice, in a foreign country, the unhappy man remained for a year and a half in close confinement, experiencing all the horrors of mind and body that can fall to the lot of humanity.

At the expiration of that time, he was sent in irons to England in a man-of-war, and consigned to Newgate; here again a long delay occurred, as many legal points were to be taken into consideration. Arising firstly, from the crime having been committed abroad; secondly, from the difficulty of collecting witnesses to prove it; and thirdly, from the long interval that had taken place since its commission.

These obstacles were, however, overcome; and the wretched prisoner, after an incarceration of more than two years, was brought to trial—Lord Ellenborough presiding as judge. There was little difficulty in proving that the hand of Captain S——r had deprived of life the woman whom he loved; but there was one who could have proved, by a document in his possession, that she was not only a consenting party, but had provided laudanum for herself and lover, in the event of being frustrated in their design. This essential witness had feelings of deep revenge to satisfy, and withheld the testimony that would have saved his hated rival from an ignominious death.

Lord Ellenborough summed up the case, and in his charge to the jury, placed mercy as a mite in the balance, against the necessity of "proving to the Portuguese nation, that murder was not to be committed by British subjects with impunity." This was the spirit of the Judge's charge; and, as might have been expected, the jury returned a verdict of "Guilty." Poor S—r was hanged at the Old Bailey at the close of 1814.

Chapter 19

To the Front

Like the overwhelming waters of a spring-tide, rose the excited feelings of all classes of society at the fearful occurrence recorded in the preceding chapter, bursting over the landmarks, both of charity and of truth, in the different versions, fabricated and circulated, concerning it; but, like other things, it was destined to occupy no more than a single line in the page of novelties, and a few days afterwards, the public mind was equally interested and excited by a diverting official manifesto from General Peacock, the Commandant, expressive of that worthy officer's incurable enmity to the crowing of cocks, and enforcing, under pain of penalties, the destruction of all such obnoxious birds within an allotted distance from his residence.

The consequence of this proclamation was a fearful massacre among the chanticleers. Every hen in the neighbourhood of the Commandant was widowed, and the feathered population brought to a diminished ratio, that would have satisfied even a Malthus or a Martineau. Some other eccentricities were recorded of this military functionary, whose long sojourn at Lisbon, far from the noise and tumult of the camp, may perhaps account for the dislike of being disturbed by a morning *reveillé*.

It certainly was whispered that not a few of the officers bore to the Commandant about as much friendship as he had evinced towards his neighbours, the cocks, and a young Irishman, smarting under some insult, imaginary or otherwise, adopted a very original method of revenging himself on the author.

Each morning the Commandant, attended by a Portuguese Adjutant, who neither spoke nor understood one word of English, made the rounds of the different quarters of the city, prying into holes and corners for the chief purpose, as it was asserted, of looking out for squalls. The Irish officer dodged his steps until he found him in a favourable position for his project, away from all English ears, and then approaching with a reverential manner, he said, with the softest tone of voice he could assume, "Colonel, you are without an exception the veriest bully in the service."

"Sir," vociferated the Commandant, foaming with rage, "what the devil do you mean."

"I mean, Colonel," repeated the young man, lowering his voice still more, and bending cap in hand most respectfully, "that by G—d, you are a bully, and detested by every one in the garrison."

The Commandant vainly turned his face of wrathful indignation from the speaker to the Adjutant. The latter could only wonder at the violence exhibited by a superior officer to a subaltern, whose gentle demeanour, and almost obsequious bearing, seemed to demand so different a return. Choking with rage and vociferations, the Commandant returned upon his steps towards his official residence, accompanied, part of the way, by his tormentor, who still in the mildest tone of subjection, and keeping at a proper distance in the rear, on the line with the Adjutant, applied some more choice epithets for the digestion of the Colonel before taking leave of him.

The best part of this story, which made the rounds of every mess-table, lay in the impossibility of the young Irishman being called to account for his impudence. He was placed under arrest immediately, by order of the Commandant, but when it became necessary to substantiate the charge, there was found to be no witnesses against him. The Commandant's testimony alone, could not of course be received, and the Adjutant was only able, and with truth, to affirm that the mild voice and respectful bearing of the young officer, was answered with loud, and violent language, and gestures by the Commandant. The lucky fellow was, therefore, released from arrest, and gained great commendation for having placed his assurance under the safe-guard of such good precautionary measures.

Having received orders to join the allied army on the frontiers, as chief officer of the Field Train department, I started as soon as the necessary arrangements could be completed of purchasing baggage mules and horses for the march. With much difficulty, and only by paying a high price, I obtained three mules, and three saddle horses; for which number I was entitled to forage by the regulations of the service; and after superintending the fitting of the pack-saddles, and the accurate poising thereon of canteens, camp-bedding, and other essentials for campaigning, I bade a final farewell to Lisbon, mounted on my English horse, one of the few that had survived the stormy passage across the Bay of Biscay in the transport *Cora*.

The third day's journey brought me to Abrantes, where several officers had halted waiting for a sufficient reinforcement to brave the dangers of the *banditti* on the march to Castello Branco. The roads in the neighbourhood of Nizza were infested by these ruffians, and only a few days previously, two of our officers had been plundered of their baggage and mules, stripped of every shred of covering, and tied up to a tree with an ingenious skilfulness that baffled all their exertions to release themselves. In this deplorable state, they must inevitably have perished, but for the timely assistance brought to them by one of their muleteers who had escaped.

Our party, however, soon mustered strong enough to bid defiance to these gleaners of the highways, and marshalling ourselves and servants in a kind of military array, we pursued our march without molestation to Castello Branco.

In this town, I had been quartered in 1808, for a period of six weeks enjoying the hospitality and unbounded kindness of the Portuguese family, where I was fortunate enough to be billeted. My host was one of the best of men, and apparently the happiest; a wife, and two pretty daughters formed his home circle, and each night he indulged his kind heart and hospitable feelings by inviting our young officers to the reunion of his own friends and neighbours. Music and dancing wiled the hours away, and the happy looks of the young were reflected in the benevolent countenance of our host.

At this, my second visit to Castello Branco, I sought the once splendid residence of my old friend. The outward walls were blackened with smoke; the window frames torn with violence from their sockets, while the dismantled rooms and fire-stained ceilings, spoke of scenes of which the tongue dreaded to ask the solution.

Between the spacious apartments, the partitions we destroyed, giving them the appearance of vast neglected storerooms, or of a building that had been gutted by fire.

Pursuing my way through this devastation, I arrived at a detached part of the house, that had formerly served as offices for menials, and guided by the not unsavoury odour of *"acho,"* reached a small kitchen, in which a woman, whom I instantly recognised as my *ci-devant* hostess, in spite of her premature old age, and care-worn countenance, was preparing food over a *brazerio*. In a low chair near to her was seated what appeared to me the ghost of my old friend Don Jozé. "*Virgem beatissima*" exclaimed the reduced matron, as she almost threw down the little *casserol* she held, to greet me with the sunny kindness of other days; but the vacant eye of Don Jozé wandered over my face without a ray of recognition. Grief and terror had long since destroyed the powers of his once vigorous mind, and when I heard the tale of woe the mother had to tell, it was no longer to be wondered at that the father's nerves had given way. Since I had seen them, they had known and felt the ravages of war.

Massena's advancing and retreating army; the pursued and pursuing forces of the British and Portuguese, had in turn cursed the land with famine and desolation. Every species of violence had followed in their steps, and every house in Castello Branco bore traces of plunder and conflagration.

On the near approach of the French army in 1810, the two daughters of my host fled in terror with the retreating army, in the hopes of reaching Lisbon. Those only who have witnessed the relaxed discipline of troops so circumstanced, can understand the insults and pollutions to which women are exposed. One of these helpless girls died on the road. The other reached Lisbon; but had never since revisited the home of her childhood. This sad evidence of the atrocities of war oppressed me like a waking night-mare during the remainder of the march.

The village of Malhada de Sourda had been chosen for the head-quarters of the Artillery Engineers, and Paymaster-General's department. It was situated two leagues from the fortress of Almeida, and only half a league from Frenada, a small village occupied by Lord Wellington and his staff. There was not a more miserable place on the face of the earth than Malhada de Sourda. The sterility of the surrounding country was as remarkable as the poverty and filth of the village which, however, afforded stabling for the horses and mules, and this was an object of such primary importance, that it compensated for the wretched accommodation of the officers.

My billet was, in point of fact, a capacious stable, with a corresponding loft above. Into the former I turned my animals, and into the latter myself, albeit my first night of possession did not pass wholly free of alarm. Numerous were the holes and apertures by which I was surrounded, and having inadvertently stepped into instead of over a cavity in the floor, I found myself suddenly transferred to the company of the mules below. They being equally astonished at my unexpected intrusion, let fly their legs in every direction to my no small jeopardy, as it may be surmised that I was only buff proof against hostilities.

At length, however, I managed to beat an honourable retreat, though not by the way I came, and the following day, not only were all holes filled up, so as to keep me in, and the rain out, but what with the assistance of canteens and camp furniture, not forgetting a partition, effected by one of his Majesty's hair-cloths, I managed to transform my loft into a respectable bed-room and dining-room.

It is astonishing to what good profit experience is turned by the soldier. Each campaign adds to his stock of resources, and this it is that in after life makes an old soldier so efficient a personage. In most cases he is a good cook, a good carpenter, and even builder; with his wits always ready to answer whatever demands may be made upon them.

At the end of the village was a monastery occupied by Colonel Fisher, who had recently arrived from Lisbon to succeed Colonel Robe in the command of the Artillery—the latter officer having returned to England in consequence of his wounds—Colonel May, the Assistant Adjutant-General of the Artillery-Brigade, Major Woodyear, and two Adjutants, Major Frazer commanding the Horse Artillery, the Paymaster-General, Stanhope Hunter, and his department, as well as the officers of my corps, the Field Train, were studded about in whatever hovels the village afforded, and wretched enough they were. In this rural retreat we were cantoned six months, during which period, what we wanted in comforts, was made up in good fellowship, for a more jovial and happy set of fellows never breathed than were thrown together at Malhada de Sourda.

Beyond the rations issued by the Commissary at Frenada, our larders had but few supplies, although occasionally a couple of mules would be dispatched to Coimbra, and return laden with a freight of wine, cigars, and other creature comforts, that tended to prolong our evening sittings until cock crow in the morning. One of the chief agitators of these orgies was a personage of no small importance at head-quarters.

The well-known Tom Marsden was a character that may be summed up under the denomination of a "gentleman horse-dealer;" one of a race nearly annihilated by the combined associations of steam and rail-roads. The Duke of York had specially appointed him purveyor of horse-flesh to the army, which involved the duty of filling up all casualties of horses and mules, that might occur in the Artillery; supplying chargers and baggage mules to those who stood in need of them, &c. This situation Tom filled with admirable efficiency, and possessed moreover the advantage of being the very personification of his vocation—was up to a trick or two; knew how to oblige a friend with a good horse, or give a "roarer" to one less favoured, and withal was a prime favourite with Lord Wellington; dining frequently with his Lordship at Frenada.

Tom Marsden may be said to have united in his person the offices of Master of the Horse and Master of the Buck-hounds. He hunted the pack kept at head-quarters, and managed the horses, dogs, and riders, with equal boldness and success. When others were in scarcity, Tom was always abundantly supplied with every thing, and as he exercised most laudably the virtues of hospitality, his quarters were always full to overflowing. A large placard over his door announced, "that gentlemen honouring Tom Marsden with a visit, were expected to bring their chair and drinking cup," an order which I have seen obeyed with alacrity by upwards of forty officers assembled there.

Upon such occasions, Tom would preface the forthcoming work by a pathetic address to his guests, praying that wherever he might "fall", there he might be laid out on a ration of straw, near to his favourite dog "Beauty." It generally happened that Tom's "fall" took place at a comparatively early hour, after which it became a matter of honour to conduct his obsequies, in strict conformity with his directions. Stretched out on straw, with his dog "Beauty" by his side, Tom would lay, until vitality and time had worked together in his favour; a combination that rarely took place before a late hour on the following day.

Until men of the present generation are placed in precisely the same position as those of the last, it will be impossible to determine upon the advantages to be derived in time of war, from *Hydropathy* on the internal system. As far as regards the moral tenue within the circle of home duties, there can be little doubt but that father Mathew has been the means of preserving many a home hearth from wrangling, and even may have helped on some of his votaries, to claim the flitch of bacon which, of old, rewarded the connubial bliss, that no angry word, for one long twelve-month, had disturbed. But in time of war! who can remember the first exhilarating touch of Old Lamego, in the days of the Peninsula, on the outward man, without remembering also that it fired him into friendship for his comrades—zeal for his country—love for unprotected woman, and sent his ardour for distinction flying like a Congreve rocket through the air?

I doubt much if a single drop of water, at such moments as I have described would not have been attended with consequences as fatal as putting on damp linen when under the influence of a raging fever. Alas! that excuses should be necessary for acquaintance with so pleasant a fellow as Bacchus; but it is so, and that reminds me of the best apology I ever heard for becoming on too intimate a footing with him. "I mean to get drunk," said Sir A. D., upon an occasion of great conviviality, "in order to make the fleas drunk; having discovered that after the first bite they fall powerless, and leave me to repose in peace the rest of the night." Certain it is that those men of the olden times, would have stared "pretty considerably," as Jonathan says, at the full allowance to which members of the modern clubs restrict themselves—*half a pint of Marsala.*

During this period of repose in winter quarters, the reorganization of the army was carried on with great activity. Reinforcements of cavalry, infantry, and artillery had been sent from England. Tents were, for the first time, provided for the troops; a pontoon-train had been prepared, and an improved system established for the protection and conveyance of the ammunition for the allied army.

Upon the Field Train department devolved the practical carrying out of these new arrangements, and it became a matter of much consideration to select from this corps, officers of sufficient experience and judgment, in whom to confide responsibilities of so important a nature; but this selection once made, it would be indeed a false humility to leave untold the gallant exertions and admirable conduct they exhibited during the whole period of their services in the Peninsula. It may be, with truth, asserted, that to these zealous and efficient officers, the Anglo-Portuguese army, consisting of upwards of seventy thousand men, was deeply indebted during the active and brilliant campaigns of 1813 and 1814.[1]

The duties of this department in the field were at all times most arduous and responsible, but especially so during the continuance of a long-contested engagement, when the least delay, or the issuing of a wrong calibre of ammunition, would have been productive of fatal results to the success of the day. There are many reasons that prevented the Field Train from assuming the conspicuous position in the service that its merits warranted. In the first place, the department wore the uniform of the Royal Artillery, which latter corps was in consequence often supposed to have performed the duties that belonged, and were executed exclusively by the Field Train, and from the same cause the merit of such services was, in many instances, wrested from that department.

Again: The circumstance of the Commanding Officer of Artillery being the organ of communication between the head of the Field Train and the Commander-in-Chief, took from the Field Train officer, the appearance of being what he really was—the sole responsible individual for the execution of one of the most important duties of the service—important, inasmuch as upon the efficiency of war material, and its prompt distribution in the face of the enemy, may depend the fate of an entire campaign.

My duties, as the chief officer of the Field Train, were, therefore, so regulated as to bring me in daily communication with the Com-

---

1. The late Sir Alexander Dickson, one of the most able, experienced, and distinguished officers, whose opinion upon military matters has never been disputed, bore testimony to the merits of the Field Train in a letter addressed to the author, February, 1816, in which he says—
"I beg to express the sense I entertain of the valuable services afforded to the army throughout the war in the Peninsula by the Field Train department under your orders."

mandant of Artillery, who, during our stay at Malhada de Sourda, was Colonel Fisher—an officer who had seen but little service beyond the routine of garrison duty at Lisbon; where he was much liked and respected for his many kind and gentlemanly qualities—to these, however, nature had not added the requisites for a rough and ready soldier, and it was soon perceptible that to throw the last warm tints over the masterly landscape he was finishing, or to shut himself up with the companionship of some favourite poet, was far more congenial to the accomplished mind of Colonel Fisher, than the matter of fact enumeration and minute inspection of articles required for the completion of a park of artillery.

Not that Colonel Fisher lacked the becoming spirit of a soldier, or neglected any of the preparatory details imposed upon his position, for the campaign that was about to open; but there is an immense difference between the elderly officer who respectably adheres to the line of duty laid down for him, with the same methodical precision that he would use on the barrack field at Woolwich, and one who possesses energy of mind and vigour of body to set difficulties at defiance, defeat stratagem by stratagem, grapple with adverse circumstances, and even turn them to good account. Such an officer Colonel Fisher was not—such an officer Colonel Dickson was.

If proofs were wanting of the rapid judgment with which the Commander-in-Chief marked out those who, by their peculiar talents, were adapted for the special uses he designed to make of them, none could be more positive than the selection of Colonel Dickson for the command of the Artillery.

It is true that private interests and feelings were to be wounded in the selection; but Lord Wellington rightly refused to place them for a moment in the scale with the good of the public service, and Colonel Dickson was called from Covalao, where he was attached to the reserve artillery, to supersede Colonel Fisher, and by doing so, to take—in direct violation of military usages—command of several officers, senior to himself in the corps. In the meantime, it must be said that the movement which metamorphosed Colonel Fisher to an invalided officer on sick leave at Lisbon, and Colonel Dickson into his efficient substitute, was marked with more of rapidity than the inactivity of five long winter months need have rendered necessary.

A few days before the opening of that march that led from the frontiers of Portugal to the soil of France, beginning in hope and ending in triumph, Colonel Fisher was summoned to render his official reports at head-quarters. Everything was at that time prepared at his own quarters in the monastery for the ensuing departure. The mules, the canteens and cooking apparatus, the tent and camp-bedstead, in short all the campaigning paraphernalia of a commanding officer's equipage. The interview with Lord Wellington was of short duration—a few minutes sufficed to explain to him that his appearance indicated a prostration of health, which the air of Lisbon would probably restore, and it may literally be said that he returned to Malhada de Sourda with his dismissal in his pocket. Two days afterwards, Colonel Fisher was on his way to Lisbon, and a few hours after his departure, the new Commandant of Artillery appeared among us.

An officer who has obtained so distinguished a name as Sir Alexander Dickson, requires little of description, but it may be stated, as characteristic of the man, that on his arrival, he appeared in an old and very shabby Portuguese uniform—which he wore in virtue of his rank in the Portuguese service. This dress he never changed during the whole campaign, and by this admirable display of tact—which by the undiscerning might have passed even without notice—escaped the feelings of jealous envy that would have rankled in the hearts of many, had he worn the British uniform while in the command of his senior officers.

CHAPTER 20

Into Spain Once More

The comradeship of military life at Malhada de Sourda knew none of those distinctions of castes that divide the feelings and affections of men under the ordinary circumstances of life. The pride of birth, and even of royal birth, was forgotten in the nobler pride of restoring freedom to nations, and peace to the world; and in this sacred cause the fraternity of arms was substituted for the distinctions of rank.

No brighter example, in this respect, could have been given than by the Prince of Orange, heir to the sovereignty of a kingdom and descended from a long line of illustrious ancestors. This Prince, although young in years, sought to perpetuate his noble name by the achievements of his own good sword. Mild, gentlemanly and submissive to his superiors in military rank, his daring courage and gallantry in the battle-field were to be surpassed by none. Wherever there was most danger there was to be found the Prince of Orange; his unaffected and kind demeanour won him universal esteem and regard; and it was remarked by all how anxiously he endeavoured to merge the rank of Prince into the position of a soldier.

Among many instances recorded of his amiable demeanour in the camp, one little trait cannot here be out of place. I was returning from an inspection of the brigades of field ammunition on a dreary winter's evening at Malhada de Sourda. It was growing dusk. I was late for dinner, and my English mare was pushing along rather too briskly for the state of the roads, when a large stone in the path stopped her progress, and caused her to roll over me in a manner that was anything but agreeable. With true feminine tact, however, she contrived to get on her legs again, without inflicting any serious injury on my person; but the fall had frightened her, and off she galloped out of sight and hearing. At the same moment, a young officer came up on horseback, and finding that I was not hurt, he started off with the greatest good humour, in pursuit of the fugitive. A considerable time elapsed before he returned, leading by the bridle my horse, which he had caught after a chase of more than two miles.

The young officer was the Prince of Orange.

General orders having named the twenty second of May for the head quarters to break up at Frenada, we bade adieu to Malhada de Sourda on that day, and fell in with Lord Wellington and his staff as they were crossing the little rivulet that separates Portugal from Spain. The morning was clear and bright, and the sun shone gaily on the fair scene of our route. In the distance were visible the battlements and church spires of Ciudad Rodrigo.

On our right lay the ruins of Fort Conception, and on our left the Agueda flowed smoothly through the broad plains of Leon. It was a gallant train of horsemen that entered at that moment on the territory of Spain.

Lord Wellington's staff ranked in its numbers the scions of some of the noblest houses in Europe, who were as eager to share in the privations and hardships of the soldiers, as to share their laurels on the field of battle. The Prince of Orange, Lord March, Colonel Gordon, the Marquis of Worcester, Lord Fitzroy Somerset, Colonels Burgh and Canning, with some others, formed the personal staff of the Commander-in-Chief. The rest of the staff was composed of the Quarter-Master-General, Sir George Murray —an officer to whom was ascribed the importance of being the only individual of the army received into the unlimited confidence of Lord Wellington—the Adjutant-General the commanding officers of Artillery and Engineers, and the heads of departments. Orderlies and led horses brought up the rear.

This brilliant cavalcade, mounted on high-bred English horses, to which a long season of repose and good feeding had imparted spirits so joyous, that they seemed to participate in the hopes and feelings of their masters, had more the appearance of a party bent on some agreeable exploring excursion, than one composed of the directing and responsible chiefs of an army on the march to scenes of war and bloodshed. That army had been some days in motion, for Graham with upwards of forty thousand men, and a pontoon train, had already crossed the Douro, and traversed the almost impassable roads of the Tras-os-Montes: Hill, with nearly thirty thousand men, was advancing towards the Tormes, and thus, exclusive of the Spaniards, Wellington was at the head of an army consisting of upwards of seventy thousand men[1] in the highest state of discipline and equipment, with every requisite supply, both of ammunition and military stores.

On the fifth day after quitting Portugal, we arrived in front of Salamanca, then occupied by a detachment of about four thousand of the enemy, commanded by General Vallette. At a distance of about a mile, Lord Wellington halted, and dismounting, as did his staff, seated himself, surrounded by his officers, on a mound that overlooked the ancient city that lay before us, glaring in the fierce rays of a mid-day sun.

The head of the light division on our right was seen advancing towards the river, over which the bridge had been barricaded by the French. Guided by a Spanish peasant, they reached a ford, which they succeeded in crossing; while, at the same moment, a troop of horse artillery and some squadrons of cavalry forded the river above them with equal success.

The enemy perceiving the danger of being cut off by the only road left open to him, commenced a retreat, but from some unaccountable delay that occurred in the town, the march was protracted until it was too late to preserve the rear-guard from the attack of our troops. The result was attended with considerable loss to the French, and six of their guns with ammunition, fell into our hands.

As these first shots proclaimed the presence of the British troops in Spain, it was a spectacle of no small interest to behold Lord Wellington, carelessly seated overlooking the scene, and too confidant in the result to feel anxiety. He talked and laughed in high good humour, either with his officers, or three or four of the peasants, who in their

1. British Cavalry	8,500
British Infantry	37,000
Portuguese Cavalry	1,800
Portuguese Infantry	25,000
Spaniards, under Morrillo, Mina, Julian, Sanchez, &c	25,000

dark cloaks and slouched hats grouped round him to communicate whatever intelligence they knew, or guessed at, of the enemy's movements. No sooner had the French disappeared, than the inhabitants of Salamanca rushed to disencumber the bridge from the barricades, and a passage to the town being thus opened, Lord Wellington mounted his horse. It was a signal for all to do the same, and in less than half an hour, the head-quarters of the army entered Salamanca, amidst the ringing of bells and joyous acclamations of the inhabitants.

In the fine old city of Salamanca our head-quarters tarried three days to afford time for the columns on the right to cross the Tormes and advance upon the Duero and the Esla, where the whole of the allied army formed a junction. During the stay of head-quarters, the enthusiasm shown by the Spaniards in favour of the British was very great. The male inhabitants offered to us without reserve all that they possessed, and the fairer portion, if less inclusive in their proffers, were not backward in their demonstrations, that were nipped in the bud by the hastening hand of time. In this respect the French had the advantage over us; they had made the most of their opportunities during the long winter months they had held possession of the city, and report whispered that in spite of the patriotism of Salamanca's fair daughters, there had been some deserters from the pure faith to Cupid's banner.

On the day succeeding our arrival, there occurred an incident which certainly determined the possibility of such report being true. A group of British officers were lounging through the corridor of the ancient Plaza, when a crowd flying before a troop of mounted *partidas,* burst into the square. All eyes turned in the direction of this unexpected movement, which the excited gesticulations and vociferous language of the populace were sufficient to explain.

In the centre of the horsemen, who were endeavouring to shelter him from the fury of the crowd, was a young French sergeant-major, whose soiled dress and bleeding forehead told the tale of his having been already very roughly handled. The mule he rode was almost in as pitiable a state as himself, for many a lump of mud and dirt, intended for the rider, had alighted on the rough coat of the animal, which hung its head and flapped its long ears at the pillory exhibition it was undergoing. Upon another mule, in as bad a plight, was seated a French drummer boy. The appearance of this youth seemed to excite the passions of the mob to a pitch of frenzy. In vain the *partidas* closed in to protect him from the storm without. The increasing pressure forced an opening to him, and dragging the soldier boy from his mule, they of French *galanterie,* that the young Sergeant major showed himself more than willing, by the sacrifice of his own life, to avert the indignities offered to his "ladye love." However, the truth of the French proverb: *"Contre la force il n'y a pas de résistance"* was here fully made manifest; and the author of these calamities was not only doomed to see his victim carried off with the certainty that her young days would be devoted to the unearthly tenement of a cloister, but also to feel that his own career of hope and honourable ambition was exchanged for the mournful existence of a prisoner.

On the twenty-ninth head-quarters quitted Salamanca by the route of Zamora and Toro. Both of these places had been evacuated by the French only a few hours before we reached them. Indeed, our advance was so close upon their heels, as to give occasion for a brilliant little affair near Morales, on the 2nd of June, between the Hussar brigade under Colonel Grant, and some squadrons of the enemy, in which the latter sustained severe loss in killed and prisoners.

At Palencia, we staid two days, and found this town crowded with our own troops, and Spanish horsemen, which caused great difficulty in obtaining billets. My lot was cast in an old fashioned building, affording, however, what was of immense importance on a march—stabling for the horses and mules; but, no sooner were the animals unloaded, and beginning to feel the agreeable difference between repose and labour, than an orderly entered the large, half-furnished apartment in which I was probably enjoying the same comparison, and announced the arrival of General O'Lawlor—an officer of Irish extraction in the Spanish service, attached to Lord Wellington's staff—who, with his mules and horses, was waiting to be accommodated in my quarters.

As the orders were imperative to turn out, on all occasions, for general-officers, there was no alternative, but to desire that my animals might be removed to make place for the General's; an order that must have appeared very unjust to poor brutes, ignorant of the nature and qualities of military precedence.

The General himself was a kind and courteous man, and offered, with a soldier's frankness, to share his billet with me; but Spanish mules and horses are less accommodating in each other's society, and as there was only room in the stable for the new comers, I declined the offer.

As ill-luck would have it, the rain poured down in torrents, and it was a hard thing upon the servants and muleteers, who were just beginning to cook their rations, to turn out again to the irksome task of re-loading animals that had been just unloaded. The necessity, however, was peremptory, and we had the benefit of a two hours drenching, before another billet could be procured.

On the following morning, at an early hour, I was roused from my slumbers by a loud "*halloa,*" that rung from powerful lungs, followed by a volley of oaths, uttered in pure Milesian accent:

"Och, Jasus!—stop thief. The thundering blackguard has hooked away my watch. Stop the rascal, can't ye!—'till I report him to the Gineral."

I threw open my window; a party of Spanish lancers were galloping past, each in his turn bestowing a jeering laugh upon a head that was thrust out between the iron bars of a window grating, immediately beneath my own, ornamented with a large-sized white cotton night-cap.

As each horseman passed in succession, a laughing *"carracho ombre'* was launched into the enraged countenance that peeped from beneath the cotton night-cap, until one, more waggish than the rest, slackening his steed's pace, and seizing a favourable opportunity, gently insinuated the point of his lance into the thick fold of the cotton appendage, and, to my dismay—for I thought the head was with it, whirled high in air the trophy that his good lance had won. A growl of indignation from the head that rapidly withdrew behind the bars, assured me that it had not been included in the booty carried off and I hastened down stairs to ascertain to what luckless wight it might belong.

I found a young Irish officer possessed the exclusive right of claiming the pate that had been so unceremoniously denuded of its covering, and it was with no small difficulty that I could preserve my gravity, as he endeavoured, as intelligibly as his emotion would permit, to enlighten me as to the cause of my first acquaintance with his white-capped head.

By his own account, he had, previously to going to bed, hung up his watch, "a fine ould family watch," with gold chain and seals, upon a brass nail near the window, which he left open—as the night was warm. The distant tramp of horses' feet in the morning had roused him from the depth of sleep into that visionary state, when home, and home relics; and time, past and present, press on the un-steadied brain; perhaps with the floating thought of time, came in concatenation that of the mechanism that marks time; be that as it may, the Irishman declared that he thought he saw his watch, "the ould family watch," flying from the wall on which he hung it! He sat up in bed—it was no dream!—horror chased from his brain the mists that had collected there, and reality offered to his straining eyes a horseman's lance, bearing through the iron bars the valued object.

The poor fellow could gain no redress for this audacious act, although more witnesses than one deposed that a Spanish lancer, tempted by the glittering bauble, dangling within his reach, did, with a dexterity, only to be equalled by his comrade's dislodgement of the cotton night-cap, transfer it from its resting place, via the aperture of the iron grating, into the safer custody of his own pocket.

CHAPTER 21

Towards Vittoria

On leaving Palencia we proceeded in the direction of Burgos, and crossing the rivers Carrion and Pisuerga, arrived in front of that city on the 11th of June. Lord Wellington had now again before him the fortress, that had so completely, by baffling his attempts, exposed the weakness of the means he had brought against it. The French had here assembled in considerable force, and on the 12th, Sir Rowland Hill attacked the advanced guard under General Reille, strongly posted on the heights of Hermosa, and forced it to retire upon the main body. Early on the following morning, a tremendous explosion, that seemed to shake the foundations of the neighbouring hills, announced that some great event had taken place, and when the smoke had cleared away, it was seen that the enemy had destroyed the works that he was no longer able to defend, and had retired beyond the river Arlençon.

Almost immediately after the evacuation of the fortress by the French, Lord Wellington, eager to inspect the defences that had defied the attacks of his troops, rode into the town, with the principal officers of his staff; dismounting from their horses, the party proceeded to the dismantled ramparts, little aware that a danger menaced, which had it reached them, might have closed the campaign with a rapidity as startling as the explosion that destroyed the stronghold of the enemy.

Scarcely had Lord Wellington and his party entered the lines of defence, when a squadron of the enemy's cavalry was seen retiring within three hundred yards of the town, partly concealed by the sloping ground. If these horsemen had obtained a glimpse of one of the red coats upon the batteries, or received information of the prize within their grasp, nothing is more certain than that they would have swept round to the front of the fortress, and in the twinkling of an eye carried off Lord Wellington and the most valuable members of his staff, prisoners of war! On such a chance as this, may the fate of nations depend!

We remained encamped two days at Villa-diego, in the neighbourhood of Burgos, and then resumed our march towards the Ebro. On the night preceding our descent to that river, we halted at Massa. It frequently happened that in order to escape from the confusion and delay, in getting billets, and the tormenting annoyance of the fleas with which they generally abounded, those among us who had tents, pitched them in some sequestered spot, in the manner of the wandering Arabs.

On the night in question, I had selected an inviting green nook for my repose, *a la belle étoile*. Colonel Dickson, and his Brigade-Major, Woodyear, had added their provisions to my stock, and after a pleasant pic-nic supper, we retired to our respective tents, congratulating ourselves on the plentiful repast nature had provided for our baggage-mules, without the assistance of his Majesty's Commissariat. They were tethered to stakes driven through the long grass near to our tents, and we believed it next to impossible that the hand of depredation could make its way to that noiseless and secluded spot, although even then, we were tolerably well acquainted with the character of the Spaniard, who has a relish for theft, which is only equalled by the delight he feels in laughing in your face, when he has robbed you.

During the war, the sale of mules and horses to the officers of the army, was carried on by the Spaniards in a manner very ludicrous. It often happened that a horse, bought in the morning, was stolen at night by some peasant employed by the seller. In a few days, the same horse was sure to be brought back again for sale to the rightful owner, by another party, in league with the first, who would swear by all the saints in the calendar that the animal had arrived that very morning from a distant part of Spain.

I had a very favourite baggage-mule named Jenny; she was worth her weight in gold on a long day's march, and would take the lead with an air of reproachful contempt, if others, less zealous than herself, stumbled, or slackened pace on the wearisome route.

Jenny was a character—and a female character of course—uniting coquetry to constancy; and gentleness to the most provoking obstinacy, whenever the opportunity occurred. To attempt with Jenny, the style usually adopted by the muleteers, of adding to her encumbrances by vaulting on her well-poised pack-saddle, was certain exposure to a kick that Jenny alone could inflict, and which warned the offender to abstain, for ever after, from similar familiarities. But if a gentle touch of the neck, a soft whistle, implored her to help the tired muleteer on his way, Jenny would come to a stand still, and with a knowing toss of the head, grant the favour that she refused to violence. Such was Jenny; a favourite with all, and it was with no small care that the stake which we thought ensured her safety, was driven into the green turf, on which our tents were pitched.

The following morning, by dawn of day, we were on the alert. Nothing can be more exciting than the early start after the night's bivouack. The hurried breakfast; the mounting on horseback, just as the first light of day gleams upon the magic dissolution of one's temporary home. The striking of the tents, and the packing of the luggage on its respective bearers. It was this last operation, which on that morning revealed the serious loss I had sustained. Jenny had disappeared. In vain her native attendant, like a second Orpheus, made the rocks resound with her name. She answered not, and our progress onwards admitted of no delay.

Nothing can be imagined more beautiful than was the descent to the Ebro, by a mountain pass of more than a league in length that led to the valley of Quintana. The staff officers forming the head-quarters of the army, dismounted from their horses, and led them down the rocky path. Lord Wellington did the same. On the left were to be seen, sometimes emerging from the morning mist, that still hung upon the mountains, and sometimes from behind the jutting rocks, the columns of the several brigades of Hill's corps, winding down the zig-zag roads below us; smiling plains, thickly studded with villages and vineyards, lay stretched along the valley. The heat was intolerable, and those who have suffered from the darting rays of a southern sun, can alone understand the avidity with which we sought the shelter of some cherry trees that lay on our sloping route.

It may be questioned if any one of the gorgeous banquets, at which the Commander-in-Chief has since been an honoured guest, has afforded him a pleasure equal to that he felt, as seated on horseback under the bending branches of those fruit trees, he cooled his parched lips with their refreshing fruit.

There are moments in a soldier's life, that by their very contrast to all he has ever experienced before, stand as time-marks in his memory, in after years. Such moments still cling tenaciously to the cell, in which past joys are registered, and I should think there were few old soldiers who do not, even at this distant period connect, by some fanciful concatenation of the mind, all that is brightest in the present, with their campaigning recollections.

An old military friend of mine never sees the early sun struggling with the mists of his highland home, without recalling his thrilling feelings in Spain and Portugal, when, at dawn of day, the drum of the *reveillé* roused him from his tent. The mists of a southern clime were seldom long in yielding to the warmth of a southern sun, and as the beautiful panorama rose gradually to view, displaying, in its progress, first the military array of tents and armed men, then, the bright landscape of richly cultivated valleys and rivers, and lastly, the cloud-topped hill, it left an impression that even now sheds a halo over the darker sky, and less brilliant luminary of his native land.

The passage of the Ebro was hailed with delight and enthusiasm by the troops. The army had now marched for a period of thirty days; during which it had traversed mountains that hitherto had been considered impassable for Artillery, and crossed broad and rapid rivers, by means of the Pontoon bridges that had been prepared previously to the march. To complete this triumph of discipline and judicious arrangements over the stern and frowning obstacles that nature presented, it must be stated that the army was in as perfect a state of health and efficiency, as when it quitted winter quarters in Portugal.

The allied army was now encamped on the smiling banks of the Ebro. Head-quarters were established at the beautiful little village of Quincoces de Yuso. It was a stirring scene. In the distance, to the left, were the long lines of tents belonging to Hill's corps; their white tops peeping through the green foliage that shaded them, while the gay colours of the soldiers' uniforms, and their shining arms and accoutrements glittered in the sun's rays, and mingled with the dark brown dress of the Spanish peasants. It was on the second day of the army's encampment that some Spaniards brought in, from a neighbouring village, a mule, to replace the loss of Jenny, in the baggage train. It was almost with disgust, that I consented to allow so wretched looking a brute to fill the place of the handsome Jenny; but the necessity was urgent, and the animal purchased at a price that appeared ten times its value.

No sooner had the new comer been ushered into the presence of Pedro, the muleteer on whom had devolved the care of Jenny, than the most expressive signs of recognition took place between them, "*Carracho*, it is Jenny," he exclaimed.

"Impossible," I said, "this ugly animal has a short tail, short ears, and hair as short as a scrubbing brush!"—Jenny had been celebrated for the length of these appendages to her person.

"*Carracho*" again exclaimed Pedro, "It is Jenny, *Signor*," and indignant at my refusal to recognise his favourite, even in spite of the docking she had undergone, he vaulted uninvited on the animal's back, as a last and conclusive test. Jenny—for it was no other than herself—resented the insult by a well-known fling that established her identity beyond a doubt, and, in consequence, was immediately reinstated, notwithstanding her loss of beauty, into the highest dignity of office.

On the 17th, the army pursued its route towards Vittoria, and on the following day, a short and well-contested fight took place at Osma, between two divisions of the French army, and General Graham's corps. The enemy sustained great loss, and was driven onwards, and on the evening of the 19th, the allied army encamped on the banks of the river Bayas, the sixth division, under Sir Edward Pakenham, alone remaining in the rear, in charge of the heavy stores, and a brigade of eighteen pounders.

CHAPTER 22

The Battle of Vittoria

The 21st of June, 1813, will ever afford to history a page of the brightest hue, in commemoration of the victory of Vittoria. The trophies of that day were more numerous than had yet been won in the many battle fields of the Peninsula, and the display of one hundred and fifty pieces of Artillery with four hundred and fifteen caissons of ammunition captured in the flight, proved the strength of the foe that British valour had overcome.

The French, upon the approach of the allied army had taken up a position about six miles in front of Vittoria, with all the advantages of ground. Their left rested upon the bold heights of Puebla and Arlanson; their centre occupied the village of Sabijana, and the high ground commanding the valley of the Zadora; and their right defended the passages of that river leading to the city of Vittoria.

The sun shone brightly on the glittering arms and accoutrements of the French army, as it formed in close columns upon the undulating slopes chosen for the scene of strife; bodies of cavalry were in rapid movement to and fro, appearing in the distance like moving masses of burnished steel, as the sun's rays reflected on their polished helmets, while, the activity of richly dressed *aide-de-camps*, as they crossed and recrossed each other at full speed, from one General's staff to another, gave promise that on that day, both valour and generalship would be tested between the contending armies.

The allied forces had, in the meantime, taken up their position, and the first movement of the day was the dislodgement, by Sir Rowland Hill, of the enemy's left from the heights of Puebla. This was effected by Morillo's Spaniards and light brigade under the command of Colonel Cadogan of the 71st regiment, after a most severe combat, during which it fell to my duty twice to bring up ammunition to replenish the cartouch boxes of our men.[1]

The loss on both sides was very considerable, and among the many that fell at this point was the gallant Colonel Cadogan. Mortally wounded, he was carried at his own request to a rising ground, from whence his brave spirit enjoyed the last satisfaction it could on earth—that of viewing the gallant 71st in possession of the heights of Puebla.

Sir Rowland Hill having thus succeeded in turning the enemy's left, attacked the village of Sabijana, and drove the French from it in gallant style. Many vigorous, though ineffectual attempts, were, however, made by them to regain possession.

It was then noon, and immediately after this success, the 3rd, 4th, and 7th, divisions, headed by Picton, Cole, and Dalhousie,

---

1. The strength of the Anglo-Portuguese army, brought into action at Vittoria, may be stated in round numbers, at fifty thousand infantry, and eight thousand cavalry. The Spaniards numbered twenty-two thousand, and had the charge of their own ammunition; that of the Anglo-Portuguese was under the author's direction, and to those who have turned their thoughts to the almost incredible disproportion that exists between the number of shots fired, and the casualties they occasion, on a field of battle, this note will not be void of interest. At Vittoria, each infantry soldier, on entering the field, had sixty rounds of ball cartridges in his cartouch box for immediate use, making a total of three million rounds. As near as possible to the divisions of the army, were brigades of small-arm ammunition to feed the expenditure; and from the commencement to the close of the engagement, one million, three hundred and fifty thousand rounds of ball cartridges were issued by the Field Train to the troops. Now allowing one half of these to have been expended at the termination of the battle, there was still a total of three million six hundred and seventy-five thousand rounds fired against the enemy. The French lost in killed and wounded eight thousand out of ninety thousand combatants; therefore it follows that only one musket-shot out of four hundred and fifty-nine took effect! and this calculation excludes altogether the injury inflicted on the enemy by ninety pieces of Artillery, which, upon the average, fired, on that day, seventy-three rounds of shot and shell each, making a total of six thousand eight hundred and seventy rounds. The cavalry was but slightly engaged during the day, but the fire of the Spaniards may be supposed to have been commensurate with that of the other combatants, as they were, at times, very closely engaged with the enemy. At every battle in the Peninsula, except Barossa, the author remarked the same undue expenditure of ammunition, in relation to the small extent of damage done; and, from whatever cause this immense waste of powder and shot may have proceeded, whether from the ground being irregular, or from the smoke obstructing the sight, or from the musket being discharged at a slight elevation, or from these three causes combined, it is a subject well worthy the attention of commanding officers of regiments.

passed at different points, the bridges of the Zadora, bearing upon the enemy's front so vigorously, as to compel him to retire upon a ridge of hills, over broken ground to the rear.

Ninety guns under the direction of Colonel Dickson, in a state of as perfect efficiency as could be displayed on the barrack field at Woolwich, were darting their destructive fire on the enemy's lines. From upwards of one hundred guns the compliment was returned, and for the space of more than half an hour, this brilliant battle of Artillery continued on both sides, presenting a spectacle of such magnificent fire-work, and attended by a thundering so terrible, as might have satisfied even Jove himself, as a display of his god-like powers.

The enemy, pressed on all sides, retreated towards Vittoria, our troops advancing on his retiring steps in admirable order.

A division of French infantry, and some cavalry still occupied the heights commanding the village of Gamarra, which was strongly defended, as well as the village of Abechuco, by the enemy.

These heights were bravely gained by two brigades of Portuguese and Spaniards, supported by the fifth division under the command of Major-General Oswald, and the villages were subsequently attacked and taken, notwithstanding the severe opposition of the enemy.

The result of the day was now no longer doubtful, and the last stroke to the total discomfiture of the French, being given by driving from the heights of Zadora, two divisions of reserve infantry that commanded the passage of the river, our victorious army joined in one general pursuit of the fugitive foe.

During the progress of the battle, the churches, towers, and roofs of the houses in Vittoria were crowded, not only with the inhabitants watching the issue of the combat, but with the ladies belonging to the French army, who were also anxious spectators of the scene. Vittoria was at that time, the emporium of all the ill-gotten wealth plundered by the French during their progress through Spain. Confident in the never-failing prowess of their arms, and blindly neglectful even of the commonest regard to prudence, the superior officers of the French army had sent for their wives and children, without one thought that the intrusion of a hostile foe, might disturb their security.

In the same pride of heart had Joseph Buonaparte, the usurper

King, left his palace on that morning, surrounded by all the paraphernalia of royalty, and pomp of power, followed by a brilliant military cortege, and confident of leading his numerous host to victory.

It was only when fluctuating reports of defeat to the French arms found their way from the field of battle, that the wisdom of being prepared for the worst, suggested itself to those who were left without protection within the walls of Vittoria; and as these reports gained more and more the strength of reality, so did the bustle and uproar of that eleventh hour increase.

Upwards of one hundred and eighty carriages stood ready horsed and packed with valuables, awaiting but the signal to take them, with their respective owners, on the road to France. The royal household, the regal jewels, the plate, the public treasury, all were in readiness to move at the confirmatory intelligence of defeat.

As evening approached, the anxiety rose to such a pitch of alarm, that all who sought escape—including the wives and families of the general officers—took refuge in their carriages. These, with a large number of baggage carts had been drawn up on an extensive space of ground, on the right of the road leading to Bayonne, and where the French had established a park of artillery. A dry, but wide ditch, alone separated it from the main road, with which it had but one communication. At this moment of feverish suspense, a body of French soldiers burst into the town, closely followed by the British troops, who effectually chased them through the gate on the opposite side, turning them out of the road to Bayonne, into the unwelcome one of Pampluna. The signal for escape was now indeed given, but too late to be available; fruitless were all the efforts to reach the communication with the road. Confusion and terror reigned around, and carriages, baggage-carts, artillery, pursuers and pursued; all stood jammed together in one inextricable mass. Escape was impossible, and as our troops now rushed like a torrent down the road, sweeping everything before them, the whole of the baggage, carriages, jewels, plate, and public treasure, became the spoil of their victorious arms.

Almost miraculously, Joseph Buonaparte effected his escape amidst the general confusion—throwing himself from his carriage, he mounted on horseback, escorted by a few of his body guards— the Colonel of whom was less fortunate, and remained a prisoner in our hands. Scarcely had the usurper monarch left his carriage when the panels of it were perforated through and through by a nine pound shot.

Surrounded on all sides by our troops, the ladies endeavoured to regain, on foot, the houses they had occupied in the town, while others sought the protection of such British officers as good fortune threw in their way. The scene was one of the most extraordinary that can be imagined; here and there groups of soldiers were to be seen busily engaged in knocking open packing cases and trunks with the butt end of their muskets, and pulling out, amid shouts of laughter from their comrades, sundry articles of female apparel, such as dresses, caps, bonnets, &c, with which they decorated their own persons. Petticoats were slipped over their heads, regardless of the obstruction such appendages offered to the use of their firearms, and many of these fellows, as some fugitive Frenchman came in sight, vainly struggled to disentangle himself from a covering that not only pinioned his arms, but rendered his cartouch-box equally useless. No *Carnival de Venise* ever displayed more grotesque figures than did this short episode in the annals of Vittoria. Lace caps covered the rough chakos of some; Cashmere shawls hung in no graceful folds over the red coats of others; while bonnets of true Parisian manufacture, crowned the tops of many of the muskets that had done good service that day on the battle field.

As night threw its shadows over the scene, all further pursuit of the enemy was abandoned, and Vittoria became the rendezvous of Lord Wellington and his staff. The inhabitants had left their houses to receive the victors with due honours, and amidst the shouts and acclamations of the populace, who rent the air with cries of *Viva los Ingleses,* we took up our quarters in those so recently occupied by our enemies.

I remember the circumstance of a wounded Frenchman being brought in from the field, at the very moment when enthusiasm was at the highest; he could not brook the sound of triumph in his ear, even in that distressed state, and turning fiercely round upon the mob, exclaimed with vehemence, in broken Spanish, "You were for the French yesterday, you are for the English to-day, and you would be for the devil to-morrow, *braves Espagnols que vous êtes."*

During the whole of the night, conveyances were bringing in the wounded of both nations, every house being converted into a temporary hospital for their reception; and here it must be recorded to the honour of the fair women of Vittoria, that never did female excellence shine more conspicuously than in their tender care of the poor sufferers. They made the lint, and applied it with the delicacy that woman only could display; they watched by the bed of agony, and dropped the tear of sympathy on the pallid cheek of him, whose sufferings had closed with his last drawn sigh!

Midnight had sounded before the bustle and confusion of the town had lulled into that quietness, which, like the calm at sea, succeeds the storm; and which remained undisturbed, save by the occasional dull sound of some vehicle depositing its suffering cargo at those houses that still remained open to receive them.

It was late before the duties I had to execute permitted me to enter the billet assigned to me by our Quarter-Master. Some trifling circumstance, that I now forget, had been the means of informing me that a French family, one of those who had regained their quarters after the general capture, were inmates of the same *casa*. A death-like stillness reigned around as I ascended the staircase leading to my apartments, and, perhaps, it might have been the recollection of all that had been suffered that day by women and children, that made my step the lighter, as I passed the corridor where slumber seemed to dwell.

The fatigues of the day required no assistance from narcotics to produce a strong disposition to sleep, which gaining ground irresistibly, I laid myself down, without undressing, to indulge in. Between asleep and awake, the din of the battle, the groans of the wounded, the laments of the dying, all returned to my confused ideas, passing, perhaps, like the flitting shadows of the magic lanthorn, but so faithful in detail, that the past was blended with the present. A groan, indicative of deep suffering, seemed to fall upon my ear; I started, and for a moment the energies of waking life struggled for the mastership; in that brief space, another, and another followed, and the heavy tread of steps in a distant part of the house, told me that something was going on, connected, perhaps, with the painful feelings I had experienced. Hastily quitting my room, I approached the spot from whence the sounds proceeded, and was soon in possession of the cause.

The corridor appropriated to the French family I have mentioned, was long and vaulted; a dull lanthorn hung at the farthest end of it, and on each side, doors opened into the sleeping apartments, according to the fashion of the old houses in Spain.

On reaching the entrance of this gloomy passage, I saw scattered, here and there, some blood-stained straw, as if it had fallen from the litter of some wounded person in his conveyance thither. As I moved onwards in the direction that I felt led to human suffering, the door of an apartment suddenly opened, and a beautiful little boy, on whose anxious countenance the lanthorn threw its dull light, bounded up to me with the question, *"êtes vous le chirurgien?"* I drew back, grieved at the disappointment my answer must give to the little fellow, and as my tongue faltered out *"non,"* my eye fell upon some straw, saturated with gore, at my feet.

"Oh Monsieur" said the child, in a voice so piteous that it went to my heart, *"c'est le sang de papa"*

What a subject for reflection did that short sentence impart, for what can offer a finer field to the theorist, than the question whether man, in his state of civilization, enjoying and participating in the blessings of social ordinances—such as they are instituted by his fellow-man—is thereby relieved from the individual responsibility of his actions. To insure to himself the advantages of the former state, he is obliged to doff all consideration of the latter, and, like a mere peg in the machinery of a wheel within a wheel, places his duty to God, and his duty to his neighbour, at the unlimited disposal of a crafty Government, or a despotic King.

Such is, individually, the position of every man who makes war on his fellow-man, without the excuse of that holy cause, which alone can sanctify the arm of violence—the defence of our own country against invasion.

Perhaps these feelings were even then in embryo, for as the little fellow gently tried to pull me towards the chamber, where his wounded father lay, I had time to consider how obnoxious might be the sight of an English uniform to one so situated, and gladly would I have retreated; but it was too late. The door was opened by my little guide, in another moment it closed behind me, and I stood by the side of the wounded Frenchman.

In a distant part of the room, there reclined, on a *chaise longue,* a pretty little woman of that class of beauty that the French call *chiffonnée*, a term that no other language can define so well, in a *deshabille* of the most costly description. This delicate little lady was evidently labouring under that malady so well understood and appreciated by her countrymen—*une attaque de nerfs.*

A French abigail, whose name, Louise, was too often apostrophized to admit of ignorance on the subject, hung over her mistress with all the assiduity that a long apprenticeship had taught her the efficacy of displaying; and *eau de Luce,* and *vinaigre de quatre voleurs,* perfumed the room, where the real sufferer lay.

Long before I had accomplished my survey of the room, into which I had been so unceremoniously ushered, my hand had received a responsive grasp of kindness from the wounded man, who was attired in the brilliant uniform of a Colonel of Chasseurs, to which was attached that symbol of French gallantry, *la Croix d'Honneur.*

By the side of his litter, the same on which he had been borne from the field by our men, stood a beautiful specimen of Spanish beauty, in the form of a young girl, whose anxious watchfulness, and noiseless attentions, contrasted most agreeably with the *mon Dieus,* and noisy selfishness of Madame. As she leant over him, binding round his forehead the damp cloths that brought coolness to his fevered brow, or gently helping him to find some position to relieve the anguish of his mutilated leg, she looked like an angel of light, shedding the balm of pity on the sufferings of mortality; but even in this moment of agony, shown by the heavy drops of sweat that chased each other down his face, the French Colonel maintained his national character of gaiety and insouciance: "*C'est la fortune de la guerre, mon ami*" said he, addressing himself to me, "*qu'importe une jambe de plus ou de moins. Vive la gloire.*" These sentences were repeated at intervals, though in a voice less firm than the speaker might himself have believed possible, and to each succeeding bravado, an equally characteristic response fell from the lips of the little *mignonne* lady on the sofa, "*Mais, mon ami, y songes-tu? Une jambe! Mais c'est beaucoup qu'une jambe; et tu étais si bienfait*" Here the tears and *mon Dieus* recommenced on the part of the lady, while the poor fellow, who thought the loss of a leg a mere bagatelle when placed in the scale with glory, lay fainting and exhausted before me.

At the same moment, a step was heard in the passage, and the door of an adjoining room opening immediately afterwards, I heard a little anxious voice repeat the question that had greeted me, *étes-vous le chirurgien?*

It appeared that immediately on the arrival of the wounded Colonel at the house, the fair Spanish girl, who was the daughter of our padrone, had sent for a surgeon; and at the moment when exhaustion from loss of blood had reduced him to unconsciousness, this welcome visitor entered with the little boy.

It required but a glance of the surgeon's experienced eye, to determine the necessity of immediate amputation of the crushed limb, and I was desired to find some pretext for removing Madame and the child from the apartment.

As I led her towards the door, holding by the hand her sweet boy, I felt by the violent trembling of her arm, that genuine feeling had, at that moment, superseded the disgusting *minauderies* of a Parisian woman; her bosom heaved convulsively, as she cast a last look on the couch where her husband lay, and I was in the act of philosophizing on the possibility of deep feeling assuming many external garbs, and yet still remaining the same unmixed essence of the soul, when the fair mourner turned upon me her streaming eyes, exclaiming with broken sobs, as the door closed upon us, "*Hélas, la belle jambe.*"

Having deposited my charges in as distant a room as possible from that in which the operation was to be performed, I returned when I thought my services would be required, and found the preparations in progress that precede the fearful process of amputation. Faithful to her office of comforter and nurse, the beautiful Spanish girl bent over the poor being whose genuine *gaieté de coeur* had sunk beneath the pressure of exhausted nature, and was thus mercifully spared the anticipation of an evil, which is sometimes more difficult to bear, even by the bravest, than the reality itself. The dread tourniquet was now applied; involuntarily I turned away my head, but one glance at the fair girl before me conveyed a just reproof for indulging in a morbid sensibility that incapacitated me for usefulness. Inspired by the divine principle of assuaging the misery of another, divested of every thought beginning or ending in self, this heroic young creature shrank not from the task that duty had imposed, but hovered like the form of charity, over the wreck which the tumultuous ocean of man's strife had wrought.

With the returning consciousness of the sufferer came also the acute susceptibility of pain. And though he bore it like a man, and a brave one too, I doubt much that at that moment he considered *la gloire* an equivalent to the pain he was enduring.

The noble Spanish girl slackened not her attentions during the whole time. At one moment bathing his temples with aromatics, at another, fanning his brow with the ever ready little fan that constitutes so essential a part of Spanish female attire. A few minutes more, and the manly limb was severed that so recently had trod, in the pride of strength, the very floor which it now lay a mangled cast-away!

The usual routine of such cases having been concluded, and restoratives administered, the patient was carefully removed into a comfortable bed, with every appearance of being in as satisfactory a state as the circumstances could admit of. The surgeon took his leave, to visit others equally in want of his assistance. The sweet young nurse took up her station for the remainder of the night at the bed-side of her mother's guest; and I retired to my apartment without being able to ascertain if Madame had heard, with becoming resignation, of the loss of *la belle jambe*.

CHAPTER 23

After the Battle

By dawn of day, I was at Colonel Dickson's quarters making arrangements for replacing the expenditure of ammunition that had taken place in the battle, both for the troops and brigades of artillery and for the several divisions of the army. This duty completed, I proceeded with a party of the Field Train to the battle plains to ascertain the full amount of guns captured from the enemy; and such was the zealous promptitude with which my department executed the arduous duty of collecting the immense mass of war materiel, that a detailed return of it was given to Lord Wellington before his despatches were written, thus enabling his Lordship to head them with the glorious intelligence of "one hundred and fifty-one pieces of cannon, and four hundred and fifteen waggons of ammunition having remained in the hands of the British army."[1]

The scene of the battlefield, as I traversed it, in the course of my duties, stripped as it then was of all illusive excitement and din of war, produced a train of the most painful reflections. Suffering was there, in all its agonising forms, from the dying wretch, whose

---

1. In the Gazette Extraordinary from Downing Street, dated July 3rd, 1813, it will be seen that this return—signed by the author as Military Commissary of Ordnance, and chief officer of the Field Train—formed a principal feature in the despatches of Lord Wellington; and yet, nearly twenty-five years afterwards, the editor, or rather compiler of the Duke's despatches, thought fit to exclude altogether the name that guaranteed, and was exclusively responsible for the correctness of the information afforded to Lord Wellington.

If truth be the aim and end of history, the author who writes for posterity should substantiate the facts he records, by the authority upon which those facts have become history.

expiring groans vibrated on the air, to the wounded soldier, who yet could look around with hope for succour.

Spaniards were there plundering the stranger, whose gallant blood had flowed for the cause of liberty and Spain; and women, if such they could be called, like wolves, were prowling over the field stripping the insensible clay, and sometimes even hastening the spirit from its "dull abode."

Impressed with horror at the sight of so many fiends in female form, I crossed rapidly the field of slaughter, and coming to a remote part of it, beheld a scene that reconciled me to the sex. A woman, young in years, and of a most interesting appearance was seated on the earth, by the side of a shallow grave, that she appeared to have but recently finished. Stretched close beside her, in the cold sleep of death, lay the form of a British soldier, over whom she leant in all the convulsive writhing of genuine grief! On an opposite bank, with eyes deeply and sternly fixed on her, reclined a wounded French grenadier—that man's face has lived in my remembrance; his hard set features expressed the fierce determination to die, rather than to complain. Yet, from the earnestness with which he gazed on the work before him, it was possible, nay probable that some chord of tender remembrance had been struck, some thought of home had subdued the natural sternness of his mind; some regret had followed the sad forebodings of the heart, that his bones, unsepulchred, would whiten on a foreign soil; unblessed, unhallowed by the tear of love.

The grief of the mourner was too sacred for intrusion; my attention therefore turned to the wounded Frenchman; and giving to him a few drops of brandy, which I found in a canteen upon the field, I promised to send him assistance as soon as possible. He scarcely seemed to notice, or to heed my words; but when, on the following day, I visited the hospital into which he had been removed, a look of gratitude beamed from his eye as I approached him.

At no great distance from the group I have described, lay a very youthful French officer, whose ghastly and death-hued countenance bespoke the extent of his sufferings; he had covered himself with a blanket, and at the moment I saw him, a Spaniard, who durst not have met him man to man in the field, was in the act of depriving him of this poor luxury; the youth grasped it with a hand, in which all the strength of his frail existence seemed concentrated, and looked the defiance that he could not breathe; I arrested the Spaniard's arm in the ruthless act; and on the following day, when my duties again called me to the field, I saw the gallant youth stiff and cold, beneath the blanket that I had been means of preserving to him.

In returning that same night to Vittoria, I met General Hay, whose anxiety had brought him from his brigade at Tolosa, where it had been halted, to make some inquiries respecting his son, who had been dangerously wounded by his side in the battle. He had called at almost every house and hospital in the city, without success, and accepted the offer of a bed at my quarters. The following morning, by daylight, the General rose to return to his division, his mind still unrelieved from suspense. In opening the window to order his horse, he saw the serjeant in whose care his son had been left, and eagerly inquired how he was getting on. The serjeant replied that Captain Hay had only just expired, at a house within three doors from that in which his father and myself had passed the previous night. The General was conducted to all that remained of his gallant son, and having given vent for a while to the feelings of a father, those of the soldier returned. Wringing my hand, he mounted his horse, and left Vittoria; to lead his men to future victories, and to meet, a few months afterwards, in an advanced age, the same honourable fate that had cut off his son in the bloom of youth.[2]

Most great battles are prolific in subjects for after talk, and that of Vittoria was not exempt; for every one had some story to tell of what he had personally seen. I remember having myself witnessed, on that day, an act of humanity, performed by an officer to whom I was sincerely attached; an officer as brave as gentle, and so truly a Christian, that no man had ever heard an oath from his lips, even in those moments of vexed feeling that try the temper most.

Sir Augustus Frazer, of whom I speak, commanded the horse-artillery at Vittoria, he was riding at the head of Major Gardner's troop, along a narrow road, with the guns almost at a gallop; when he saw a wounded French officer lying in the centre of the road. Another minute, and the ponderous weight of the guns would have crushed the sufferer into the earth as they passed over him; but

---

2. This lamented officer was killed on the 14th of April, 1814, at St. Etienne, before Bayonne, gallantly repelling the sortie made by the French from that fortress.

anxiety to save gave Sir Augustus Frazer the strength to do so. With the rapidity of thought he threw himself from his horse, dragged the Frenchman to the bank that skirted the road, and remounting with the same rapidity, had barely time to escape the fearful death from which he had saved an enemy.

During the heat of the action, Deputy Commissary-General Booth, accompanied by Mr. Larpent—who had just been exported from England in the civil capacity of Judge Advocate to the army—most narrowly escaped paying a severe penalty for the curiosity of seeing the fight. These amateurs, both of them very conspicuous—one from the enormous black feather that he wore, and the other from a still more enormous white feather—squatted themselves upon a mound of earth, protected in front by a little thicket of stunted trees, and beyond that by our own troops; here they amused themselves by viewing from a distance the show, doubtless feeling as much personal security as might have been indulged in at a review in Hyde Park The sight of our soldiers in front had banished all thoughts of danger in the rear, from whence, however, a party of French dragoons bore down upon them, attracted by the importance attached to feathers of such long proportions. The Assistant Commissary General was indebted to his feather for his escape, for having left both hat and its appendage in the hands of the dragoon who would have seized him, he managed to slide down the hill into the little thicket beneath, which afforded him a refuge. The Judge Advocate was less fortunate; retaining his magnificent head-gear, he lost his liberty, and was marched off a prisoner in great triumph by the dragoons, who imagined they had effected the capture of a general-officer judging by the length of his feather.[3]

Colonel Burton, of the Welch Fusiliers, had been appointed Commandant of Vittoria, and by the help of the working parties, with which he supplied me, I completed the task of parking the guns and ammunition captured from the French. When this was done, I received orders to transfer them over to the Spanish Governor of Vittoria, and to join the artillery battering train at Passages, where preparations were making for the siege of San Sebastian.

---

3. Mr. Larpent was sent to Bayonne as prisoner of war, but Lord Wellington, requiring his services as Judge-Advocate, effected his exchange for a French officer of rank.

During the period of collecting together the war materiel at Vittoria, upwards of one hundred and sixty private carriages were brought into the park. Some of them were fitted up in the most costly manner, with velvet and silk linings, and as they were only encumbrances in the park, and totally useless to the army, I made them over to Colonel Burton, suggesting that they might perhaps be advantageously distributed among those inhabitants of Vittoria, who had suffered from the depredations of the French. He gladly acceded to the proposal, and it was not until after the fall of San Sebastian, that I heard of the large treasures in money and jewels that had been found within the linings, and other parts of the carriages I had so unwittingly disposed of.

There were also discovered, at the same time, some curiosities of the female *boudoir*, so peculiarly ingenious that Sir Colin Campbell—the permanent Commandant of head-quarters—thought it his duty to hand them over for the inspection of the Commander-in-Chief; where-upon His Excellency, for some mysterious reasons that were not made public, ordered, without loss of time, an escort of the Royal Irish to convey the French ladies to their lords and masters.

Very shortly after the battle of Vittoria there appeared in the artillery orders, promulgated by the Assistant-Adjutant-General—Colonel May—a notification from the Master-General, Lord Mulgrave, that his Royal Highness the Prince Regent had been graciously pleased in consideration of the very striking and unexampled circumstance of the whole of the British artillery having been brought into action at the battle of Vittoria, and the whole of the enemy's artillery having been captured in that glorious victory, to grant to all the officers, entrusted with the command of divisions or brigades, an allowance for good service in the following proportions: to the officers commanding divisions each 10s. per diem; to the officers commanding brigades, each 6s. per diem; and to Colonel Dickson, as commanding officer of the whole, 20s. per diem.

Notwithstanding the high degree of military merit that must always be attached to the names of Robert Gardner, Webber Smith, Hugh Ross, Norman Ramsey, and other officers who commanded as Captains of Artillery on the plains of Vittoria, it may perhaps be asked why the artillery—valuable as were its services—should have been selected for special reward, where each corps vied with each other in conspicuous gallantry. None were more surprised at the circumstances than the fortunate officers who were so selected, but whatever might have been the justice or injustice of thus marking out the officers of artillery for a special sign of approbation from the country, it is undeniable that the Field-Train should have been included in the grant; for the high state of equipment which had "enabled the whole of the British artillery to be brought into action," was essentially contributed to by the able exertions of the department of which I was the chief officer.

It is unnecessary to observe upon the unity that exists between a soldier and his means of warfare, without the efficiency of which, his exertions are paralysed; and in that same close connexion did the Field-Train stand united to the Royal Artillery.

The following opinion on this subject was given by Lieutenant-General Sir Julius Hartman K.C.B., of the German artillery—than whom no officer is possessed of greater experience in the military profession.

> The artillery to be well and efficiently served, must have an active and well organized Field-Train department. It is a branch of the same tree; the honour won by the former must redound to the latter; and, therefore, in my opinion, rewards and remunerations should be equally shared.

Many accidents took place on the field of Vittoria, owing to the immense quantities of ammunition that lay scattered over its extent. The Spaniards, in their search for booty, opened several tumbrils, in the hope of finding concealed treasure, and careless of the sparks that dropped from their inseparable companion, the cigar, often occasioned an explosion, of which they were themselves the victims.

Upon one occasion, a catastrophe was averted by the presence of mind of an officer of the Field-Train on duty, which in its effects would have blown up the whole city of Vittoria. A tumbril containing live shells was discovered to be on fire in the midst of the captured park of ammunition. There was a moment's hesitation; for fearful was the alternative by which alone could be saved the number of human beings within reach of the terrific explosion that must inevitably follow the ignition of the shells. An immense mass of combustible matter lay loosely scattered around, and upwards of one hundred thousand pounds of powder. The loss of another moment would have been fatal, when the officer above mentioned sprung into the burning tumbril, and having thrown out the live shells beyond the reach of the fire, took in his arms the last—of which the fuse was already ignited—and carrying it thus to an adjacent deep ditch, rolled it to the bottom, where it exploded harmlessly.[4]

It has often been my lot to witness the beneficial results of presence of mind, and also the lamentable results produced by the want of this valuable quality and essential attribute even to valour. Many bold hearts, who have been fore-most in the path of danger, have fallen victims to causes that required but a small portion of energies they possessed to have averted; but so is man constituted, that too frequently according to the cry of fear, or of triumph, that re-echoes around him, so are his physical and moral energies paralysed or drawn forth; and it is as true, that the stoutest hearts have been known, in cases of sudden surprise, to respond to the craven who first gave the signal of alarm, as it is, that dispositions, naturally weak and cowardly, have been rallied into daring achievements, by the presence and co-operation of the brave.

On the evening that preceded my departure from Vittoria, I went to say farewell to my fellow-lodger, the French Colonel, who had been gradually progressing towards recovery since the amputation of his leg. I had visited him almost every day, and the acquaintance between his little boy and myself had ripened into something very like affection on both sides. At parting, the Colonel pressed my hand with kindly warmth, expressing the hope that we might meet again as friends. Madame almost forgot her affectation when thanking me for my attentions to her gallant Lord; and my little friend roared fairly out, when I bestowed a last kiss on his cheek. And so we parted, who a few days before would have cut and hacked at each other, with all the animosity of fighting dogs, at the word of command.

In passing along the corridor, more than half subdued into the melting mood, I saw the light and graceful form of Donna Flora, our

---

4. The late Earl of Mulgrave, when Master-General, observed, in allusion to this officer's services, that, "the Board of Ordnance and himself very highly appreciated his conduct and services throughout the war, which they considered entitled him to every encouragement the service could bestow; but, that there existed no precedent to guide the Master-General and Board in granting him any mark of distinction." This remark was made immediately after the unprecedented grant to the officers of artillery at Vittoria.

fair young hostess, waiting at the end of it as if to speak to me. It is unnecessary to say that I had improved to the utmost of my power my first acquaintance with this fair young being, that had commenced on the first night of my arrival in the apartment of the wounded Colonel. I had also been the happy means of saving her from insult and violence, when an attack was made on her brother's house by his fellow-countrymen, under the impression that he was sold, as they termed it, to the French interests; for such was the position of Vittoria, that although its inhabitants had appeared more than reconciled to the French yoke during the time they were in possession of the town, no sooner were they succeeded by the English, than a counter-revolution of feeling took place, and all those who were even suspected of favouring the French, were violently assaulted in their own houses, and many were even murdered by the excited populace.

As Donna Flora saw me approach, she put her finger to her lips is if to impose silence, and beckoning me on, I followed her into a little room, where two Spaniards were seated wrapt in their large cloaks. No sooner was the door closed, than the girl threw herself at my feet, and with passionate vehemence, declared she would not rise until I had promised to comply with her request, whatever it might be. I confess that I was sorely puzzled; for at that particular time, party spirit ran so high that I feared lest her demand might comprise more than it was in my power to concede. While still hesitating how to compromise matters with the fair petitioner, I found my difficulty's considerably increased by a new supplicant. One of the Spaniards, whose large *sombrero* only left enough of his countenance visible to show its extreme youthfulness, at this crisis, joined his urgent entreaties to Donna Flora's, and thus hemmed in between beauty and distress, I found no other means than to surrender.

The outer works once gained, the other Spaniard who had sat apparently unmoved, and indifferent to the success of the supplicants, now rose, and with the ease and dignity that distinguishes, in most cases, the noble Hidalgo, introduced himself to me as Don Miguel Malafra; one, who had, alas, for Spanish patriotism given such proof of submission to the yoke of France, as to accept the office of a Prefect under that Government. The newly aroused vengeance of his countrymen against all Spaniards so situated had left him but one alternative—escape; and Donna Flora, his near relative, with all the wit of woman, when closely pressed for systematic stratagem, had not scrupled to name me as one likely to aid and abet in the enterprise. The plan that my acquiescence was to mature, was, that the Conde should assume the disguise of a muleteer in my service, and by this means traverse Spain, now to him a hostile country, and seek protection from the French Government. The whole difficulty of the case as regarded the compromise of a British officer's position, rushed at once to my mind; and yet, as so many Spaniards of rank had been in the same renegade phalanx with the Conde de Malafra, without incurring punishment, I could not but think it hard that he should be singled out—the victim perhaps of vindictiveness more than of justice.

Notwithstanding my promise, however, hesitation got the upper hand. I remained silent, and the result might have been very different, had not the younger Spaniard, who saw my embarrassment, removed from a very fair brow the large *sombrero,* and turning to me a pair of dark eyes, almost concealed by a profusion of clustering curls, implored me in the name of woman to save her husband.

When the citadel is carried, it is useless look out for new means of defence, and so in this instance; the heart had given way, and the head was therefore put *hors-de-combat.* I consented to be blown up, if necessary, to show my devotion to the sex, in whose name I had been summoned to surrender, and in half an hour afterwards, the Conde and his fair spouse, Donna Flora and myself sat down to a delightful *petit souper* where we discussed the preliminaries to be observed on the morrow's departure.

The sun was fast sinking in the west on the following evening, when I left Vittoria on my way to Passages. The nature of my situation at head-quarters facilitated the arrangements I had made during the day to insure the safety of Don Miguel and his wife, the latter having also procured the dress of a muleteer to accompany her husband in his flight.

A larger number of mules was allowed to me than to any other officer holding the same rank; and I was, therefore, enabled to send on, in advance, my camp equipage, reserving three mules for my own personal effects, that were to accompany me on the road. A German sergeant who was attached to my party—an upright trustworthy fellow as ever lived—was admitted into the secret, and he managed to load the animals so lightly, as to allow of the additional weight of my noble muleteers.

When all was ready, the Conde and his wife issued from the stable with their respective charges, taking up their position in the rear of my saddle horses. I could not help glancing round to see how the noble lady played her new part, but the dark cloak and slouched *sombrero,* so completely concealed both figure and face, it was impossible to discover the deceit.

Another glance at the lower window of the house we were leaving, showed me Donna Flora kneeling before a little shrine dedicated to the Virgin, praying, as she had promised to do, for the protection of our party.

She turned her beautiful face, bathed in tears towards us, and looked a sad farewell. And thus we parted for ever.

The second evening brought us to Villa Franca, where we found Captain Norman Ramsey's troop of horse-artillery, and a brigade of cavalry under General Vandeleur. The former gallant officer was in arrest under circumstances of a peculiar nature. Lord Wellington had met him in the valley of Araquil, on the day succeeding the battle of Vittoria; and had given him orders to put his troop in cantonment in a neighbouring village, and not to move until he received further direction from himself. Early on the following morning, a staff officer, of the cavalry division to which Ramsey was attached, rode to demand the assistance of the troop at the advanced posts. Ramsey explained his position in reference to the orders he had received from Lord Wellington the previous night; but was told that change of circumstances had produced a change of orders, and under this impression, Ramsey led his troop to the advanced post.

With an exuberance of displeasure, Lord Wellington visited this offence, if offence it could be called, totally unmindful of the previous brilliant services of the offender; for Norman Ramsey was one who yielded to none in bravery, talent, and every other quality that constitutes the soldier and the gentleman. The shaft had, however sped, that was to make him a victim; his troop was transferred to the next senior officer, and almost heart-broken at such a sequel to the reputation he had so nobly earned in the many battlefields of the Peninsula, Norman Ramsey was awaiting the mandate that was to send him back to England.

My first object on arriving with my party at Villa Franca, was in obtain some comfortable nook, without creating suspicion, for the night's repose of my muleteers. This was effected by the agency of the German sergeant, who managed to secure to himself the next best quarters to my own. When all was still, he exchanged them for a bed of clean straw in the stables with the mules, and conducted our patrician muleteers to the enjoyment of his own snug roost.

The next morning, I was breakfasting with Norman Ramsey, and the officers of his troop, now commanded by another, when General Vandeleur arrived. Upon entering the room, he went up in Ramsey, and grasping his hand with a brother soldier's warmth, said:

"The object of my visit, Captain Ramsey, is to inspect your troop."

"My troop, General, is mine no longer," answered poor Ramsey, with deep emotion.

"I am glad to say you are mistaken, Captain Ramsey," rejoined the General, "for I am the bearer of orders from head-quarters that authorise me, as I before said, to inspect your troop. The command of it is restored to you."

Ramsey, overcome by his feelings, turned away and wept, while every officer present, and none more cordially than Captain Cater, who had superseded him, gave vent to their joyful feelings at this happy termination; yet, notwithstanding this restoration to favour, the shaft, as before stated, had sped from head-quarters, and Norman Ramsey, whose name had appeared with distinction in the despatches of Vittoria, and who had distinguished himself in every brilliant action in the memorable campaign of 1813, was omitted in the brevet that came out after Vittoria, and left the field at the termination of the war in Spain, without one honorary distinction having been conferred on him.[5]

On leaving Villa Franca, we continued our route to Passages through Tolosa. The road was so unfrequented, that by degrees my companions began to throw off the alarm that they laboured under during the first day's march, and the dark-eyed little Spanish dame would sometimes relax in attention to her sluggish charge, and even ventured to chat with me when I got off my horse to walk by the side of herself or husband.

---

5. Major Norman Ramsey found a soldier's grave on the plains of Waterloo.

If a human figure appeared in the distance, the German sergeant gave a pre-concerted cough, which was the signal for us all to resume our respective places in the front and rear.

Thus we journeyed on in safety until we arrived at Passages, where difficulties would have thickened around us, but for the skillful management of our friend the sergeant. My billet at Passages was in an old tumble down house, overlooking the harbour, and as full of long passages, iron gratings, and trap doors, as any locality ever selected by Mrs. Radcliffe for the theatre of her monstrosities. There was an old wooden terrace in front of the house, literally overhanging the ocean, and in the still hour of night, how sweet it was from that old crazy resting place, to view the myriads of stars that lit the southern sky, reflected in their deep bed of azure blue! but dearer even than this to the sentimentalist, were the dark holes and corners that offered security to those who required it.

The ground floor, if such it could be called, once appropriated as store-rooms, but now unoccupied, save by a few articles of old furniture, became the object of our sergeant's speculations, and consequently my quarters. A little kitchen was occupied by the culinary apparatus of my canteens, under the special guidance of José, a Portuguese cook, with so little of good and so much of evil in his composition, that to this day I am inclined to believe that Satan sent him as one of his *chef-d'oeuvres*, to "sink, burn, and destroy" whatever came within his reach on earth. The next chamber was appropriated as my own bed-room, with indeed but scanty furniture, for the whole of my camp equipage, bedding, &c. was transferred to an inner room, in which I had placed Don Miguel and his Donna Marguerita.

The sergeant had exacted, on the part of the refugees, the most complete seclusion in this one apartment and my occupations were of such an out-door nature that but little scope was given for surmise in the old house that we inhabited in common. So things went on, and in the meantime were concluded the operations of disembarking the heavy ordnance and materiel for the Siege of San Sebastian, as well as the equipment of the guns and mortars for the batteries, the whole of which laborious duties devolved upon the department of the Field Train.

Every hour that I could dispose of in the midst of my numerous vocations, was devoted to relieve the monotonous confinement of my Spanish guests; and every evening, after nightfall, found me either listening to the specious reasoning's of Don Miguel, in extenuation of his political conduct, or to the soft accompaniment of his lady's guitar, as she sang the deeds of Spanish patriotism or Spanish chivalry.

Alas! that they should live in song alone! The perfume of the flower has been extracted, but the root that bore it is exterminated from the soil.

When danger has surrounded us for a period, without our having sustained any injury, we grow callous to its continuance, in the' belief that the security of the past is a guarantee for the future. Sometimes we even forget altogether our position of danger, and advance nearer and nearer with a kind of irresistible fatality, to meet the evil that at first we made so many efforts to avoid. The sequel of my Spanish friend's adventures was an illustration of this truth. In the meantime, I was called upon to quit my quarters in the old crazy house for others in easier communication with those of Sir Thomas Graham and Colonel Dickson. This was the first leak sprung in the bark that I had hoped would have steered my poor refugees safely into port; for although I left them in my old quarters, under the special care of our friend the sergeant, there was another in my establishment, who necessarily had become a sort of demi-confidant; and that other was José.

CHAPTER 24

San Sebastian

The batteries being fully armed, and the magazines formed for supplying them, the artillery under Colonel Dickson opened fire upon the fortress of San Sebastian on the 20th of July.

Our naval force upon the station consisted of only *La Surveillante* of forty guns, commanded by Sir George Collier, and the *Lyra* sloop—Captain Bloigh—a force totally inadequate to prevent the garrison from receiving supplies from Bayonne. From the former ship, a party of as gallant fellows as ever lived, was sent on shore to work a battery of six twenty-four pounder carronades, under the command of their first Lieutenant Dowell O'Reilly.

It was the night preceding the attack that I took possession of my new quarters, and anxious, if possible, to transfer Don Miguel and his wife to my new abode, I took a lamp to explore the lower regions of the house, and ascertain its capabilities for my purpose. In descending the stairs, I was greeted with a shout of boisterous mirth, united with the tones of a sharp fiddle; and, following the sounds, I found myself in a large room, appropriated to a grand entertainment.

Tallow candles stuck in bottles, as substitutes for candlesticks, illuminated the fête; large barrels of cider—for the premises were originally intended for this commodity—were unceremoniously stowed away into the corners, to make room for the dancers, with the exception of one, that served as gallery to the orchestra. On it, in triumphal display, stood the scraping fiddler, while upwards of thirty blue jackets were footing the double shuffle of the sailor's hornpipe, till the beams shook and cracked in sympathy.

Along the ceiling ran a double tier of slung hammocks, and

this latter circumstance left me in no doubt that these jolly fellows were quartered in the same house as myself. I had scarcely time to give a regret to the annihilation of my plans for the refugees, when the Lieutenant in command stepped up, and giving me Colonel Dickson's compliments, informed me, that by the recommendation of that officer, he had brought his men to my capacious premises. I certainly wished the Colonel in one of the cider barrels for his good counsel, and in one of them he certainly might have been, without receiving any injury, for the blue jackets had transferred the whole of its contents to the safe keeping of their leathern belts. I was kindly asked to sanction, by my presence, the installation of the sailors into their shore-slung hammocks, and we kept it up merrily until the dawn of that morning, when we commenced our operations against the fortress of San Sebastian. And now having paid due attention to the happy merriment of our Jack tars, let me try to give a faint outline—for description must ever in such cases fall short of reality—of their noble, yet characteristic bearing in the little battery they served.

It was early on the morning succeeding our fun, that I volunteered to show them a short cut to their battery, and headed by the fiddler, who scraped away to the tune of *Jack's Alive*, we came in sight of the French soldiers upon the ramparts; and much they must have been amused at the sight of the blue jackets cutting capers, and playing every kind of antic that joyous hearts could devise; whilst when a shot boomed over the head of one of the party, the lucky fellow who escaped was made to bend, while his comrades played leap frog over him, and then the never-tired fiddle burst forth with *Jack's Alive*, or *Hearts of Oak*.

The sailor's battery was altogether so gallantly worked, that the artillery and Engineer officers used to drop in by turns, either to say a word of approbation to the men, or to be amused by the original and quaint ways of these amphibious soldiers. Nothing daunted them; nothing put them out, and even if a murderous shell fell, with its levelling vengeance in the little battery, "*Jack's Alive,*" was instantaneously struck up by the enthusiastic fiddle, to staunch any pang that the loss of one of these gallant fellows, might have inflicted on the rest. Thus three days and nights of incessant firing, on both sides, passed away. On the right of the sailors, was a battery of twenty

twenty-four pounders, worked with such skill by the gunners of the Royal Artillery, that the great breach of the fortress was practicable on the evening of the 23rd, a day, alas, that was fraught with direful results to our gallant tars. Up to that time, the casualties throughout the batteries had been comparatively trifling, owing, in a great measure, to their skilful construction by the Engineers, who had afforded all possible protection to the gunners, placing traverses, &c, to save them from splinters of shells, and other accidents.

The French had, in San Sebastian, four immense mortars, from which they threw shells of fourteen inches in diameter—hitherto none of these monsters had found their way to the batteries, but as they passed over our heads, the heavy rush they made through the air, and the terrific noise of their explosion, made us distinctly recognize them, amidst the thundering of all the other guns. The tars had christened them "the babies," and as each "baby," with its own peculiar cry, ranged beyond the mark of their battery, the sailors cut capers at their escape, and the fiddle played.

It was about eleven o'clock on the morning of the 23rd, when one of these awful shells, thrown with fatal precision, appeared in the air, descending like a mighty destroyer, in the direct line of the sailor's battery. The monster alighted on the back of a poor fellow, who had thrown himself on his face as the only chance of escape, and exploding at the same instant, killed, or dreadfully mutilated, seventeen of these noble-spirited champions of England's wooden walls.

The tide of mirth now flowed no longer; the survivors looked at each other in sad astonishment at the sudden thinning of their ranks, and the tones of the scraping fiddle were exchanged for the deep groans of those few in whom life still lingered. There was a boy of the party, who was the beloved of all—handsome, gay, and gallant; and so young, only fifteen, that his messmates would not hear of his accompanying them into the battery, always trying to find him some duty, that was to detain him within doors; but Ben Harris was not to be kept away from danger; his young heart panted for glory, and he found it, poor little fellow, at a fearful sacrifice. He was found, at a considerable distance, with both his legs blown clean off. I never shall forget the tenderness with which his shipmates carried him into hospital, where he received every care, but the shock was too great for one of his tender years and he survived but a short period.

The good and gallant O'Reilly was blown right through the embrasure, by the rushing whirlwind that accompanied the monstrous shell in its downward flight. Although taken up senseless, he was found to have sustained no serious injury, nor outward wound, yet the early termination of his gallant career at no very long period afterwards, led his friends to believe that he had never recovered from the effects of that concussion. After this disaster, the sailor's battery assumed a completely different aspect; the men worked at their guns with the same activity, but in silence; the merry joke was heard no more, and on revisiting the cider premises that had witnessed the joyous revelling of those whose eyes were now closed in death; I saw that some hand had assigned a humble place against the wall to the now silent fiddle.

The battering train force employed against the fortress of San Sebastian was thus disposed of. On the right of the attack, along the Chofre sand-hills, were twenty twenty-four pounders, four sixty-eight carronades, four ten inch, and six eight inch mortars. On the left, against the fortified convent of San Bartolomeo, were six eighteen pounders, under the direction of Colonel Hartman, of the German artillery. Up the Monte Olia, we had dragged, with great labour, the six eight-inch mortars from the Chofre sandhills, and from the above eminence we looked into the enemy's batteries of the Mirador, and Monte Orguello.

The several batteries were worked under the directions of Lieutenant-Colonels May and Frazer; Majors Dyer and Webber Smith; and Captains Dubordien, Parker, &c, the whole under the command of Colonel Dickson.

The Engineer department was commanded by Sir Richard Fletcher, ably assisted by Colonel Burgoyne, Majors Ellicombe and Smith, the latter, an officer who had much distinguished himself in the defence of Tarifa, had been selected to draw out the plan of the siege, and to superintend its details.

On the second day of the firing, the artillery lost an officer of great promise in Captain Dubordien, who was killed by the splinter of a shell. On the day of the 23rd, a smaller breach to the right of the main breach was rendered practicable, and preparations were made for the assault before daybreak on the following morning. During the night two thousand men from the fifth division, were placed in readiness in the trenches, but the attack was deferred, in consequence of the conflagration of the houses immediately joining the breach, and during the day of the 24th, the guns from our batteries were employed in destroying the new defences raised by the enemy. In the dead hour of that night, the same party, headed by their gallant leaders, were reassembled in the trenches waiting their signal to advance.

And here it may justly be permitted to remark upon the injudicious arrangements of our first assault on the fortress of San Sebastian. In the first place, the hour elected, was one of complete darkness; a circumstance that carried with it so much of evil, that it ought not to be passed over lightly. Without, for a moment, doubting the innate courage of the British soldier, common sense points out the error of allowing men the power of shirking danger, without being exposed to the wholesome discipline of the eye of comradeship, which alone suffices, in many instances, to make men brave. The same soldiers, who would respond to the cheering cry and bright glance of their officer, under the broad glare of daylight, by rushing to the summit of a breach, might show less enthusiasm in seeking death, if the veil of darkness were to conceal alike their deeds of valour, or the absence of them. In the case in question, the troops had the additional disadvantage of receiving a check to the ardour they at first felt, by the postponement for twenty-four hours of the dangers that threaten, at all times, a storming party, and which certainly did not add to the enthusiasm of the attack.

Long before dawn of day, on the 25th, the storming party issued from the trenches. The leading column was commanded by Major Fraser, of the Royals, headed by the forlorn hope under Lieutenant Campbell, of the 9th regiment, and accompanied by Lieutenant Harry Jones, of the Engineers, who volunteered as guide to the breach. The road from the trenches to the points of attack was bad in the extreme, being upwards of two hundred yards in distance, over sharp pointed rocks, and deep holes of sea-water, that the receding tide of the Arumea river had left.

The Governor of the fortress, General Rey, had not been neglectful of gathering together his powers of destruction against the assailants, and as the latter advanced with as much rapidity as the difficulties of the path would admit, they were exposed to a terrific fire of musketry and shells from the ramparts, while, in front, a heavy discharge of grape showered from the battery of the Mirador, which flanked the approach to the breach. Yet still our men rushed on, headed by their brave officers, whose cheering tones rang audibly through the disordered columns that the narrowness of the uneven road had caused. The forlorn hope made a desperate effort to mount the breach; they partly succeeded, but few survived the attempt, and their gallant leader fell wounded in the fruitless effort to maintain the position. Lieutenant Jones, of the Engineers, was the first to show the way to the summit closely followed by Major Frazer of the Royals, whose loud cry of "Follow me, my lads," was distinctly heard amidst the tumult of the storm, until death froze it on his lips. The foremost men of the Royals pressed closely on, and some few stood by their intrepid officers, but the remainder of the advancing column, awed by the overwhelming fire to which they were exposed on every side, hung back, and turned their muskets upon the enemy on the ramparts. Unsupported by their comrades, the foremost men fell one by one upon the breach, and Lieutenant Jones, misled by the darkness into the belief that his footsteps would be closely followed by the stormers, bravely leaped from the breach into the town below—a distance of upwards of twelve feet. Had his expectations been realized, the fortress of San Sebastian had been our own; but they were not so. And Jones stood alone on hostile ground, a wounded prisoner.

After these discouraging attempts to gain a footing on the breach, it would appear that no combined efforts were made to effect it, yet it was evident from the fate of those gallant fellows who lost their lives on its summit, that such was practicable, and had the noon day's sun shone upon the men at the foot of the breach, there is little doubt but that Lieutenant Jones would have been gloriously followed by a victorious storming party.

The increasing intensity of the enemy's fire raked, with fearful force, our ranks. Darkness still prevailed, each moment added to the confusion, and the stormers, panic-struck at the hot reception they had encountered, endeavoured, amidst the tourbillon of musketry, bursting of shells, and whistling of grape, to regain the trenches. But these were almost as difficult to attain as the summit of the breach. The narrow road stood choked up by the assailants in one dense mass, and it was only when the demon of destruction had fully glutted his appetite, that the diminished numbers of our men opened the means of retreat to the trenches.

The trenches once regained, and the intelligence of our failure promulgated, our batteries reopened a continuous and tremendous fire upon the fortress; the very guns appearing to sympathize in the revenge we were taking for the events of the night.

The grey dawn was just peeping through the eastern sky, and the surrounding objects beginning to emerge from shadowy perceptibility into the tangibility of their accustomed forms, when Colonel Frazer of the artillery, visited the twenty four-pounder battery, then actively employed against the fortress. His eyes naturally turned in the direction of the scene of the previous night's failure, and through the curling smoke that lightly wreathed through the morning air, he thought he perceived a figure on the summit of the breach. Again it was concealed by the thick flakes of smoke that followed the returning fire of the fortress, and again as the smoke curled off into the blue air, it assumed a more distinct appearance. As the morning's light increased, the outline of the figure became clearly perceptible, and Colonel Frazer could then distinguish that it was a French officer, making sundry telegraphic signals with his sword to the English batteries. The singularity of the circumstance caused Colonel Frazer to stop the firing; which was responded to by a similar cessation from the fortress, and an officer was despatched forthwith for an explanation of this extraordinary proceeding; under the security that was offered by the continuance of the Frenchman's position on the breach, his sword pointed to the earth.

The annals of war present, it is true, many noble actions that proclaim abnegation of self. Many traits of personal heroism, that draw the burst of admiration from our hearts towards the hero, without allowing us time, even had we the inclination to inspect the soundness of the root, of which the action we admire is so beautiful a flower. Perhaps in most cases we might find 'ambition for distinction,' the little bulb from whence great actions spring; but in the present instance, the officer, upon the breach of San Sebastian, risked a thousand times his life in the sacred cause of humanity.

Under the walls of the fortress and strewed along the strand, lay our wounded officers and soldiers. The shells from our batteries bursting over the walls of the fortress, fell upon these poor defenceless creatures, killing and wounding the already wounded, while the shots also rebounded from the walls among them. The spectacle of so much suffering was not to be endured even by their enemies, and a noble spirited young French officer stepping forward to make known their distressing situation, sought the dangerous and conspicuous position on the breach, as the best means to acquaint us with the fatal effect of our own guns on our wounded countrymen.

In consequence of this information, one hour's truce was agreed upon by the belligerents, and a very curious and interesting scene occupied this short period. British and French soldiers were promiscuously engaged in carrying off the sufferers, and it was a subject for reflection to see the ease with which the French soldiers, each encumbered with the burthen of a wounded man, managed to ascend the same breach that that so many had found to be impracticable. It is true that broad daylight was now substituted for the cover of night.

The French made no opposition to the British soldiers taking into their own trenches as many of their countrymen as they could carry off; but those taken by the French in the fortress, became of course prisoners of war. The hour expired, the contending foes returned to their respective strong-holds, the guns recommenced their thundering, and thus may be said to have terminated the first assault on the fortress of San Sebastian. An unsuccessful enterprise, that cost us, in killed and wounded, upwards of five hundred soldiers, and fifty officers; but worse than even the loss of so many gallant fellows were the disheartened, crest-fallen looks that pervaded the ranks of our men, when the full extent of our signal failure was made known. A settled gloom, not unmixed with shame, lowered on every brow, and though unexpressed, there was not one who did not feel how much more might have been done than had been done.

It may easily be imagined that such a feeling in British soldiers rapidly engendered another, that of retrieving the past by a glorious future, and all hearts panted with the one desire to be led a second time against the walls of San Sebastian. In the midst of these aspirations, the movements of the French army caused Lord Wellington to order the whole of the guns, stores, &c, to be sent immediately to Passages for embarkation, and San Sebastian was left in a state of blockade only. The operation of removing the battering train to Passages, and its subsequent embarkation, was effected in all its details by the Field Train department, and I consequently found myself once more located in my crazy quarters overlooking the harbour.

CHAPTER 25

The Escape

My absence from Passages had cut off all communication between myself and the Spanish refugees, except on two occasions, when that the German sergeant had been over to San Sebastian, to tell me how things were going on with them. From him I learnt that Don Miguel had thrown aside the disguise on which his security depended; and that his frequent absences from home during the hours of evening had destroyed all hopes of his preserving an incognito in the neighbourhood. I heard too that he had quarrelled with my cook, José, and it was with a presentiment of coming evil, that I knocked at the door of his apartment on the first night of my return to Passages. It was opened to me by a lovely woman, in the costume of the Andalusian ladies of rank; nor is it to be wondered at that I started back, unable to trace in the beautiful creature before me any resemblance to the young muleteer I had left in that apartment. I trembled at the change, for I saw broken down at one fell swoop all the benefit that the continuance of our well-conceived plan might have insured; and although, at the first moment, it was exclusively on their own account that I was alarmed, it was impossible for me to conceal from myself that my own position was not slightly embarrassing, in harbouring persons who unequivocally had been employed in the interests of France. Before I could recover from my surprise, a whistle under the window caused the signora to bound towards the terrace, which led, by a pair of rickety, wooden stairs, to a little landing-place beneath. Her fair hand threw down a cord, and following her steps, I saw a figure, by the retreating twilight, leap from a small boat, moor it carefully, and in another moment Don Miguel stood before us. To say the truth, we were both embarrassed, though perhaps from different causes, and scarcely could I find patience to listen to his plausible reasons for an act that seemed to me little short of madness. Forgetting that he had owed his safety to the very disguise and seclusion that were now both relinquished, he imagined that mixing with the inhabitants of Passages, like any other individual, would multiply the facilities of escape; and in this belief, had purchased a boat, in which himself and wife made daily, or rather nightly, excursions on the water, preparatory to that last, that was to convey them in safety, as he hoped, to the French coast.

It had not entered into Don Miguel's speculations that a Spanish boatman was an indispensable companion, and that the whole coast was scouted by Spanish vessels engaged in a scrutinizing blockade. In vain I pointed out the prudence of remaining quiet, at least until the movements of the Spanish forces were more accurately known, which might then allow of an escape by land to Bayonne, without approaching their hostile lines. In vain I pointed out the impossibility of escaping the scrutiny of a blockading force by sea. Obstinacy had planted his staff determined not to yield to reason; and thus I left them.

Preparations for an early renewal, on the following morning, of the embarkation of the Ordnance stores, kept me until a very late hour from my quarters. The night was moonless, and the irregular streets of Passages were so shrouded in darkness that I carried, as a necessary protection, a lanthorn to guide my steps.

The sound of voices in earnest conversation, and at so late an hour, made me, for a moment, hesitate whether to advance or retreat, and during that moment the guttural sounds of José's broken Spanish struck upon my ear.

Curiosity, and some strange feeling, undefinable, yet mysteriously powerful, caused me to retreat behind the jutting corner of an old building; but the colloquy, whatever it might have been, was closed. The parties walked away, their voices lowered to a whisper, and I had no alternative but to return, with curiosity unsatisfied, and suspicions strongly excited, to my own quarters. The door was opened to me by José, and though I turned the light of my lanthorn sharply on his face, in the hope of finding some traces that might solve my doubts, nothing was discernible beyond the half grin of quiet cunning that usually lurked there.

Early on the following morning, before leaving my quarters, I went to my Spanish friends to warn them of the danger that I believed threatened them, and to entreat them to resume their secluded life, until the dark clouds of their destiny had passed away. Donna Marguerita was occupied in concealing within a curiously wrought leathern belt some valuable jewels she had brought from Vittoria; while her husband, with fevered anxiety, told me that on the proceeding night, he had seen from a little window overlooking the narrow street, two men of very suspicious appearance in close conference with José; that a secret presentiment whispered that he was the subject of that conference, and that rather than live the prey to a thousand fears he had determined, on that night, to attempt an escape to the French coast. The boatman was engaged, the bark moored beneath the window, and to the blessed care of Virgin he would confide the rest.

During that day the embarkation of the Ordnance stores was completed, and my orders having been to repair to head-quarters at Lesaca, an opportunity was thus offered, not to be neglected, of getting José out of the way. I gave him directions to go off instantly to prepare my quarters at Lesaca; but I could not help fancying that there was at the time a sardonic laugh in his eye, that said as plainly as if he had spoken it, "I am a cleverer fellow than you are."

At sunset he started with one of my mules, and never did I feel much more relieved than when I saw his back fairly turned on my poor refugee guests. On that very day intelligence had been received of the arrest of two Spaniards of rank within the Spanish lines; both of whom had paid the penalty of their political backsliding with their lives, and this circumstance had increased my anxiety for the safety of my friends.

At about ten o'clock, I repaired to their apartment. The night was calm and beautiful, and as the rippling waves broke lazily and loud against the little boat beneath, it sounded, to my imagination, like a funeral dirge, moved by the prophetic spun of the future. A figure wrapped in the dark cloak and flapping sombrero of the Spaniard, reclined indolently awaiting the party he was engaged to accompany. There was a pause of deep emotion, that wrung the hearts of that little party as they stood, gazing for the last time on the old wooden terrace, that looked too frail to bear even the weight of the delicate form, who was first to lead the way. One pressure of the hand, a stifled sob, a sigh, and the little boat, under its light sail, pressed onwards through the blue waters.

On my arrival at Lesaca, on the following morning, I found that José had played me false, and taken off, not only himself, but part of my baggage, and my best mule also. I could have borne my misfortunes more philosophically, had it not been for the anxious thought that would intrude of his absence being connected with the flight of my poor friends; and I caused him to be sought in all directions, but without avail. I never saw him afterwards!

The object of my going to Lesaca was to re-organize the several brigades of ammunition for the field, which the numerous actions that had taken place with the enemy—particularly those of the Pyrenees—had nearly exhausted.

From the 25th of July to the 2nd of August, the belligerent armies, with the exception of the blockading force at San Sebastian, under General Graham, had been in constant movement, during which period no less than ten actions had been fought; and perhaps there never was a similar test of the superiority of generalship than the mountainous locality of the Pyrenees afforded. On one side, the directing presence of the experienced Soult; on the other, the discerning, combining, and time-seizing spirit of Wellington. As force moved against force, retreating, advancing, dodging; as each Commander endeavoured by *finesse,* to outdo his skilful antagonist, the position of the armies represented in their different movements the scientific progress of a well-played game of chess, where each piece acts the parts assigned to it, under the powerful combination of man's intellectual agency. At the conclusion of these days of sanguinary hostilities the armies resumed their first position; the French occupied the hills about Ainhoa, the heights of Sarre, St. Jean de Luz, and St. Jean Pied de Port.

The line of the allied army extended from the pass of Roncesvalles to the mouth of the Bidassoa; the light division occupying the heights of Santa Barbara near to the little town of Vera.

CHAPTER 26

San Sebastian Falls

Orders were now given for the renewal of the attack on San Sebastian, and for the re-landing of the guns and stores, that for security had been embarked on board of transports in the harbour of Passages. The old guns, however, were found to have done their duty too efficiently to be in condition to begin again.

The unceasing vomiting of destructive missiles at the first attack on San Sebastian had not only caused the metal to droop at the muzzle, but had so enlarged the vents of the guns, that few of them were at all serviceable. We, therefore, waited for a fresh battering train from England, which arrived on the 20th of August, and also an abundant supply of small-arm ammunition. All was once more bustle and expectation; fatigue parties from the line, the artillery, and the navy, assisted in the disembarkation, and the scene presented one of stirring interest; nor was the picturesque wanting—the country boats we put in requisition, covering the blue waters of the little harbour, were manned, as Paddy might say, by Spanish women, whose dark expressive countenances, long plaited hair falling almost to the feet, and animated gestures, added a magical touch to the picture, that without it, would only have spoken to the heart of turbulence and strife.

During the suspension of the siege, the Governor of the Fortress had caused the defences and works to be repaired. New obstacles to the besiegers had been thrown up, and both men and ammunition were daily dropping in from Bayonne, owing to our naval force being inadequate to prevent it. On our side, the preparations for the premeditated attack were carried on far more vigorously than for the first. Sixty-three guns were planted on the right, and thirty-two on the left, making a total of ninety-five pieces of heavy ordnance, manned by the gunners from the field batteries, and amply supplied with ammunition. So matters stood till the 23rd, when the fire was opened on both sides, continuing with but little interruption until the 31st. Several times within that period, Lord Wellington visited the batteries in person, and for the last time on the 30th, when having carefully examined the state of the fortress, he gave orders that the assault should take place at eleven o'clock on the following morning.

Notwithstanding the dilapidated appearance of the outward defences, and inviting aperture of the gaping breach, the ingenious inventions of the besieged, to frustrate their assailants, were formidable; and as the sequel will show, accident alone effected what had baffled the almost super-human efforts of that terrible assault. Immediately behind the breach, a fall of twenty feet was the only means of entrance to the town beneath. This was defended by a high wall, crenelled for musketry, while the flanks of the summit of the breach, were defended by three lines of traverses, to prevent access to the connecting line of the ramparts. Mines were prepared to blow up the first adventurous spirits that might gain too firm a footing. Several pieces of Ordnance lay concealed, but ready to send forth their deadly missives on the assailants, and the heavy guns from the Mirador scowled upon the columns as they advanced from the trenches to the attack. From an eminence to the left of the howitzer battery, General Graham looked on, during which time I was with him, and therefore an eye-witness of the whole progress of the assault.

It was some time past eleven, when the Forlorn Hope, headed by the brave McGuire, rushed sharply to the breach. Close at its heels followed, like an impetuous torrent, the leading columns, under a fire of shot and shell that brought to the earth heaps of killed and wounded. As each succeeding party fell, so did another, and another, rush on with fearful shouts over the bodies of the slain, gaining the summit of the breach, and falling lifeless on it, as soon as gained; for the fearful leap below impeded further progress, and the impetuous assailants from the strand, could only cling to the crumbling walls, unable to advance, until the mighty current from behind forced them in turn upon the breach, in turn to die.

From the position in which General Graham stood, during this anxious and awful time, masses of our gallant fellows were to be seen ascending the broken fragments of the breach, and disappearing the moment afterwards to make room for succeeding victims, and yet no progress had been made. The breach and strand were strewn with heaps of slain, and up to that point, their gallant blood had flowed in vain. Occasionally the waving of an officer's sword, and the desperate efforts that followed, caused a momentary gleam of hope that was as suddenly checked by the increased fire of the besieged; and again the foot of the breach was covered with a fresh layer of unsuccessful dead.

To replace these losses, General Leith, who directed the assault, sent forth fresh columns of men, in rapid succession, but as these pushed with vigour from the trenches, the guns from the Mirador tore up their ranks, even before they gained the foot of the breach. Upwards of two hours and a half had elapsed since our gallant troops had been exposed to this terrible carnage, inflicted by an enemy, with whom they had no power of grappling in return.

At this crisis, it has generally been supposed that Sir Thomas Graham directed that our batteries should open fire upon the traverses, which flanked the great breach, and behind which were concealed the grenadiers, whose deadly musketry had contributed so much to the destruction of the besiegers. That such a measure was adopted is true, but it is equally so that the suggestion was made in my presence to General Graham by Colonel Dickson, whose experienced eye, and knowledge of the precision exercised by his gunners, made him foresee the advantages to be derived from it. Accordingly, the concentrated fire of fifty pieces of heavy Ordnance was turned upon the enemy's defences.

It would be difficult, indeed impossible, to describe the workings of the veteran Graham's stern countenance as he looked upon the sad destruction of his brave troops, but even this was for a moment forgotten in the interest that a new feature in the scene produced.

The sun shone with a brilliancy that gave to the burning sands in front of the batteries, the appearance of a spangled carpet, when suddenly there seemed to rise from it a close column of soldiers, arrayed in the dark uniform of the Portuguese.

Shooting rapidly to the right, they bore down towards the Arumea river, directly in front of the Mirador battery, while an officer, preceding by some yards the rest waving his sword and cheering on his men, plunged into the river that divided them from the small breach of the fortress.

As if paralysed at the bold attempt, the guns from the Mirador, and Monte Orguello ceased to fire; the smoke cleared off, and all eyes turned to the river, in which, above their waists in water, were wading, in close marching order, the devoted band.

A moment's pause ensued. Alas! it was but a moment, for the next brought a fierce flash from the Mirador, followed by a roar of fearful import, which showed too clearly that the momentary lull was but to insure the certainty of destruction by a more deadly aim. The white foam of the Arumea danced high into the air, while a dense cloud of black smoke rolled over the head of the column. Scarcely had it gained transparency, before a second discharge, more terrible than the first, fell in among them. An Oh! burst involuntarily from General Graham's lips, as he looked upon the murderous havoc made in the ranks of those brave men. Still, however, the survivors pushed on to the shore, and though assailed by a sharp fire of musketry from the ramparts, the gallant Major Snodgrass and his brave Portuguese followers succeeded in gaining the smaller breach of the fortress.

Yet still the death-winged missiles of the besieged continued with increasing intensity to carry destruction to the besiegers. All that human bravery could effect had been effected by our troops, and not an inch of real advantage gained. At this moment of feverish anxiety and uncertainty, a tremendous explosion, succeeded by several others, that seemed to shake the foundations of the earth, suddenly changed the aspect of affairs. A howitzer shell from our batteries had struck an expense magazine in the rear of the traverses, igniting an immense mass of combustible matter, live shells, &c. and blowing into the air numbers of the grenadiers who were placed behind the traverses to bar the entrance of the stormers from the town.

In every direction these hapless beings fell by the force of the explosion; legs and arms, heads, and headless bodies, showered over the ramparts among our men, who, shouting with exultation, rushed with frenzied enthusiasm to every crevice that offered admittance, proving how much the occurrence had contributed to renew the ardour of the attack. The ringing voice of the gallant Colonel Hunt, in leading on his heroes of the light division, was heard amidst the clamour of the fight, and the confusion of the enemy having paved the way to victory, the assailants rushed in like an impetuous torrent, at every point of entrance. The French contested the ground step by step, but in vain. The fortress was won; and as the British troops poured into the town, the only retreat left to the enemy was within the fortified position of Monte Orguello.

Thus, after a protracted siege, fell the Fortress of San Sebastian, leaving in its fall reflections of the most painful nature, whether we reflect on the noble men who shed their blood in the almost ferocious bravery that marked that assault, or whether we reflect on the whirl of evil passions that marked the foot-steps of the victors after the assault. Of the former, there were some, who will ever be remembered by those who knew them. One of the foremost of these was the brave McGuire. His beautiful countenance, as he lay stretched in the sleep of death at the foot of the breach, wore a sweet smile; and a calm serenity was spread over it, which seemed to say, "I have exchanged the bloody strife of man for the peacefulness of Heaven!"[1]

Who can ever forget McGuire who led the Forlorn Hope at San Sebastian?

The Engineers suffered severely. The commanding officer, Sir Richard Fletcher, who had gone through all the battlefields of the Peninsula, from the year 1808, with the regard and esteem of all men, fell, with several officers of his corps, before the breach of San Sebastian.

The pen shrinks from a description of the scene that succeeded to the capture of the fortress. On every side, in heaps, lay the dead and dying, while the frantic shouts of the incensed and excited soldiers, as they rushed into the town to glut their pent-up feelings of revenge upon everything that came in their way, mixed with the heavy rolling of a terrific thunder storm that swept down from the mountains. Nature seemed herself to mourn, not only over the

---

1. Early on the morning of the assault, McGuire was seen dressed with unusual care, as if for some great occasion. Some one remarked upon it to him, when he replied, "When we are going to meet all our old friends whom we have not seen for many years, it is very natural to wish to look as well as possible."

extinction of some of her favourite spirits on that day, but over the influence that had been wrenched from her by the demon of revenge over the hearts of men.

For eight days succeeding the fall of the fortress, did the gallant Frenchman Rey, and his devoted garrison, hold out within their last remaining lines of defence; but sickness, famine, and the total destruction of their last bulwarks, necessitating their proud spirits to bend down: they surrendered prisoners of war,[2] and filed out with the honours of such, on the 9th of September, from a position that had taken us two months to subdue.

In a few short hours, the stillness of peace had replaced the din of war, but not so were the ravages of man to be obliterated; the town was in flames, the wretched inhabitants houseless and beggared, while many a defenceless woman with agonized heart, or maddened brain, bore witness to the still more horrible results of war.

---

2. The French officer, whose fearless exposure on the walls of the fortress, after the first attack, had been the means of preserving our wounded from the danger of our own guns, was restored unconditionally to liberty by Lord Wellington.

CHAPTER 27

The Death of a Lady

The Ordnance stores were again to be embarked at Passages, and glad to escape from the spectacle of misery that every step presented, I found myself, towards evening, in my old quarters, overlooking the little harbour from the wooden terrace where I had last seen my Spanish friends.

The exciting scenes of San Sebastian had almost banished them from my mind, but when I entered the little room, where I had passed with them so many hours, I almost started to find it empty, and involuntarily my eyes turned to the wide expanse of ocean before me, as if I held it responsible for the safety of those, who had confided so much to its keeping. But how changed was the aspect of that ocean from the smiling face it wore on the night in question; scowling thunder clouds shed their dark reflection over what was then the deep blue water, and as the mighty waves came rolling in from the great Atlantic, chased by an equinoctial gale, each little bark and transport that rode at anchor in the harbour, shook and rocked to the wild music of the elements.

I stood on the old terrace, looking at the heightening storm, and watching, with intense interest, the many little sails that came dropping in to seek protection from the raging sea without. One by one they braved the buffeting of the waves, and landed their dripping owners on the beach, where many an anxious wife and mother stood to greet the welcome return. The wind had now risen to a fearful height, and far as the eye could reach, the fretted, agitated waters, rose like a huge bubbling cauldron, when distant far was seen a *chasse-marée*, or country boat, making to the shore. Every eye turned to the object with intense anxiety, not unmixed with strong forebodings that neither seaman's skill, nor tight-set boat could bear against that gathering storm.

The mariners collected on the shore, some to indulge in their own speculations on the fate of the distant object, others with a view to render assistance, if practicable. My elevated position from the terrace, and English telescope, brought plainly to my view the endangered bark. It was a fearful sight to witness the frail thing at one moment tossed on the summit of a rising billow, the next plunged into the abyss below, disappearing altogether between the engulfing waves. So passed away some minutes, hope and fear alternately prevailing, as the bark still rode on, diminishing, at each plunge, her distance from the shore. A roll of mountain waves now came hurling on her stern, and a shriek of terror burst from the assembled women, as the avalanche swept over the tiny atom—a deadly pause followed—and then a shout of gladness as the boat popped up her head once more. As nearer and nearer she approached the mouth of the harbour, so did dangers thicken around her. The rolling waves that dashed with frantic fury against the outward piles, rebounded back at the obstruction offered; and, as if influenced by revenge, formed into whirling eddies, threatening destruction to whatever might approach.

Again the wind, that had momentarily lulled, poured forth the low and distant howl, that ushers in the ungovernable blast, and in another moment the little sail flapped in ribbons over the now unmanageable and death-doomed boat. With one bound she reached the mouth of the harbour, but death was foremost in the race, and at the same moment that by the growing darkness three human figures were distinctly seen, with arms outstretched to shore, the relentless waves struck on the side the gallant boat, which sank to rise no more. A scream of horror rang from the lookers-on that was re-echoed, as if in mockery, by the hissing surge. But why does every heart beat again with hope as a small dark spot becomes more discernible on the bosom of the waves? One moment it is borne up on high, the next invisible; yet still it re-appears, and nears the strand, while the thrilling voices with which the men vociferate, *"Carracho,"* and the women *"As Dios mio,"* tell plainly that the frail strength of a human being is exerted against the strife of elements.

Some brave fellows push off a boat in the direction of the object; a rope is thrown, and caught, and in a few seconds, a rescued man stands among his deliverers on the shore.

Turning from the dark storm without to the comforts of my canteen within, I sat me down to moralize upon the caprices of destiny. My mind pondered over the unequal measures meted out to man, and from which he traces the fiat, not only of his physical existence, but that of his moral also. In the wreck that I had witnessed, three human beings had suffered equally the terror of approaching death; two of them had been launched into that vast eternity, of which the element that betrayed them is, to mortal sight, the type. One had been saved—for what purpose? For what fate? Reserved to good or evil? To glorify on earth the divine hand that raised him from the "overwhelming waters?" Or to add another link to the chain that rivets Satan to the human race?

On the following morning, on leaving my quarters at an early hour, my attention was arrested by a crowd collected on the beach, and approaching to learn the cause, I found that the tide had thrown up the corpse of a woman, one of the victims, doubtless, of the previous night's storm, for accounts had already reached Passages of the total wreck of twelve vessels on the coast. Wrapped in a coarse cloak, the unconscious form lay in the arms of two boat men, the face entirely concealed by a mass of dark luxuriant hair, that fell, saturated by the heavy sea-water, like a funeral shroud over the inanimate clay, while from beneath the rough serge covering, peeped two exquisitely formed Andalusian feet, cased in materials too rich to belong to other class than that of gentle blood.

As I followed in the crowd to a neighbouring *posado*, where the body was to be deposited, I learnt that it had already been identified—by the man who had been saved on the previous evening—as that of a lady who perished with his fellow-boatman in entering the harbour of Passages. The hostess of the *posado* came out to receive the melancholy procession, and the still dripping body was placed upon a bed until the arrival of the Alcalde, who had been summoned to superintend the proceedings. The entrance of this dignitary was the signal for the removal of the cloak, and no sooner was this done, and the dark hair parted from the corpse, than the delicate and beautiful features of Donna Marguerita were exposed to view.

Round her waist, concealed by the black mantilla, that clung to her form in heavy folds, was the curious leathern belt, in which she had placed her valuables on the last day we met, and which the Alcalde now proceeded to open. A parcel of detached papers, bearing the direction of "Donna Flora," fell from the faithful deposit. One paper more the leathern belt contained, directed to myself. At the wish of the Alcalde, I opened it, and drew forth a woman's cambric handkerchief, steeped in blood. It told a tale that required not the confirmation of the few written words that were enclosed,—"*La sangue di marido asesinado!*"

All the information the boatman could give was, that a lady, apparently in great distress of mind, had engaged himself and another to take her in their boat to Passages. The rest we knew too well!

When the last mournful directions had been given respecting the interment of the body; and when the crowd had dispersed, to gather again together at the next passing object of idle curiosity, I gave to the Alcalde as much information regarding the hapless Don Miguel and his wife, as was consistent with my own position, and asked permission, which was easily granted, to be the medium of forwarding to Vittoria the papers addressed to Donna Flora by her unfortunate relative. They were unsealed, and open; and as I knew they could only relate to those circumstances with which I was acquainted, I did not hesitate, on my return to my quarters, to peruse them.

Once again, and for the last time, I found myself in the room they had occupied; the door leading to the terrace was open, and behind it, like a framed picture, lay the sea, as calm and as blue as on that night when the little boat waited beneath the window; while the rippling waves that now struck against the landing place, reminded me of the requiem they then seemed to chant over those beings that futurity was committing to their agency.

Tears had turned to blots the unconnected and scarcely discernible words that lay before me, traced by the trembling hand of Donna Marguerita, and yet the purport was too plain. The revengeful José had been the traitor; leagued with the boatman, the latter had run the little bark on the hostile beach of Andaye, where the Judas was himself in waiting—and not alone.

Under an escort of Spanish *partidas,* the unhappy fugitives were conducted to a near post of the Spanish army, where the Conde was tried for treason on the spot, and summarily shot in the presence of his agonized wife.

I was present at the interment of Donna Marguerita, and caused the handkerchief, that her enthusiastic affection for her husband had dipped in his blood, to be laid beside her in the silent tomb. *"Requiescat in pace."*

CHAPTER 28

The 95th at the Bridge of Vera

During the assault of San Sebastian, Marshal Soult attacked the position of the allied army at Vera, in the hope of being able to bring relief to the distressed Governor of San Sebastian. It is difficult to assign any reason for Soult having deferred this attempt until the moment when it may be said that the assailants were in the breach, unless that his information respecting the progress of the siege was at variance with the fact.

Before reaching Oyerzum, from whence a good road led to the beleaguered fortress, the French Marshal had to force the passage of the Bidassoa, to pass the lofty mountains of San Marcial, the Pena de Haya, and the heights of Vera, opposed at every step by an army, superior in strength to his own. The consequence was a long and sanguinary struggle, its terrors heightened by a tremendous hurricane, not infrequent in the wild and elevated regions of the Pyrenees.

The combat waged fierce and bloody on these mountain tops. In the distance, for many miles, the hills and rocks looked alive with the moving groups that crowned them. As far as the eye could reach, the dark smoke curled densely on their sides and summits, while the pealing musketry reverberated in sullen repetition through the echoing crags. Here and there the dark red fire might be seen flashing from the cannon's mouth, its deep roar mingling with the shouts of the allied troops, as they drove the French down the mountain slopes they had too rashly ascended, forcing them to recross the boundary stream of the Bidassoa, swollen into a dangerous torrent, by the rush of descending waters, impelled by the hurricane above.

The loss on both sides was severe, that of the allied army being estimated at nearly three thousand; and of the French at four thousand men. But far more than the loss of four thousand men was sustained by the enemy in this desperate onset. The morale of the French army had been already weakened by a succession of defeats; and here was another, affording, as it seemed, an unnecessary display of declining strength. Driven to the very threshold of their own country, the soldiers felt the humiliation of their position; no longer imbued with the daring spirit that animates an invading army, they beheld themselves on the point of becoming, by stringent necessity, the defenders of their own soil from invasion.

A foreign foe was already on the frontier mountains, looking down with the laugh of triumphant derision on the broad plains of France; hence the wild impetuous rush to protract, at least, the dreaded encroachment. A movement that probably originated more from the vehement desire of action, than from any reasonable hope of averting definitively the impending evil.

On those mountain heights stood the Spaniards, no longer flying in terror before the French troops, or skulking to their mountain fastnesses like outlaws in their native land. No longer defenceless victims to the brute force of a savage multitude that despised their weakness, and held cheap their courage; that time had passed away, and a goodly array of well-armed men, in all the strength of discipline, stood prepared to glut a retributive vengeance in their turn.

The Portuguese likewise—they, for whom the French had evinced so utter a contempt—they also stood on those mountain tops, a brave and daring band, not only looking down upon the distant plains of France with hopes of a nearer acquaintance with them, but prepared to tread their way through paths of blood, if necessary, to reach them. In proof of this, so desperate was their bayonet charge at the bridge of Lesaca, that the French, humiliated at their repulse by men they had so despised, vehemently asserted that British soldiers had fought in the uniform of the Portuguese.

What a glorious tribute from an enemy to British valour! at the same time showing how the good effects of British discipline had gradually extended to troops, that at one time were more dangerous than useful as auxiliaries in the field. Here then was a powerful army, strong both in numbers and efficiency, eagerly waiting for the coming crisis.

The sanguinary strife of the preceding months had produced a daily association with death, that had weakened its terrors in the minds of those engaged in it. Each felt that his turn was perhaps the next, and a kind of apathetic indifference was the result. There was also another cause to reconcile survivors to the loss of friends, in despite of the excellent fellowship that existed between all ranks of men in the Peninsula, and pre-eminently among the "choice spirits" of the light division. The death of an officer gave a step of promotion in the regiment, and therefore the senior Captain, who stepped into a majority, or the senior Lieutenant who obtained his company, found in that circumstance a healing balm to his regret.

It was of usual occurrence to hear the young officers, when assembled after an engagement, congratulating themselves on the promotion that had perhaps fallen in among them, with the explosion of some murderous shell.

In the 95th regiment, there were two brothers, the eldest was a Captain; the youngest a Lieutenant in the same battalion, and such was the avidity of the former for promotion, that although an excellent fellow, he would have seen all the officers in his regiment spitted like larks, if such a process would have given "a step," as he used to term it, either to himself or to his brother "Joe." At every fresh casualty that occurred—and there were many, for the gallant 95th was always in action—the Captain would exultingly exclaim, if the deceased was a superior officer to himself "poor fellow! he was a good fellow, *but,* it is a step for me." If junior to himself, his fraternal affection found an equal pleasure in saying, "poor fellow! he was a good fellow, *but,* it is a step for Joe," and so frequently were these expressions used, that they became play-words in the regiment.

During the heat of the combat at the bridge of Vera, a ball struck the Captain to the earth, but as he related the story himself, not very long after, it is unnecessary to add, that promotion had not yet done with him.

For a long time he lay unconscious of the war that waged around, nor recovered his senses until all was over, and a sergeant and some men had approached to remove the bodies of their comrades from the ground. Although faint and unable to stir from the effects of his wounds, he was still able to remember that the sergeant advanced to the spot where he lay, and pointing with commiseration to his apparently dead body said: "Ah Jack, there lies our poor Captain!" The soldier apostrophised, quickly retorted with a laugh: "Poor fellow! he was a good fellow; but it is a step for Joe!"

It did not fall to the good fortune of all, on that day, to be removed from the field of suffering in the manner of this gallant lover of promotion. Many lingered, in hopeless agony, until death came like a friend to their relief; others were brought into hospital, on the third day, and yet recovered, although the pangs of starvation, and exposure to the weather had terribly aggravated the condition of their wounds. Some poor fellows were never found, nor afterwards heard of, having no doubt fallen victims to the plundering fiends that infest all battlefields.

An instance occurred of a brave officer of the 34th regiment who was seen to fall wounded among the mountain brushwood; the spot was marked by the lifeless bodies of some soldiers of his regiment. At the cessation of the combat, a party was sent to find the wounded man, headed by the individual who had seen him fall. The place was identified by many tokens, but he they sought was no longer there.

In vain they explored the neighbouring hills, and tore away the dwarf trees, to which he might have crawled for shelter. The search was unavailing, although it proved that he had been there, for a torn pocket handkerchief, bearing his initials, was found hanging to a bramble bush, close to the spot where he was last seen.

For a long time afterwards, it was hoped that the poor fellow had fallen into the hands of the French, and would be spared to recount the history of his escape; but time at length crushed such hopes, and it was then conjectured that some wolfish being had stripped the sufferer, and hurled him down the precipice into the torrent beneath.

At the bridge of Vera, a party of the 95th gallantly defended the pass, and Captain Cardew, a veteran officer of the regiment, nobly fell in this encounter with the enemy. He was much beloved; and as conspicuous for valour in the field, as for his gentle courtesy out of it. I had received orders to repair to Lesaca, the head-quarters of the army, on a particular duty, and arrived just as the sale of poor Cardew's goods and chattels was in progress. Truly it is a melancholy sight to witness the regimental process of the disposal of articles, that look as if they formed part and parcel of the owner himself.

As I entered, the half worn-out jacket, and still glittering *chacot* were held up to view by the military auctioneer. Such objects usually go in the regiment, and bidders were not slack in their endeavours to obtain some relic of their lamented comrade. In some short moments, the limited wardrobe was dispersed in divers hands, and with the exception of the sword and watch, reserved as mementos for sorrowing relatives, all other things fell piece-meal into the hands of those, who were in daily intercourse and friendly association with the deceased.

Only a few hours before, and the gallant Cardew stood, on that very spot, reconnoitering with his glass the mountain heights at the foot of which he now lay a mangled corpse. But such is the fate of war. His death was the birth of grief to some fond hearts; but to his regiment "A step for Joe."

Chapter 29

The Crossing of the Bidassoa

On the morning of the 7th of October, the allied army moved against the French, and after a day's hard fighting, effected the passage of the Bidassoa, causing the enemy to retreat back to his position. Nothing could surpass the conduct of our troops on that occasion; and though the complicated and difficult details of warfare, carried on amidst the gigantic mountains of the Pyrenees have been already described by historians as accurately as the locality will permit, there were patches of home scenery, so to speak, that could only fall beneath the individual eye.

The dark green jackets of Barnard's rifles, as they fought their way in climbing up the steep and rugged hills, whose summits were crowned by the enemy; the bright red and white colours of the 43rd and 52nd, as they crossed, in close column, the valley which divided the heights they had quitted from those they sought to gain; and then, throwing off their kits, in single file, wound up the narrow broken paths that led them to the fierce expecting foe, whose peppering fire from above seemed only to infuse fresh vigour into those unrivalled "Light Bobs;" the aspect of the Spaniards, whose sombre hues made it difficult to distinguish them from the brown rocks, over which they clambered with the characteristic agility of the inhabitants of mountainous countries,—all these were brilliant lights and shades in the great picture of nature's wilderness before us.

The 52nd, led by Major William Mein, on reaching the brow of the mountain, formed rapidly into line, and without firing a single shot, advanced in double quick time against a column of the enemy, which had only a few minutes before driven a regiment of

Portuguese Cacadores over the other side of the rugged declivity. The soul-inspiring cheer that rang from the ever foremost 52nd, struck terror into the ranks of the French, they wavered, as British steel advanced. Then turned and fled towards one of their great redoubts; they were so closely pursued, that some of the 52nd actually entered the redoubt, with their flying foes, upon which the latter again started forth from the opposite side, making, at the top of their speed towards a second line of redoubts and entrenchments.

On the right of the first redoubt, was a deep and thickly wooded ravine, in which a body of three or four hundred of the enemy was concealed; but being discovered, some companies of our rifles advanced at a running pace, by a little footpath, parallel to the ravine, to intercept their sortie. The French within the ravine also ran to reach the opening first, and a regular race took place between them. The view holloa of the rifles, as they spied their enemies through the trees, rang through the air, and with renewed spirit they bounded over the narrow foot way, reaching the mouth of the ravine at the same moment as the French. The latter, panic-struck at so close a proximity with the green jackets, threw down their arms and surrendered as prisoners of war. Their commanding officer was a fine lively young fellow, and it was difficult to prevent him from jeering and laughing at the volley of "*carrachos*" that the Spaniards fired at him when within their power. Moreover, they were so disposed to handle him roughly, that we recommended him in kindness, to bridle his tongue, as no influence would have been available in protecting him from the carbines of the Spaniards. With ourselves, he was both courteous and gentle in return for some kindness that was shown to him. His arm had been broken by a musket ball, and I remember that one of our young officers converted his own pocket-handkerchief into a sling, while others tore up theirs for bandages, until surgical assistance could be had.

The result of this day's fighting, though the loss on both sides was severe, was the opening of the passage of the Bidassoa to the allied armies, and thus, a firmer footing was gained upon the frontiers of France.

After the victory gained in the passage of the Bidassoa, the headquarters of the army removed to Vera, a small village still more embedded than Lesaca in the mountain wilderness. My billet was in the house of the parish priest, and in these days of religious contumacy, when, in our favoured land, it is a matter of frequent occurrence to witness the feuds and dissensions that embroil the church, when shepherds and their flocks seem united but on the one point of seeking causes for disunion, in such days as these, memory furnishes a refreshing contrast in Padre Oliveira, the parish priest of Vera. Upon a stipend that would sound strange to the ears of our well-paid Rectors, this holy man was rich among his parishioners, but above all, he was rich in the charity that he dispensed spiritually and temporally in his attached flock.

The modest parsonage was close to the little church, whose tiny steeple, as it reared its head among the stupendous rocks and elevated mountains, was no unfitting representation of pygmy man, in communion with the mysteries of eternity. The Padre's home was under the guidance of a sister, many years younger than himself; an arrangement that removed from the little dwelling the comfortless aspect that domiciles exhibit, in nine cases out of ten, when deprived of female vigilance and care. Next to his parishioners, the simple-hearted man loved best his bees; from bees to flowers, the step is short, but with him it led to still higher researches, and as a botanist and naturalist, Padre Oliveira was held in no mean repute.

The little apartment allotted to me was scrupulously neat. It had been furnished by himself, and although plain, evinced a degree of taste, showing how much alike, though perhaps differing in nation, language, and religion, are those in whom purity of mind dwells as an habitual principle, diffusing its mild effulgence over every minutiae of life. Such purity as this dwelt in the good Padre, and he and his mountain home were well suited to each other, protected by the little church that looked like a link in that dreary nature between himself and a more beautiful world.

The room that I occupied led by a narrow passage to a door that opened on a little flower-garden; beyond it was the church. The autumn was already considerably advanced, and in those mountain regions the rushing wind howled in mournful cadence, shaking the dry leaves into noises that sounded unearthly in the stillness of the night.

I had several times fancied that I heard the sound of footsteps in the passage leading to my room, but the gusts of wind would return with terrific violence and drive such thoughts away. At length, from long continuance, these hurricanes ceased to disturb me, and I slept soundly to their boisterous lullaby.

The placid equanimity of my worthy host seemed proof against all storms, either from within or from without, and his sister, the quiet Agnese, was like the waters of a lake on a summer evening, that deep and motionless receive the reflection of external objects on their bosom, but are incapable of disclosing of their own. No characters are so difficult to fathom as the apparently apathetic. The more complete the stagnation of the moral existence, so long as the ordinary events of every-day life have been alone concerned, the more terrific has been known the sudden rousing of the soul to violent action by some untouched spring; but to return to the good curate and his quiet sister. Few had been the words exchanged between this young woman and myself beyond what the courtesies of civilized life required, and in truth there was something in her manner discouraging to a nearer acquaintance.

Unlike the generality of her countrywomen, Agnese was delicately fair, with a profusion of flaxen ringlets, her light coloured eyes were only remarkable for their passionless lustre, and as she flitted from room to room, in pursuance of her domestic duties, invariably attired in a flowing dress of white fustian, she appeared the very personification of the "Lady of Avenel," or the better known, because more modern, "*Dame Blanche*". There was also a strange expression in those pale eyes, as they wandered from object to object, without seeming to know where to rest; shunning the look that would have detained them for a moment on their un-quiet progress.

Between the reverend father and his young relative, there was as little of congeniality as between herself and me. The daily duties of his profession took him much from home, but on his return, no step of joyful recognition bounded to his fraternal embrace, the presence of youth was unfelt, with all its gladdening attributes, that usually break down the barriers that age and sober reason would raise against them; the quiet Agnese was there, but cold, passive, indifferent as an automaton under the control of machinery.

At the hospitable, but frugal, evening meal, I was sometimes a guest, and should have been so more frequently, but for the strange feelings that the presence of Agnese invariably produced in me; her whole appearance was so strange and unearthly, she ate so sparingly, that imperceptibly, I had identified her in my imagination with the female Ghoul in the Arabian Nights, picking rice by single grains in the day-time, and satisfying her cravings with less delicate fare at night. At an early hour, the Padre usually concluded his day of usefulness by a short prayer, the benediction of Heaven was invoked on the inmates of his dwelling, and we severally retired to be rocked into repose by the bellowing winds from the adjacent mountains.

November, dreary November had set in, and Vera was still the head-quarters of Lord Wellington, but since the successful issue of the 7th of November, the army had been thrown into a position still nearer to the French territory; and although nothing was positively made known as to its intended movements, there was sufficient to guarantee the certainty of an aggressive advance upon the enemy being in contemplation. In support of this assurance, the first days of November were employed by Lord Wellington in moving the several corps of the army into position, preparatory to his attack on Soult, and every breast beat high with expectancy that the approaching crisis would lead to the immediate invasion of southern France. We had received orders to march on the 9th from Vera, and mine excellent host had indulged his kind nature by preparing sundry articles of dainty fare for the occasion. The weather had become mild and rainy, and the monotonous trickling of the water from the roof, had replaced the noisy howling of the wind. Again I fancied that each night brought the return of those sounds I had attributed to the creaking beams of the old house shaken by the blast. One night I felt assured that footsteps were approaching. I listened attentively, they seemed to recede, a door opened, gently closed, and all was still. The following night, at the same hour, I heard the same sounds; again I listened, they became more distant, a door opened and closed. Curiosity was too powerful to remain unsatisfied. I, therefore, opened my own door, and stole—I am half ashamed to own it—on tip-toe to the end of the passage. Another moment assured me beyond a doubt that two persons, of different sexes, were together within a few yards of where I stood. The voice of Agnese was of too remarkable a quality to be mistaken for another's. It was a thin and wiry voice, such as might have been expected from so chilling a reservoir—but who was he, the visitor to a young girl's virgin chamber at that unholy hour? I heard him whisper. Could it be in accents of love to such an icicle as Agnese! Again I listened. She spoke with all the warmth of awakened passion—yet still her voice grated harshly on my ear, as some voices do, leaving a chiming knell that vibrates painfully on the nerves.

Unwilling to play a protracted part of eaves-dropper, I retreated to my own apartment. Not a sound disturbed the stillness of the night, beyond the dull pattering of the rain upon my windows, and the sullen blackness of the sky was un-cheered by a single star. Long and patiently I watched for further tokens of the nocturnal visitor's presence, but sleep will beset the faculties of the most curious; and so in my case. After tiring myself out with speculations and surmises, all of them, it must be admitted, most unchivalrously prejudicial to the fair Agnese's fame, I fell asleep, and so ended my disquisitions on the subject.

During the whole of the next day, I was occupied in extensive arrangements for completing the several mule brigades of small arm ammunition that were to move with the troops, and therefore had little time to ponder on the events of the preceding night, or even to see my host and his sister, until the hour of supper. It was with no kindly scrutiny that I bent my eyes on Agnese, as she coldly and silently performed the honours of the table during this evening meal. My feelings towards her were changed to positive dislike, from the innate conviction—a kind of presentiment that is always conclusive to the heart, because it springs from the heart—that she was betraying the confidence of her unsuspecting brother.

The conversation turned chiefly upon my approaching departure; the state of Spain; the increasing resources of the allied army, and tottering position of Soult, driven back to the verge of his own frontier boundary. From politics we travelled onwards to the condition of the Church of Rome in Spain; her decadency in concentrated force since the first invasion of the French, which, however, had only tended to the increase of her power; for, in those days of trouble, each parish priest invested himself in his restricted circle, with the authority and infallibility that in ordinary times, were arrogated by the Pope exclusively; and thus the discipline of the church was maintained in all its rigidity.

Notwithstanding the benign nature of my host, it was not difficult to see that he looked upon me as a heretic, though destined perhaps at the eleventh hour to be received into the bosom of the Holy Church; and he much lamented that I had not had the benefit of frequent conferences with the holy brother Antonio, a member of the Franciscan Monastery on the road to Araquil, whose erudition and piety were celebrated throughout the whole of northern Spain. As the worthy man pursued his eulogium of brother Antonio with all the warmth of religious zeal and admiration, my eyes accidentally turned on the countenance of Agnese. Was it indeed her, or another? I gazed and gazed again; the paleness of her cheeks had given place to a tint of vermilion; the usually insipid eyes were lit up with a fire that seemed to expend itself in rays of dazzling light; she was beautiful to look upon; but there was something awful in her beauty.

After our little party broke up, I found myself in my sleeping chamber, entangled in a maze of wild thoughts; the fatigues of the day were, however, an effectual counterpoise even to my curiosity, and I fell asleep, in spite of all my resolutions to solve the mystery that perplexed me. Perhaps I should never have been the wiser on the subject, if chance, that ready waiting-maid to fortune, had not helped me ever beyond my expectations or desires.

The grey dawn of a November morning was just tinting the gloomy sky, when the closing of a door roused me from my sleep. I started up; and this time went to the window, that overlooked the Padre's garden. A tall figure habited in the frock and cowl of a friar, was rapidly moving in the direction of the church that formed a boundary to this small plot of ground. With a key he turned the lock of the entrance door and disappeared within its walls. Here then was another step gained towards the development of this strange mystery. Yet could it be possible, I asked myself, that a young girl, brought up in the simplicity of a rural life, and the rigidity also, of the Roman Catholic faith; should receive a nightly visitor, and that visitor in the garb of a monastic fraternity? Both reason and feeling argue strongly against the probability of such a circumstance, and I felt relieved by my reflections, and determined, for the future, to set down all mysterious movements that I might see, to the account of some mystical religious observances, that my heresy prohibited me from being initiated in.

On the afternoon of the same day, I returned from the completion of my duties to partake of an early farewell dinner with my host. Orders had arrived for the breaking up of head-quarters on the following morning. The whole army was in motion, and a great battle was evidently on the eve of taking place. With such a prospect in view, it may be supposed that little room was left in the mind for subjects unconnected with it, and it required nothing less than the extraordinary events that occurred during the last few hours of my stay at Vera to have riveted them in my memory with a strength that time has not weakened.

On entering the little parlour that served both as dining-room and study to the Padre, I found he was not alone, and it required but a single glance at the tall figure that meekly rose, and saluted me, to recognize the friar that I had seen under such ambiguous circumstances. My simple host smiled triumphantly at the surprise I was unable to conceal, and which he attributed, poor man! to my reverence for the name by which he introduced his guest,— the reverend brother Antonio.

Had the eulogium I had already heard passed upon this individual been confined to the external man, it would have fallen far short of the truth, for rarely, if ever, had it been my lot to witness so perfect a delineation of human beauty. The shorn hair, that marked his holy calling, might almost have been deemed a *ruse* of art, to display the intellectual contour of the head; while the lofty forehead, polished as Carrara marble, and fringed with the thickset sable locks, spoke to the imagination of abstract science, midnight vigils, and the student's toil. Nor were the features of the countenance less perfect than the head; the eyes dark, luminous, and searching. The nose of the truest Grecian mould; the mouth and chin full, and what a Lavater might have named voluptuous; yet the vacant, brutish expression of the voluptuary was not to be traced in that brilliant and beautiful face.

I learnt from my host that the sudden illness of his sister was the cause of the friar's visit to the house. Agnese had expressed a wish to see the holy Antonio, to whom the guidance of her religious principles had been entrusted by her brother, and the latter was the more anxious to accede to her wish, from Antonio being versed in the science of medicine, and in the qualities of healing herbs, that were never known to fail, when administered by himself.

To lessen the anxiety of the brother, the friar consented to remain until the evening, which came too soon to put an end to the charms of his conversation. The variety of his knowledge was as surprising as the depth of thought, which he seemed to have bestowed upon every subject. His beautiful quotations from classical authors were relieved by an equally perfect conservancy with modern languages and their literature; his manners were a mixture of the frankness that springs from nature, and the polished reserve which characterizes the man of good society.

On the subject of politics, he evinced the independent spirit that spurns at tyranny, and claims for the human race the heaven-born gift of freedom. On that of religion, his liberal mind admitted no pale of division between man and his Creator; and the flush that for a moment lighted up the cheek of our pious host, as if in gentle reproach at the unexpected boldness of such an avowal, was answered by a warm effusion of blood over the beautiful countenance, which seemed almost to speak the words: "All men are brothers."

So completely had this singular person carried away my best feelings in his favour, that when he rose to take his leave, and after cordially embracing his friend, extended his hand to myself, I confess that all thoughts of Agnese, and deception, were wafted from my mind like chaff before the wind.

The night that precedes the commencement of a march is always one of bustle and excitement; and, on this occasion, my time was occupied until the last moment in looking over the returns of ammunition in the field for the ensuing conflict. This pressure of official business prevented me from taking repose that night, and led to a discovery that initiated me into one great feature of worldly knowledge—a distrust in appearances.

Twelve o'clock, that hour for all dismal stories and hob-goblin terrors, was striking by the church clock, and my pen was seeking the ink-stand in a lazy, and half-tired manner, when my ear caught the sound of footsteps in the passage, followed by the closing of a door. I jumped up, determined this last night to make the most of my time, and following the sound, found myself once more playing the part of Paul Pry at the door of a young lady's apartment.

Again I heard, at intervals, the voice of Agnese, but in faint and feeble tones, while suppressed moans, the evident tokens of severe suffering, showed that the malady of the patient had gained ground since the previous evening. The deep voice of the friar announced that she was not without the aid her situation required; and I, therefore, returned to my own room, and tried to resume my writing, but an unaccountable agitation rendered this no easy task, and propelled by an irresistible impetus, I retraced my steps to the passage. At the instant that I reached the door of Agnese's apartment, a faint cry, not to be mistaken, the first that weakness utters on the threshold of this world of sin and sorrow, rang clearly and even sharply through the air. It was the first and last evidence of life!

Another hour elapsed, and the door leading to the garden opened gently on its hinges. I hastily extinguished the light that might have betrayed me, and stationed myself at the window. The night was so intensely dark, that it was impossible to discern the nearest object; but while vainly straining my eyes to catch the tall figure of the friar, a dull light suddenly fell upon a patch of earth beneath the church wall at the extremity of the garden. It was evidently produced by a dark lanthorn, and by a strange misconception of its effects, the deed that darkness was intended to conceal, was rendered visible. The tall figure of the friar was no longer shrouded in the gloom of night, and without being able to account for it, my blood ran cold as I looked upon him.

The earth was saturated with the heavy rains, and it required but little exertion to make an aperture in her moistened bosom. A shovel in the friar's hands performed this work most expeditiously, but guilt is seldom accompanied by self-possession, and even this accomplished hypocrite tarried in his work, to look around in fear. At length, the task was done, and a little grave stood yawning for its intended occupant. Nor did it wait long. Another hurried look around him, and then, drawn from beneath the cowled frock, an infant—murdered, there is little doubt, by the author of its being—was transferred to that silent bed.

The friar, after replacing the earth, and trampling it to a level surface, stood for a moment motionless. How were his thoughts engaged in that brief space?

CHAPTER 30

Battle of the Nivelle

Before sunrise on the morning that opened with the event recorded in the last chapter, I left Vera, and before the close of the same day, the battle of the Nivelle had added its lustre to the British arms.

On that morning the two belligerent armies again stood in hostile array amidst the stupendous mountains of the Pyrenees. The rich valleys of France lay stretched below to stimulate both sides; the one to a victory that would lead to those smiling plains; the other to a victory that would save them from an invading and triumphant foe.

The combatants stretched along a chain of mountains, extending over nearly fifteen miles, and were more numerous on both sides than in any former action of the Peninsula; the French counting eighty thousand, the Anglo-Portuguese and Spaniards ninety thousand men.

Our artillery, under Colonel Dickson, consisted of ninety-five guns, in a perfect state of efficiency, besides a mountain battery of three-pounders, directed by Lieutenant Robe. The latter were not, perhaps, capable of doing much mischief, but the moral effect they produced of alarm as their shot came tumbling down from the cloud-topped hills, was fraught with consequences still more important.

The able historian, who has handed down to posterity the workings of that mountain strife, has fertilized the crags and rugged cliffs of the Pyrenees with the brave blood that bathed them. What more could be added to the already recorded tales of daring deeds that passed in those grand recesses of nature's solitude, where even her sternest barriers were spurned and conquered by the resolute and enthusiastic ardour of our British troops.

Where all are nobly brave, it seems almost a wrong to specify a part, but just as among the beauteous stars of Heaven, we look most at those that shed the brightest light, so may we without detracting from the rest, single out from among the heroes of the Nivelle, Colborn's light brigade. Gigantic rocks were fitting tombstones for such men.

The victory of our troops was complete; the forces of Soult were driven from their position, and on the same night, San Pé became the head-quarters of Lord Wellington, and his first stepping stone on the soil of France.

On the morning that succeeded the battle, I rose early from my bivouac on the mountain of Sarre, and prepared to start, in pursuance of orders, for the ground lately occupied by the enemy. My duty was to ascertain the extent of the artillery captured, and the means to be employed for collecting it; and mounting my horse, I advanced in the direction of a range of high mountains, which appeared in the distance accessible only to the chamois and mountain goat.

The difficulty I found in ascending to the summit of the first ridge of hills was well repaid by the beauty of the view, which opened over an extensive line of country. Mountains and vallies lay in wild confusion, while the deep ravines, clothed with amber-coloured carpets of wild broom, relieved the sober tints of pine and fir with which that country abounds. The recent rains had swollen the mountain streams into torrents, and in many places, where their course was impeded by the jutting rocks, that boldly rose in perpendicular heights, the waters, as if indignant at the obstacles presented to their progress, rushed furiously in their fall from crag to crag, in every beautiful variety of shape and hue.

On reaching the valley, pure and placid streams branched out from their raging bosom, and winding through the fertile plains, appeared, from the heights whence I viewed them, like silver threads in the sun's rays. The sides of many of the mountains weir thickly wooded with all the varieties of foliage that distinguish Pyrenean scenery, and although approaching winter had thrown over nature a veil of gloom; yet here and there autumnal beauty lingered.

The ascent and descent of each mountain now became more and more arduous and intricate, as if nature, in this vast retreat, had intended to exclude her enemy, man; and it was after several hours, in which I had made comparatively but little progress over the short firs and stunted shrubs which covered the ground, that

I found myself on the summit of a high mountain, overlooking a valley, which arrested my attention.

The waters of the Nivelle intersected a broad and fertile plain, and on every side lofty mountains reared their towering heads, one above another, forming a natural boundary that seemed to preclude all possibility of egress from the valley. It was a spot that Johnson might have selected for his Rasselas. Dotted here and there upon the surrounding heights were huts, curiously and carefully constructed of turf, and of trees closely interwoven together. I quickly recognized them as the work of men who were adepts in campaigning life, and taking a rugged path that led in the direction of these temporary abodes, I found myself in the midst of an encampment of the enemy. The scene was one of interest; here and there lay stretched, in the appalling stillness of death, the victims of the preceding day's strife, and in the distance might be heard the noisy merriment of those who were perhaps destined, before many days were over, to meet with a similar fate.

I soon found myself surrounded by French soldiers, who, at the first onset were disposed to survey me with no very kindly feeling; but as soon as it was established satisfactorily to them that I was alone, and perhaps separated like themselves by the chances of war from the main body of the army, a cordial welcome was proffered me. The hard features of the grenadiers relaxed from their severity, and an officer politely offered me to partake of his flask of brandy, which was all he had to offer. The poor fellows were sadly in want of provisions as well as surgical assistance, and I promised, if it lay in my power, to send them relief.

The wounded lay in groups of three and four on the ground; some of them had their heads bandaged up with handkerchiefs, that showed by their crimson dye, the severity of the wounds they covered. Others had torn strips from their clothes to support a mutilated limb; others, again were too far gone to alleviate their miseries by such means, and were seeking insensibility to suffering, through the dram-bottle of that most unfeminine of the feminine gender yclep'd *vivandière,* whose spiritual aid was all the sufferers had to solace them here below.

Having reiterated my promise to send whatever assistance fell in my way, I was preparing to examine the redoubts, where the guns were in position, when a weak voice, in suffering accents of entreaty, pronounced a few words in English, that made me turn to the spot from they came. Against a bank I saw reclining, a wounded veteran officer, in the uniform of a Chasseur regiment. Care, rather than time, seemed to have ploughed deep furrows on his high and thoughtful forehead.

A few white hairs, thinly scattered over a head, that for its form might have been coveted by the speculative Spurzheim, contrasted strangely with his black eyebrows, and dark, unshaven beard. The shadows of death were gradually overspreading his countenance. As I approached nearer to the place where he lay, another object became visible, which the bank had before concealed; on the other side of the wounded man, lay a large black poodle dog, of that peculiarly clever breed that puts to the blush the boasted supremacy of man's intellectual faculties over the brute creation. Upon his master's drooping eye, the animal gazed with an expression of deep devotion and despair.

As I leant over the bank, which supported the sinking frame of the old soldier, he tried to raise himself, and placing his hand upon his breast, as if by the movement to delay the inward progress of dissolution, he said to me, "If you are an English officer, you can give me comfort in my dying hour. Yesterday I had a son, we were in the same regiment, and fought side by side; twice he saved my life by turning aside the bayonet that threatened it, and when at last I fell, he tried to bear me to a place of safety, but at the moment, the enemy bore down upon our ranks, and I was separated in the *mêlée* from my gallant boy. Should he be a prisoner in your army, for the sake of humanity, endeavour to discover his destination, and convey to him these papers."

With a feeble effort, the dying soldier placed in my hands a packet addressed to *"Maurice McCarthy, sous-lieutenant au 8ème regiment de Chasseurs."* The clouds of approaching dissolution were rapidly gathering over his face, as he still endeavoured, at broken intervals, to give some clue to guide me in my search.

He was an Irishman, had entered the French army after the rebellion in Ireland, and had served with Napoleon both in Italy and Egypt. I stayed with him as long as it was possible, but the call of duty was peremptory, and I was obliged to quit the poor fellow to pursue the object of my journey.

He grasped my hand when we parted, and as I turned to take a last look at him in the distance, I could see the close contact, into which the faithful dog had brought himself with his master's body, as if to mingle warmth with the frigidity of life's last struggles.

My object in exploring the ground that had been occupied by the enemy was to ascertain the quantity of artillery that had been abandoned, which consisted of fifty-two guns, and a considerable quantity of ammunition. The extent of ground I traversed in the performance of this duty was not less than thirty miles, and through this remote wilderness, I met with many parties of our own soldiers, who would have found it difficult to give a good reason for being there. Perhaps, a little farther on, some secluded hamlet showed what were the evil propensities that had brought away these marauders from the ranks of their brave comrades, for every violence that can disgrace human nature was committed by them on the defenceless inhabitants of the mountains.

In one of these small clusterings of humble dwellings, I saw three little children grouped round an object that was almost hidden by their close embrace. It was growing dark, but in so vast a solitude the sight of these tiny creatures produced an interest too strong to resist, and dismounting from my horse, I approached close to them. A bleeding corpse was the object of their infantile solicitude. A man, still young in years, lay stretched on the earth; his dark hair clotted in the stream of blood that had poured from a bayonet-wound in his breast. I looked round, every door was open, and the inmates fled. The eldest child, who at first ran away with fear at seeing me, now cautiously returned, and pointed to the door of a cottage that had been, perhaps, the happy home of his lifeless parent. I entered;—a young woman was weeping in that bitterness of anguish that knows no relief, sobs and groans choked her utterance; but I heard enough to be convinced that the knot of English marauders—for they had forfeited the name of soldiers—I had fallen in with, about a league from the spot, were the perpetrators of the horrible deed that had rendered this dwelling desolate. The exhaustion and miserable condition of the survivor gave too just a cause for apprehension that the husband had sacrificed his life in the vain effort of defending his wife from outrage.

It was midnight when I entered the village of San Pé, the

head-quarters of the Commander-in-Chief and Marshal Beresford, where I found a billet allotted to me in a small farm house. A blazing fire was quickly prepared together with a good repast, for which my long ride had sharpened my appetite. In the house where I was billetted, there was an ample supply of forage for my horses and mules, nor did I scruple to apply it to their wants, as forage was at that time very difficult to obtain.

The discovery of my supply was productive of a circumstance which I relate, merely because it throws a *trait de lumière* confirmatory of the character that has so often been drawn of the Marshal, who commanded the army of Portugal. I was sitting in my room, when a Commissary dressed in all the gaudy profusion of feathers and gold lace, that distinguished that department of the Portuguese army, made his entry into the yard below, and attended by five or six peasants, proceeded without any previous communication with myself, to dismantle the granaries of their contents. I demanded by whose authority the forage was thus carried off, as I knew that by the regulations of Lord Wellington, no seizure could be made of any article without the sanction and presence of one of the municipal authorities of the commune; and in the absence of such an authority, I protested against the illegal transfer of the property.

No answer, however, was vouchsafed to my demand, and it was only upon my firm refusal to permit the seizure to take place, that my visitor withdrew, and immediately returned with a summons for me to appear instanter before his Excellency the Marshal.

Upon my arrival I was ushered into the presence of the great man, whose chafed and angry brow seemed to have gained additional height and breadth for the occasion. As he scowled upon me from the summit of his athletic form, with eyes that kindled at the opposition I had unwittingly offered to his authority, he reminded me of the picture I had often dwelt upon with terror as a child in the story of *Jack and the Ogre*; poor Jack under the bed was not in greater jeopardy than I appeared. exposed to the raging wrath of Marshal B——d.

With a voice shaking with passion, his Excellency demanded my reasons for opposing his orders, and could scarcely bear to listen to my defence, which was simply that "no municipal authority having appeared to sanction the taking of the forage, I had adhered to the regulations laid down by the Marquess of Wellington, which rendered such a proceeding essential."

"The Mayor of the Commune was in attendance upon my Commissary," thundered out the Marshal at the conclusion of the sentence.

"Pardon me, Sir," I said, "there was no municipal officer present, nor did your Commissary even mention your name as sanctioning the seizure."

"Sir," vociferated the Marshal, who had arrived at the very tip top of his constitutional thermometer, "do you mean to say I lie?— Confront the Mayor with him, and let him then deny the presence of that authority."

A movement was made towards the door, and in crept the personage, who was to confirm my guilt.

Scarcely could I preserve my gravity, as this important witness made his way through the throng of officers that surrounded the Marshal. His lean carcase was barely covered with a jacket of the coarsest texture, from the sleeves of which his elbows peeped, without, however, imparting to their owner that peculiar air of *bon ton* and independence, that is so often characteristic of a man "out at the elbows." A shirt, the original colour of which was scarcely discernible through the mass of dirt that encrusted it, was confined round his unshaven chin, by a ragged cotton handkerchief. His legs were bare, and a huge pair of wooden *sabots* completed the appearance of Monsieur Le Maire.

It the first time that I had trod the soil of *la belle France*, and my ideas of municipal authorities were so identified with the sleek rotundity and shining cloth which distinguish that respectable community at home, that it was with unfeigned simplicity I replied to the Marshal's impatient query of: "Now, sir, will you dispute my words?" by appealing to his Excellency, whether he himself, unless acquainted with the fact, "would have believed that man to be a Maire."

It is well-known that Lord B——d was a sincere lover of a joke; indeed his propensities, in that line, obtained for him, in the 48th, the appellation of "the Joker." Whether my appeal touched some chord that vibrated agreeably in his breast; or whether reason had come to his aid, and pointed out the impossibility of my being gifted with a spirit of divination, I know not, but his Excellency was pleased to unbend his brow, and to dismiss me.

Chapter 31
St. Jean de Luz

On the 17th, head-quarters moved on to St. Jean de Luz, a populous little sea-port, twelve miles from Bayonne; here we established ourselves in the billets that had just been vacated by Marshal Soult's staff, and it might have been expected from that, and other causes, that the townspeople would have regarded us with no very friendly feeling. Such however was not the case; nor was there any reason to doubt that this outward demeanour expressed a sympathy towards us that was unfelt. The greatest .mention was paid to our comforts, and after a very short residence .among them, we were looked upon far more in the light of friends than invaders of their country.

One reason for this was doubtless the proclamation issued by Lord Wellington in crossing the frontier of France, to the effect that the smallest infringement on the rights and privileges of the inhabitants would be visited by punishment of the severest nature. Again, the natives of that remote part were passive spectators of the events that had sprung from the enthusiasm of the capital, The name of glory had not found its way to their mountains, and their only acquaintance with the clash of arms was derived from the passage of armed men through their peaceful vallies. On such occasions, the supplies of the country were put in requisition to maintain them. Scarcity prevailed, and the inhabitants suffered; while, on the contrary, the presence of the British troops became, through the proclamation of Lord Wellington, the guarantee of security to the inhabitants; the owners of the produce of the country received full value for it when purchased for the army, and confidence was maintained, unbroken, between the parties.

After the battle of the Nivelle, Soult had retired to the entrenched camp in front of Bayonne, extending from the Nive to the Adour. Lord Wellington pushed his advanced posts within two miles of the enemy, and in this attitude the contending armies remained for the space of one month. During the greater part of this time, the rain fell in torrents, and the road became impassable for artillery; but there was plenty of occupation in preparing bridges to cross the rivers in our front; re-equipping the guns, and replenishing the exhausted stock of the field ammunition. This work was facilitated greatly by our proximity to Passages, where the Ordnance stores were landed, and other things were landed also; to the great comfort of the officers at St. Jean de Luz.

For instance, many were the delicate patties of game and venison that came from the fair sex to their warrior Lords, with knitted purses, sashes, braces, socks, and even night-caps. The Commander-in-Chief was perhaps the least of all likely to be forgotten by his wife, in this general bazaar of love-tokens from home; and it was reported at head-quarters, that not only had the Marchioness sent out for her liege Lord's special use a plentiful supply of fleecy hosiery, but that he had liberally dispensed these treasures around him, to those whose frames were less iron-bound than his own.

So frequent was the arrival of vessels from England and Ireland during this period, that even fresh beef and vegetables found their way across the Atlantic to our tables. Upon one occasion a remarkably fine beef-steak was brought on shore at Passages by the Captain of a trader, and sent on to Sir Robert Kennedy at St. Jean de Luz with a barrel of native oysters. The steak had travelled all the way from Falmouth, and, as I afterwards found, was anxiously expected by the worthy Commissary-General, who had been apprised of its safe landing at Passages. By some mistake the dainty morsel, and the oysters also were left at my quarters; I was out, the cook at home, and knowing that I expected friends to dinner, he naturally enough concluded that these additions to the larder were in honour of the circumstance.

Accordingly, at the appointed hour, the beef steak made its .appearance, artistically served with oyster sauce, to the no small astonishment of myself and gratification of my guests, who did ample justice to its merits. The last was in the act of disappearing, when a messenger arrived from Sir Robert Kennedy, praying restitution of the delicacy, that had been left by mistake at my quarters. It is needless to say that—as in many other cases of still deeper import—the appeal was made too late to be of service to the appellant, although it does not often happen that delays are productive of as much advantage to either side as was derived by ourselves in this innocent appropriation of Sir Robert Kennedy's property.

St. Jean de Luz, after a short time, assumed all the appearance of a fashionable watering place. The breakwater that projected far into the sea, was crowded daily as a morning lounge by Lord Wellington and his brilliant staff; by the gentlemen of the Guards, and though last, not least, by many fair ladies, wives and maidens; some of whom had taken compassion on the state of celibacy to which the sons of Mars were doomed, and had arrived from England to solace them by their presence. Among these kind creatures, the Commander-in-Chief was the object of universal attention, and many a handsome "gentleman» guardsman was treated with indifference, if a look or a word from Lord Wellington was likely to be the reward. And yet, in alluding to the *gentlemen* Guards, it must be allowed that they had far more than their appearance and cognomen to boast of. Bravest of the brave in the field when called upon; they proved that neither luxurious homes nor habits can diminish in the smallest degree, the noble attributes of British manhood.

But neither *woman's smile* nor *tempter's wile* had power to wrestle from the Commander-in-Chief one moment of that watchfulness, essential to the development of those great events which were bursting into light under his auspices. His active mind did not sleep on the knowledge that an enemy—and a formidable one—lay within arm's reach; and every precaution that wisdom could adopt, and every arrangement that combination could suggest, were quietly progressing during this season of apparent rest.

St. Jean de Luz was only within a few hours ride of Passages, the depôt of our prisoners, and I determined to go over there for the purpose of ascertaining if the veteran Chasseur's son, Maurice McCarthy, was among their number.

The sun was rising in all the splendour of a sky, as I took the road to Passages, which led through the bosom of a deep ravine. On either side, the green-clad hills rose in picturesque irregularity, while here and there, a patch of cultivated land, on the steep declivities, bore witness to the industrious labour of some rustic. Nature seemed to have just doffed her night-cap, and exchanged the calm look of sleep for one of her sunniest smiles. It was one of those mornings that live in the memory; a morning, when thoughts float as lightly on the surface of the mind as gossamer threads on the light atmosphere around, when youth and spirits rush impetuously beyond the land-mark of reason, and when even age and sorrow imbibe a temporary forgetfulness of the world's cares. It was on such a morning that I bent my course towards Passages, throwing the bridle over my horse's neck, that he also might share in the happiness of nature, and forget for a while the thraldom of man's yoke. We journeyed on together, occupied with our respective thoughts, until, at the summit of a long and steep hill, Passages appeared in sight, sunk, as it were, in the depths of the earth beneath us.

There is, perhaps, no port in Europe more singularly or more romantically situated than Passages; surrounded on every side by mountains of remarkable height, the town itself stands barely raised above the level of the sea, which rolls sullenly into the basin formed by nature to receive it. The descent from the eminence on which I stood appeared terrific, and I, therefore dismounted from my horse, and tying his bridle to the projecting branch of an old tree, proceeded to reconnoitre the safest means of descending the steep road before me. A branch path interrupted the beaten track, and as the rude steps cut in the green turf denoted that it was frequented by foot travellers, I turned into it, believing that it might lead me to some public route, more adapted to my horse's powers than that in which I had left him.

The winding of the path afforded me, at each turn, a succession of varied and enchanting views. Below, perpendicularly below, was the town of Passages, reposing, as it appeared to on the bosom of the deep blue waters. The path I was pursuing became steeper and steeper; and, at a sudden bend which it took, I was led into an avenue, thickly shaded with the leaf of the umbrageous cork tree.

It appeared to lead to some habitation, for the hand of care was apparent in the paling, that protected me on one side from the yawning precipice beneath. The murmuring of a mountain brook invited me to quench my thirst in its clear waters, and as I followed mechanically the course of the little stream into which it flowed, I came unexpectedly in sight of a small chapel, round which, in rude and un-carved materials, lay the last outward signs of man's pilgrimage on earth. I advanced to take a nearer view of these quiet regions of the dead, and to contemplate the offerings that decked the graves of many. If children only were to bring their tribute of fresh flowers to deck the spot where a fond parent lies, there would be something inexpressibly touching in this association of their infantile grief, with the equally perishable emblems of their love. But the heart turns in loathing from the husband, the lover, the wife, the friend, who profanes the mystery of grief, by lifting up the veil that conceals it from the gaze of others. The act proclaims the insufficiency of the sentiment suffice to itself, which therefore seeks in action the vehemence that a state of passiveness denies. The hand that can place upon the tomb of love a flower, has never been raised to Heaven in the utter helplessness of despair. The heart that can blend one thought of verdure with the darkness of the grave, has yet to feel those depths of darkness that surround the truly wretched.

I was turning to retrace my steps, when I saw a procession slowly enter the avenue through which I had passed; on a nearer approach, I found it was composed of a military party, bearing a comrade to the burying ground in which I stood, and I fell back to witness the sad rites that were to consign a fellow being to the earth. The coffin, upon which was placed the military cap of the departed, rested upon the shoulders of four miserably clad and pallid objects, who, from their ragged apparel, I concluded to be French prisoners. The soiled blue attire of some, who walked in mournful procession behind the coffin confirmed this supposition, and the whole party were surrounded by a detachment of our own men, who formed the escort.

The funeral convoy entered by the gate through which I had passed, and was met by a venerable priest, who issued from the ivy-grown porch of the little chapel. The service of the dead was then read, the coffin lowered down into the grave, and the party took their departure from the spot with the same decent sadness of exterior, that marked their entrance. I followed to inquire some particulars of him who had just been consigned to the silent tomb, and learnt from the sergeant of the company that the poor fellow's name was "Maurice McCarthy," that he had been desperately wounded at the battle of the Nivelle, and made prisoner at the close of the day with several others of his regiment; that every care had been taken of him, but that the agitation of his mind, in consequence of the fate of his father, who served in the same regiment—the 8th Chasseurs—had aggravated his dangerous symptoms, and that after severe suffering, he had expired on the previous day.

A bitter pang crossed my heart, as I reascended the mountain for my horse, and reflected upon the early fate of the poor fellow I had come that day to seek. To die a prisoner and alone, was in itself a fate demanding the deepest sympathy; but here was a combination of moral and physical anguish, the mind consuming the body, in the ashes of its own volcanic elements.

I led my horse down the rocky descent that led into Passages, and entered a small *posado,* which announced its reception of travellers. It was more than chilly. I ordered a fire, not meaning to return until the following day to St. Jean de Luz; and the same night, taking out of my pocket the papers confided to my charge by the dying chasseur, I perused, by the light of my lamp, the following history of a life, that reconciled me in some degree, to the fate of the young soldier whose interment I had that day witnessed.

> Heights of Zara, November, 1813
> To Maurice McCarthy
> Sous-Lieutenant huitième régiment de Chasseurs
> Should these lines meet your eye, my beloved Maurice, the hand that traced them will be mouldering with the dead. Our late defeats, the strength of the pursuing army, have left us little beyond the choice of a soldier's death, or an inglorious retreat. That the first will be my fate, a mysterious presentiment assures me; and heart-rending as the task has been, I have prepared for it, by leaving to you the sad knowledge of the causes that have made us aliens to our country; and of the misery that has marked my cursed existence, and blighted the first young blossoming of yours. There is a world, my Maurice, beyond the grave! There we shall meet.

October, 1813

To retrace the weary steps of time, my recollections must rest upon the one 'green spot in memory's waste'—my native land. No sooner had the long-sown seeds of tyranny and oppression burst forth into that luxuriance of blood and violence that rendered the French Revolution an unparalleled epoch in the annals of civilized nations, than the cry of liberty resounded from the shores of France, and was re-echoed through the native hills of Ireland. The sound thrilled to the heart of every lover of his country, and they were not wanting to whom the crown of martyrdom would have been welcome, to insure the liberty of Ireland. Through all ranks, the electric spark of patriotism ran, and, united in the same phalanx were to be seen the descendants of kings, and the humble peasantry of the soil. Each was alike imbued with the same grand and absorbing feeling, the deliverance of their 'fatherland' from the yoke of foreign oppression.

It has been proved how impossible is the task of organizing and preparing a nation for active measures, against the unequal odds of awakened suspicion, treachery, counterplots, and all the hostile array that can be produced by a stable and determined government, backed by a well-paid soldiery. In every district, select committees were appointed to represent the feelings of the mass, and as one of the leading features in the policy of the Government was to crouch in ambush, until the safe and sure moment for the annihilation of its prey, so were these committees allowed to work their own ruin by growing careless of detection.

"My father was an Irishman, but had passed his early days in England, where he had learnt to admire and cherish her institutions; venerate her religion, and appreciate her freedom. His first and best affections were blended with her name, and, on returning to his paternal inheritance in Ireland, with the wife of his love, an Englishwoman and a Protestant, he felt the sacrifice he was making of inclination to the duties to his native land.

My only brother and myself accompanied our parents. I

was the eldest, and nature had united in me all the characteristics of the people of my country. Violent and revengeful, my earliest infancy presented the fearful promise of the crimes of my manhood. Impatient of control, my pursuits led me to the haunts of the wildest characters of our neighbourhood, and surrounded by the worst associates, the evil propensities of my nature hardened into determined vice. In vain did my father warn me with all the sternness of a parent from my course of profligacy. In vain did my gentle mother, with weeping eyes, bid me for her sake renounce the errors of my ways; the demon of evil prevailed, and suffering alone was ordained to work out my repentance.

I have mentioned that I had a brother; he was two years my junior, and beautiful in person as in mind. Oh! the agony of such a recollection as his name brings to my memory. All that I ever knew of softness then, was gazing on my brother's face; and I remember that in our days of boyhood—when, for a moment, my doubled passions found repose from exhaustion—I would hurry back to his room, and if asleep, cherish the short-lived tranquillity by bending over his innocent and placid brow. Phelim! my hand starts in tracing thy name, and my heart is turned to ice. I think I see a pale form pointing to some unknown place, as if to say, 'there we shall meet.' But why do I dwell on these fantasies of the brain, when time wanes, and I have so much to tell? Maurice, hear me to the end, and curse not my name when I am gone.

It was in the year 1792, that I became a member of 'the Society of United Irishmen,' the nominal object of which was to cement a complete internal union of the people of Ireland to resist the weight of English influence. Treason and disaffection were universally disseminated, emissaries were sent to all parts of the kingdom by by 'the United Irishmen,' to disperse seditious hand-bills through every county. In the following year, the most dreadful outrages were committed under the sacred banners of Liberty and Religion, and soon open rebellion called for the most active measures from the Government. The mass of the people were provided with pikes and bludgeons; the Protestant houses were plundered for arms, often burnt, and their inmates cruelly murdered; and such was the panic that loyal subjects deserted their homes in the disturbed counties, taking refuge in their respective county-towns, or in the metropolis.

"My frequent and prolonged absences from the paternal roof alarmed my father, who was himself, an object of suspicion, from his adherence to the cause of Loyalty and Protestantism; but I carefully avoided declaring my associations, nor even in my brother's mind, awakened the slightest distrust of my political designs.

In the immediate neighbourhood of our home stood the cottage of my father's foster-brother, Michael O'Brien. In Ireland, this connexion is considered to bind, in bonds of the closest affection, the two beings who have drawn from the same source nature's first gift, and O'Brien's devotion to my father was of that pure and high-wrought cast which tinges the feelings of the lower Irish towards their superiors. His wife had been dead for many years, and his only child, a girl, had been brought up as the plaything of our home. Beautiful as an angel was the little Ellen O'Brien, with all the arch playfulness of Irish childhood mingled with the bashful reserve that my mother's precepts had instilled. Her disposition was like my brother's, and partook of the sweet ingenuousness of his nature. Even in her earliest days of infancy she would turn to him for refuge from the turbulent violence of my uncontrollable feelings.

Years passed away; the boys were transformed to men, and the little Ellen to a lovely woman. It was on my return from college, where my untutored mind had grovelled low in profligacy and vice, that the natural beauty of Ellen O'Brien met my enraptured gaze. I had never, in fancy's wildest dream, seen a form so exquisitely bright, and the admiration I attempted not to conceal, was received with that careless indifference that rendered her still more captivating in my sight. With a feeling of wild jealousy, I turned to my brother's countenance, expecting to see in it the reflection of those feelings that had rushed with overwhelming force through my being. It wore the calmness that was its peculiar character, and his eye, beaming with tender affection, rested alternately on Ellen and myself.

I turned away, never to know peace again; one all-absorbing passion held me fast, and cursed me. Oh! the agony that followed! for mine was not a fancy to be wafted from the mind by the first passing breeze of novelty, but I was doomed to suffer and to feel alone. No kindred flame lighted up the beautiful cheek of Ellen. She heard me, pitied me, and spurned me.

From that day existence became a weight from which I laboured to escape, and every dark feeling of my mind blackened into hatred of my fellow-creatures. On the same day that the cup of happiness had been dashed for ever from my lips, I met my brother. I would have hurried past him, but he stopped me, and as our eyes met, I saw in his an expression of tender sadness that I did not then understand. Oh! why did I ever learn its import?

I saw Ellen no more. She was removed from the home of her childhood, and I concluded that, by her own wish, she had been placed beyond the power of my importunities. Vainly did I seek her, and maddened by the force of contending feelings, I plunged deeply into the agitated ocean of revolution, and became a traitor and a rebel.

During the years 1794 and 1795, rebellion had risen to the most fearful height, and it was found impossible to allay the spirit of outrage that actuated the people. 'The united Irishmen' were in the foremost ranks of the rebellion, and their activity succeeded, in many instances, in seducing the military from their allegiance. To this society—destined as I madly thought to regenerate Ireland—I was bound hand and heart, and hailed with frantic joy the approaching crisis that was to sever the bonds that united her to England. The whole county of Cork was in open insurrection; yet still my father, with all the determination that was shown at that period, by numbers of the Irish gentry, refused to quit the home of his ancestors, and prepared to defend, to the last extremity, his property against invaders. Little did he think that his elder son was destined to be the destroyer of his race— the blood-hound to track the prey! A meeting was convened of delegates from the many secret committees throughout the country, and I received a summons to attend as agent to 'the united Irishmen.'

The rendezvous was given in the subterranean passage of the old monastery; some parts of the building were still standing, while rude masses of stone, heaped under the mouldering walls, gave evidence of the ruin that time had wrought upon the rest. The road leading to this remote spot was wild and lonely; and the chill air of a November evening breathed through the murky atmosphere. I wrapped around me my cloak, which bore the badge of our confederacy, and impatient from excitement, traversed the dark and silent plains. While thus advancing, the fog seemed to gather round me, and the path I had taken was no longer discernible. I hesitated whether to proceed, when a feeble light from afar awakened my attention. It was in the direction of the monastery, and from its elevation might almost have been mistaken for a star emerging from the denseness of the fog; but upon a near approach, the rays became more vivid, and falling on the objects beneath, enabled me to ascertain that they proceeded from an aperture in that part of the monastery, which had escaped, in some degree, the ravages of time.

That we were betrayed, was the first idea that presented itself to my mind, and I hurried onwards to apprise my confederates of their danger, and to disperse them, if possible, before it was too late. With hasty steps, I traversed the uneven ground, where prostrate pillars and broken arches told of former splendour. All was silent as the tomb; and it was only as I wended down the stone stairs that led to the vault, wherein treason was to hold her vigils, that I remembered how my impatience had anticipated the hour of meeting, and that I had some anxious moments to pass before the arrival of my confederates. Cautiously I groped my way back to the open air, and still the same light, issuing from the turret above me, excited my surprise. Mounting on a projecting part of the edifice, that was thickly covered by a luxuriant ivy tree, I discovered an outer staircase that led apparently to that part of the building from whence the mysterious light proceeded.

With difficulty I extricated my feet from the creeping plants that concealed it from view, and as I slowly moved upwards, a voice riveted me to the spot where I stood. 'Phelim,' it gently uttered, 'do not engage yourself against such desperate men, for my sake, for our boy's sake, give up your intention to denounce them to the Government. Who will protect your Ellen and her child, if, in these dangerous times, you exchange your peaceful home for the violence of civil war.'

My brain grew dizzy as I listened. It was Ellen—the Ellen of my ardent love who spoke. I advanced, with frantic impatience to the aperture, where still flickered the light that had so fatally allured me. My eyes rested on a scene that maddened my senses to delirium. On Ellen's knees rested the head of Phelim—my brother—her eyes were fixed on his with all the fond expression of reproach, that fear for the safety of a loved being can infuse, while at the same time her foot rocked, at measured intervals, the cradle of her first-born—the child of Phelim.

Feelings of the darkest rage boiled in my breast, and my heart heaved with the hope of being justified in an act of vengeance by the answer I should hear. Its pulses beat quick and loud, and vainly I strived to calm its rioting, so that I might hearken to what the enemy of our cause would say. His words fell low, and hesitatingly. My name, suspicion, rebel, fell like molten lead on the fibres of my brain; a low whistle sounded from beneath, I bounded to the signal, and that night planned my hellish scheme of vengeance.

Important intelligence had been communicated from Dublin of the successful demonstrations of the partisans of liberty; and in every county it was expected that similar proofs would be given of zealous adherence to the one great cause. A general attack was ordered to be made upon the Protestant landholders, and even upon those suspected of harbouring political opinions opposed to the reigning democracy.

Twenty-four hours had scarcely passed away since the meeting of the delegates at the monastery, when an armed force, composed of the most desperate of the country, was placed at my disposal for the execution of the previous night's project. Among the obnoxious was my aged father; but he had, by a life of unfeigned benevolence and good-will towards his neighbours, inspired even the depredators with a sentiment of respect. To obtain fire-arms was the grand object of the rebels, and as he was known to have prepared himself for resistance, it was proposed that his house should be first visited—not for the object of plunder—but to take possession of the weapons that were supposed to be concealed.

Night had no sooner covered the earth, and prepared it for dark deeds, than we sallied forth, two hundred men strong, under the banner of 'Liberty or death.' The remembrance of that night appals my mind with horror. Oh! that I could blot it out from the page of life!

My father made a resistance worthy of his noble bearing; inch by inch, he, and his faithful servants disputed the violation of the domestic hearth; but numbers prevailed, and as the ruffians rushed impetuously onwards, inflamed by the opposition they encountered, I vainly endeavoured to check the violence of their progress. At the moment that the first report of fire-arms announced the commencement of a sanguinary conflict, the sound of a trumpet burst on our ears, and a body of cavalry advancing into the court-yard dashed with fury upon the assailants. The attack was as vigorously repulsed, until the very floors of the apartments streamed with blood; and pierced with bullets, the devoted Michael O'Brien fell on the body of his master, whom he had vainly to save!

The rebels defended themselves with desperation against the military, shouting, as an incentive to their violence, the name of 'Phelim McCarthy.' The superiority, however, of the soldiers prevailed, and the issue of the conflict was no longer doubtful; when a tremendous cheer burst from the direction of the road, and a large force of well-organized and well-armed men appeared on the scene of action. The discouraged band of rebels rallied at the well-known cry, and with fresh vigour, joined in the slaughter of the English foe. Night was far advanced when the work of blood was over, and the victorious rebels, led on by myself, advanced, flushed with success, to the monastery.

The moon had just risen, and was shedding her first pale rays over the turret that contained the objects, both of my fiercest hatred, and most passionate love. I enjoined silence to the infuriated rabble, who were thirsting for the blood of the informer, and advanced alone to the staircase, to which my dark destiny led me on the preceding night. Ascending rapidly, I stood once more on that spot, where first I marked my victims. Once more I gazed upon the face of Ellen; she was asleep, and the light of the rising moon played on that sweet countenance that lay nestled in the bosom of Phelim. My heart turned to gall at the sight. I sprang from the aperture to the wall beneath, and cheered on my followers. A dense smoke rose in columns round the turret, and one blaze of fire soon pointed, in thousands of spiral forms, to the great canopy of Heaven. The fresh breeze of night, for a moment, separated the flames, and, in that momentary glance, I saw—oh, God! my brother vainly endeavouring, with one arm, to place his child beyond the power of the flames, while with the other he closely pressed Ellen to his heart. My brain grew mad. I rushed through the burning element—from stone to stone I leapt, till the blazing woodwork stopped my further progress; yet still I braved its fury, and reached the aperture.

'My brother,' he exclaimed.

'Thy murderer,' I shrieked. Oh! once before I had seen the same sad yet soft, look with which now he gazed upon me, the last that ever beamed from that beautiful eye.

A report like thunder echoed through the lofty arches, and as I still clung, in madness, to tottering wall, my brother with one desperate effort placed within my grasp his child! At the same moment, the whole edifice fell in one mass of smouldering ruins. How I escaped, I know not, for weeks passed away, and I retained no recollection of that night of crime. I know that a woman nursed me into life, and gave a mother's care to the sweet boy of Phelim and Ellen—that I fostered him, loved him, have lived for him, and on the battlefield have encountered death for him. If in these last few lines, my Maurice, you recognise some faint outline of my love for you, let that love guide your remembrance of me when I am gone. Think of me as I have been to you, the fond hither, the faithful friend. One who has endeavoured to cherish in you the virtues you received from your parents; and to instil into your young mind abhorrence of the violent passions that have agitated my stormy life. Farewell! there is a world beyond the grave. Phelim—Ellen—Maurice, *there we shall meet.*

The church bell struck the hour of midnight, and roused me from the reverie into which I had been plunged by the contents of the papers before me. I replaced them in my pocket, in the hope that, by one of those strange fatalities that issue from the wheel of chance, I might be brought into contact with those to whom they might be of interest. I retired to bed, but not to rest, my disturbed spirit was haunted by image of love, sorrow, crime, in fearful array, the offspring of my evening's occupation, and I felt glad when the dawn of morning broke upon the darkness of my chamber, and in some degree dispelled the thoughts that had driven sleep from my eyelids. I hastily rose, and ordering my horse, retraced my steps to St. Jean de Luz.

CHAPTER 32

Fighting After St Jean de Luz

The first outbreak that took place between the hostile armies was on the 9th of December, when the divisions under Beresford and Hill drove the French from their advanced posts on the Nive, while Sir John Hope, with the left wing of the army moving from St. Jean de Luz, attacked the posts in front of their entrenched camp, and forced them to retire within its lines.

In the early part of the day, a curious incident occurred to relieve the monotony of hard blows. At a short distance from the high road leading to Bayonne was the Château Anglet, the property of a French gentleman, whose confidence in the strength of the French army had blinded his eyes to the possibility of its defeat. In conjunction with this ill-timed security, every thing was left in the chateau as might have been expected in a time of profound peace; and the owner had the happiness, moreover, of exercising both his patriotism and hospitality in favour of General Villatte, who, with his staff, occupied the château as *quartier-general;* with so efficient a garrison, away with fears for the safety of the fortress!

On the route of our troops from St. Jean de Luz, the skirmishing had been very sharp within a mile of the château, which was in itself an object, when once espied, not likely to be passed by without a closer acquaintance with it. The flank companies of the 4th regiment having approached, under cover of the hedges, close to the rear of the mansion, made a rushing entrance at the back; while at the same moment a numerous party of French staff-officers fled precipitately from the front door to the gate where their horses stood in readiness. So great was their flurry and confusion that some had left their hats behind them—others their swords.

They had evidently been surprised, and as it turned out, at a moment that must have been particularly *mal à propos,* as the intruders found an excellent *déjeûner a la fourchette* prepared for the General, who had snatched from glory a few leisure moments to invigorate the outward man. Chickens, cutlets, and other delicacies were pounced upon with no gentle avidity by the hungry soldiers; nor could the strict orders that had been issued by Lord Wellington, prevent the transfer from the table to the pocket, of every silver spoon and fork within reach. Nor did they stop there, for the château was rifled from top to bottom of every valuable and portable article, in an incredibly short space of time.

An hour afterwards I saw a corporal of the 4th regiment lying dead under a hedge. A crimson damask cushion supported his head, whether the luxurious booty was carried off by himself, or placed there by some friendly hand, I was unable to determine.

The 10th was a day of severe fighting, for Soult tried hard to recover his lost position, but was opposed by Sir John Hope, whose valorous bearing on the field was most conspicuous. The result of the conflict was the complete defeat of the enemy.

The fighting of the next two days was attended with similar success to the allies, and on the 13th, Soult, driven to desperation by such continued failures, passed through Bayonne in the night, and burst with all his strength upon Hill's corps, in the hope of breaking through the position of the allied army. The struggle was tremendous, and more than once the success of the day fearfully doubtful. The troops, on both sides, fought with a vigour that had perhaps never been surpassed; but the indomitable front presented by some of the British regiments, turned again and again the tide of fortune in their favour. During many hours, Hill's corps, consisting of less than eighteen thousand men, bore the brunt of an engagement with forty thousand of the enemy, and although the French were seen to give way at several points, at others they still retained sufficient strength to continue the conflict.

Positions were taken and retaken at the point of the bayonet. The 92nd, under the gallant veteran Cameron, was at one time nearly overwhelmed by the force of numbers, and obliged to give way; but it was only for a moment; again reforming their skeleton ranks, they returned to the charge with bagpipes playing and colours flying, led on by their Colonel, sword in hand, over the bodies of their slain comrades.

With a shout that rose above the shrill tones of the pipes, the veterans charged, in ranks two deep, the mass before them, and regained the up-land ground they had lost. Such noble efforts were not made in vain. At every point the enemy gave way, and the sixth division coming up with Lord Wellington in person, was just in time to render still more decisive the victory that Hill had already won. Closely pursued by the allies, the French Marshal retreated with the greater part of his army to the Adour, leaving a garrison of ten thousand men for the defence of Bayonne.

The heroism displayed on both sides during these five days' fighting was not confined to the action of hostility between man and man. Patience, under the severest trials, formed no inconsiderable feature of it. To march over roads knee-deep in mud, to lie exposed, during inclement nights, to pouring rain, were evils in themselves almost sufficient to damp the glowing ardour of enterprise; but it was not so. Animated with the generous spirit of comradeship in dangers and privations, the officers did not point out the way of bearing them, but in their own persons showed how they were to be borne, and the soldiers nobly followed in the wake of such glorious examples.

It may almost be doubted, much as the mind dwells with enthusiasm on the deeds of brave men, whether the reckless exposure to which Sir John Hope subjected himself, was not carried to an extent that wisdom might censure as inexcusable in a General, on whom rested the responsibility of directing movements in the field. Be that as it may, nothing can deteriorate from the splendid parade of gallantry his warlike figure presented, moving wherever the fight was thickest, cheering and encouraging the troops. The pen of a Napier has rescued from the oblivion of time many names that threw a lustre over the battle of the Nive, and it is to be lamented that modesty did not permit that historian to record that the veterans of the 43rd were led on by himself to the glorious distinction they obtained. As long as chivalrous bravery is honoured and esteemed, such men as Beresford, Hill, Kempt, Barnard, Colborne, Pringle, Barnes, Cameron, and many others, will shed an un-fading splendour upon generations yet unborn, through the genius of that brother hero. The result of these five days' fighting, which cost the French upwards of six thousand, and the allies five thousand men, gave to Lord Wellington the free and undisturbed possession of the country extending from the Pyrenees to the Adour, thus laying bare before his victorious army, the southern plains of France.

Chapter 33
A Tragedy

After the battle of the Nive, St. Jean de Luz again assumed its jaunty appearance as head-quarters of the army. The breakwater again thronged, and many amateurs arrived from England to learn the art of war in snug quarters. Some few came also from the holier and dearer motive of gazing once again on those whom the fortune of war had spared throughout the perils and dangers of so many battlefields; while others again were drawn to St. Jean de Luz in the hope of solacing, by their presence, some beloved relative, who was perhaps slowly recovering from wounds received at the battle of the Nive.

Among these sufferers was a youth too interesting, both from his merits and early fate, to be forgotten. The short life of this gallant boy had been full of romantic incident and change of fortune, and was recounted to me by one who had watched it from its earliest dawn.

His father, the only son of a wealthy Yorkshire Squire, brought up with every indulgence that could tend to weaken the powers of self-denial, and strengthen the natural inclination of youth to the indulgence of the passions, had formed, in early life, an attachment to the daughter of his father's gamekeeper. Such intimacies are more difficult to conceal in the midst of village gossips, than in the populous districts of large towns, and reports were soon spread far and wide, sadly prejudicial to the pure fame of the country girl.

The Squire heard the rumours, and merely tracing in them some fleeting cause for the frequent absences of his son from home, determined to plead in favour of a reputation, which had hitherto been spotless among the village maidens. His task was, however, anticipated by one who had watched with anxiety, increasing to agony, the altered mien of a beloved child; and on the same day that the proud Squire proposed cautioning his heir against an intimacy that would also diminish his importance in the neighbourhood, the aged gamekeeper boldly, but with a breaking heart, came to the Hall to demand, as man from man, the only atonement that could be made for the seduction of his innocent child.

With a light and joyous step, the young man bounded into his father's study at the moment when the tear of insulted feeling and honest indignation stood un-wiped in the eye of the old faithful servant. "He had lived too long," he said, "to hear his Mary's honour bartered for with gold."

The young man's brow glowed with the flush of generous warmth as he grasped the shrivelled hand that would have recoiled, as if from a serpent's touch: "Nay, hear me," he exclaimed, while for a moment his eye rested on the incensed countenance of his father. "My errand here was to proclaim the truth, and openly avow that your dear Mary," turning to the aged gamekeeper, "has been for three months past, my lawful wife."

Some years had elapsed since the event we have just recorded. The Squire had dragged on a cheerless and desolate existence; the son of his affections had been sacrificed to wounded pride, and in a distant part was earning, by the sweat of his brow, the daily maintenance of himself and Mary. The old gamekeeper lay in the churchyard close by, and the sweet boy that often stole away to deck the old man's grave with flowers, had never even heard of another grand-sire than he, so loved and honoured by the cottage group.

But even this chequered happiness was to find an end. The once strong health of Mary's faithful guardian and protector gave way; his cheek grew pale, and his frame each day looked more and more attenuated; the daily bread became more sparing, and at last, poverty in its heaviest form weighed on the once happy inmates of the cottage.

Under this prostration of misery and helplessness, poor Mary resolved to make known her husband's declining state of health to his father. Their first advances for forgiveness had been met with resolute denial; but time is a crucible, by which men's hearts are tested with unerring truth and few there are who do not either lose qualities, or gain them, in the process. The father's had undergone a change; affection yearned for the blessing that even pride but faintly opposed; and the dying son was again restored to the scenes of his early youth, and perilous first love.

But death's shaft had sped; nor the delight of renewed affection, nor gratitude for the delicate attentions lavished on Mary and his boy, could arrest its progress. He died some weeks after his return to the parental roof, and felt there was no need of recommending his loved wife and child to the kindness of his father.

If affection can be transferred from one object to another with an increase of force to what we love the last, it was so in the case of this bereaved father and the little Henry. Years wore away; the grieving Mary had found a rest from sorrow by her husband's side, and the little cottage urchin was now the Eton boy, and grandsire's heir. It is rare, indeed, that we are not made to feel sooner or later the penalty of former errors, even though it should reach us through ramifications that seem to have no connexion with them.

Like Norval of old, the youth had heard of battles, and his young heart beat high to earn a name beyond the dull sounding one of a country Squire. In vain the doting grandfather used first persuasion, then argument, then force. The proud boy spurned the latter, and stealing clandestinely from the gates that had been closed in anger upon his father, proceeded to London on foot, and offered himself as a volunteer in the — regiment, then under orders for the Peninsula. His youth and appearance soon brought forth a disclosure of the truth, and after some necessary negotiations between the Colonel and the grandfather, the latter acceded to the wishes of the lad, and he was Gazetted to an ensigncy in the regiment.

From that moment, the young soldier's life was one brilliant, but alas! too short a career of intrepidity and gallantry. At Salamanca, Fuentes d'Onore, Vittoria, and the Pyrenees, the steady bravery of his youthful figure, leading to the charge a band of veterans, drew (he burst of applause and thrill of admiration from the sternest breasts. Susceptible as nature's gentlest child to every vibration of love and tenderness, he was equally an adept, by nature's art, in the most delicate intricacies of the path of honour. Ready to take and to return the harmless joke, or happy jest, bold would have been the man who sought for more, at the expense of the high-spirited young Ensign.

With such excellences of mind, combined with almost perfection of person, can it be wondered at, that, after the battle of the Nive, when the Sergeant of the company to which he belonged, brought him into St. Jean de Luz badly wounded in that breast, that had never yet palpitated but with sentiments of virtue and of honour, tears ran fast from eyes unaccustomed to weeping, and that but one deep settled gloom followed the announcement of the intelligence to all who knew him? It was some weeks after the battle of the Nive before I again saw the youthful warrior. The first warm rays of an early southern spring had brought him from his quarters to breathe the invigorating air. But he was not alone: a man, bent down with care more than by age, sustained the weak and tottering steps of the youth. The pale cheek of the once robust young soldier was spotted in the centre with a hectic flush that foretold the early tomb: that spoke of high-wrought feelings brought into flower too soon to blossom long. Each day I saw them thus—the grand-sire and the grandson—but one day I missed them, although the sun shone bright gaily. I called to inquire the cause, and found that this lovely bud of chivalry and honour had drooped to its parent earth.

The grandfather was left alone. A few days afterwards, I saw him at Passages, and it seemed as if a century of time and suffering had settled on his lofty brow since last we met. I stood upon the shore, gazing on the receding vessel that was carrying back to England this last of an honoured race. He stood upon the deck, one hand placed on his bursting heart, the other extended over the black pall that covered the remains of his beloved grandchild, as if to shelter him still from the storms of this world.

CHAPTER 34

Murillo's Spanish

During the lull of hostilities after the battle of the Nive, our advanced posts, and those of the enemy were within short distances of each other, without either party suffering the smallest annoyance from the proximity. Sentries were relieved, and patrols went their prescribed rounds, frequently exchanging courtesies and kindly words.

Not so with the Spaniards. Murillo's troops, encouraged by himself to look on France as the land of promise, on which might be wreaked the full debt of vengeance owed by Spain, made frequent inroads across the frontier, plundering the inhabitants and committing the most wanton atrocities on the defenceless. Lord Wellington's judicious proclamation was treated with disregard by all the Spanish Generals, Mina himself being nothing backward in exciting his troops to rapine and plunder. The Basque provinces were in arms to repel the aggressive violence, and Soult ably took advantage of this emanation of indignation to excite them to a mountain warfare that would have aided, in no small measure, his own views.

A few days before the termination of this eventful year, I was surprised by a visit from my former host, the Padre of Vera. I had often thought of him, and not less frequently on the scene I had witnessed in his mountain-home, on the night before we parted. The good man was sadly changed, and his once tranquil countenance wore an anxious, excited expression, that strongly reminded me of his sister.

Glad of the opportunity of requiting some portion of the hospitality he had shown me, I prevailed on him to become my guest for a few days; and in that brief space, I became initiated into the knowledge of some of the atrocities that had been committed by

Murillo's troops; atrocities that were never even heard of at the head-quarters of Lord Wellington, and that could only find issue to the light of day through such channels as that which brought them to my knowledge.

It was long before I could bring myself to ask tidings of Agnese, and even then, before there was time for an answer, the name of the friar Antonio escaped my lips in the same breath. The Padre looked up, as if surprised to hear from me the combination of those names, and a flush of crimson dye overspread his usually pallid countenance. "Name him not," he passionately exclaimed, as for a moment the incensed feelings of frail mortality rose with resistless force above the habitual subjection of the spirit. "Name him not, the accursed!" With this vehement injective seemed to have exhaled, in some degree, the poor Padre's ebullition of wrath, and crossing himself with lowly reverence, he effected the mastery of his feelings sufficiently to acquaint me with the following circumstances.

After the battle of the Nive, Murillo's Spanish division was placed in cantonments on the mountain heights. Under the pretence of scanty provisions, these lawless marauders invaded the surrounding villages, committing murders, and other revolting crimes on the defenceless people who inhabited those secluded legions. The Convent of St. Cecilia, situated within the valley of Bastan, offered an allurement to the wild passions of such men as these; and their General himself, the blood-thirsty, savage-hearted Murillo, was more ready to lead on to crime, than to oppose his authority to check it. To this convent then, a fierce horde of Spanish soldiers repaired at an hour of darkness well suited to the guilt that was to be consummated.

The difficulty of gaining ingress to the building was an obstacle to be overcome by one, who held within the walls a sway, that had been already subservient to the ruin of many a wretched inmate. That impious guide to the brute passions of the Spanish soldiers was no other than the friar Antonio. But this monster of human iniquity had yet his price, for which he had bartered woman's life, and woman's honour. There was one fair girl in the convent, who had been the friend in childhood of the lost Agnese; like the latter, she had become the object of the licentious friar's wishes, but unlike her friend, had repelled with loathing his repeated attempts to undermine her virtue.

Determined, at all risks, to possess the object of his unholy thoughts, Antonio entered into a league with Murillo's troop of ruffians, and disguised as one of them, led the way, through the darkness of the night, to the convent.

In the mean time, Agnese, during a lengthened visit to the convent, had received the confidence of her youthful friend, and listened with feelings of distracted jealousy and indignation to a recital of the faithlessness of him she had loved with so much peril to her soul. Maddened with contending passions, Agnese took the determination of unfolding to her brother her own lost condition, demanding from him vengeance on the head of the guilty Antonio, and permission to seek the forgiveness of Heaven by a life of penitence in the Convent of St. Cecilia.

The Padre's feelings must have been terrible at the disclosure, to judge by the violent paroxysm of emotion the recital of it produced. The habitual serenity of his nature had given way beneath the shock, and where only gentleness had breathed before, was now perceptible no small measure of the Spaniard's violence, and unextinguishable feelings of revenge.

In these latter feelings, however, his unfortunate sister had no share. Her still tender years, and apparent contrition, while pleading in her favour, only added to the fire of hatred that burned fiercely in his breast against Antonio; and at the same time that schemes of revenge that might bring to retributive justice the wily liar floated in his thoughts, he listened with patient forbearance to the tale of guilt his sister had to tell, and warmly acquiesced in the sacrifice she contemplated of her young life to the expiation of her sin.

On the night of that same day which saw the penitent Agnese received by the Abbess and sisterhood into the convent of St. Cecilia, a body of armed men, guided by the villain Antonio, descended from the mountains to the peaceful valley, through which the convent-bell was sounding for the hour of prayer. The friar's cowl was quickly thrown over the military garb he had assumed, as the ruthless band stole with stealthy steps to the front entrance of the building.

With meek and holy accents the friar claimed admittance of the porter from within, an aged man, to whom his voice was known, and who had orders to admit the reverend brother on his sacred missions to the sisterhood. As the ponderous iron gate opened slowly to admit this rare specimen of Satan's workmanship, the soldiers burst from behind into the lofty hall that led to the cloisters of the women. The friar had disappeared, and in his stead a tall athletic soldier, more demoniacal in purpose, more relentless in execution than the rest, led the way to the chapel, where the intended victims were engaged in prayer. Over the scene that followed time has not even yet thrown the shadow of oblivion, for it remains to this day a tale of horror for the winter's hearth, remembered by many an aged native of the Pyrenees. None of those helpless women escaped the brutal violence of Murillo's soldiers. The convent was set on fire in many places, and when the peasants from the neighbouring mountains, attracted by the flames, repaired to the scene of rapine, they found the edifice a burning mass of ruins.

Among the few who rushed in the wildness of despair through the devouring element was Agnese; the wretched girl had recognised in the foremost of that ruffian band, the demon Friar—had shrieked his name again and again, until the vaulted ceiling echoed with it, and received his stab of vengeance in the bosom where his image was too faithfully enshrined.

Still preserving consciousness through the terrors that surrounded her, the unfortunate Agnese sprung, when all was over, through the smoke that densely closed upon the appalling scene, and gaining strength by despair, cleared the burning timbers, and found refuge in the open space of the court-yard. It was here that the mountaineers had assembled, and here that they discovered the bleeding and apparently lifeless form of the Padre's sister. They raised her from the earth, and bore her to her mountain home at Vera, where, in her brother's arms, she finished her miserable existence.

CHAPTER 35

Bayonne

The. glorious campaign of 1813 received its last laurel by the victory of the Nive, which completed the triumph of that eventful year.

The head-quarters of the army were still at St. Jean de Luz, where Lord Wellington awaited the result of negotiations then pending between the foreign powers of Europe and Napoleon, and upon which results depended the advance of the army under his command upon the territory of France.

In the meanwhile, the French loyalist party began to show itself more openly, in consequence of the despondency into which the retreat from Moscow had thrown the partisans of Napoleon. Adversity and failure are the tests of popularity, and the sanguine temperament of the French nation could ill brook the change from glorious conquest to ignoble defeat.

The spell of invincibility attached to Napoleon's name was broken, and with it fell the enthusiasm that had sprung from it. For the first time, it was discovered that the strength of the nation had been squandered in pursuit of the chimerical visions of ambition; that the blood of hundreds of thousands had been sacrificed to the aggrandizement of the few. These late discoveries, originating in the adverse circumstances that had placed an impassable barrier to Napoleon's onward course, had the effect of multiplying the difficulties of his position.

The Royalists, on the one side, were no less zealous to restore to legitimacy its rights, than the Ultra-Republicans to destroy an individual despotism, that had not even the tinsel mantle of glory to conceal it. Between these two extreme parties, stood another, far more numerous, whose members were characterized, some by indifference, others by love of change.

With an eye of scrutiny, Europe looked on the contending elements thus bound up in the French nation, and terms of peace were placed at a proportionately greater distance from its rulers' grasp.

While thus awaiting the signal "to march, or not to march," St. Jean de Luz was as gay and agreeable as ever; dinners, soirées, and balls beguiled the time, and sutlers swarmed like flies on a summer's day, in the well-founded hope of making cent per cent by their champagne and claret. Even hock found its way from the "Banks of the Rhine" into the possession of these gentlemen vendors, who sold it for a "consideration."

The time thus sped merrily along; and Christmas-day was not only hailed with as much fun and frolic as could have welcomed it in England, but roast beef and plum-pudding lent their aid to the illusion that we were, *de facto,* at home. Hospitality and conviviality went hand-in-hand; of the latter, some judgment may be formed by the regulation adopted to disperse the guests, which movement was only to take place when the empty champagne bottles met in the centre of a long dinner-table, forming an uninterrupted line of communication between the President and Vice-President.

The life and joy of these joyous parties was Captain Moray, *aide-de-camp* to the Quarter-Master-General, and beloved by every one as perhaps no other was. Young, handsome, brave, gentle, and ingenuous, this officer was the centre, round whom all others gathered. The very sound of his laugh was catching; and many a sour face was irresistibly led into a smile by its contagious harmony.

We arranged a rendezvous one evening at Fontarabia, a little town between St. Jean de Luz, and Passages, which afforded quarters to some of the officers; among others, to two of my earliest friends, Colonels Nichol, and William Mein, the former commanding the 43rd, the latter the 52nd regiments. To these gallant brothers, the honour of our visit was intended; accordingly, we sallied forth on a very ugly night on our expedition. It was so dark, that at first we only advanced our horses at a snail's pace, which neither accommodating our appetites nor high spirits, these last got the better of prudence, and we started off pretty briskly, reckless of the consequences.

As thus we pushed along, my horse, which was upon the off side, plunged with his two forelegs into the centre of a wet ditch, and having deposited me therein, almost up to my neck in water, scrambled out on the opposite side, and pursued his way rejoicing at his loss. The loud halloo that I gave was the only indication my companions received of our having parted company on the road; and when they at length returned, guided by the sound of my voice to the spot of my immersion, we all laughed so immoderately that a considerable time elapsed before I could make the necessary exertions to relieve myself from the unpleasant position. When this was effected, I had no alternative but to mount *en croupe* behind one of the party; for my steed had not been sufficiently complaisant to proffer his assistance, and thus we journeyed on to Fontarabia.

We found our gallant hosts in excellent quarters, at the house of a French family, where they were looked upon, to use their own phrase as *"les enfans de la maison-"* and surely if gentleness, simplicity, and truth, are qualities that inspire affection everywhere, none could deserve a larger share of it than Colonel William Mein of the 52nd.

This officer entered the service at a very early age, as a subaltern in the 52nd, and served with that distinguished regiment through all the campaigns of the Peninsula. At the storming of Ciudad Rodrigo, he fell severely wounded while leading on to the attack, the Grenadier company of his regiment. Still suffering from the effects of his wounds, he rejoined it the day preceding the assault of Badajoz, and his re-appearance among the veterans of the 52nd afforded a genuine testimony of his worth, for the whole regiment turned out to welcome him with three ringing cheers. On the following night, he led his company to the attack, and was struck down amidst heaps of slain, where he lay without signs of life, until a friendly hand removed him from the scene of carnage.

The spirit of chivalry that burned in the hearts of the men of the light division, effected a quicker cure to their wounds than did the Leech's skill, and it was not long before the gallant soldier again appeared at the head of the regiment on the hills of the Bidassoa; and though severely wounded, continued to follow, at that signal victory, in the pursuit of the enemy, until fainting from exhaustion, he was carried to the rear.

The battle of the Nive was the last scene of strife in which this brave man took a part. Shot through the neck and shoulder on the second day's fighting, he was taken to Fontarabia, and was slowly recovering under the skilful and kind care of Dr. Gunning, Surgeon to the forces, at the time that we bethought ourselves of enlivening his retirement.

On arriving, I found that my horse had preceded me, and was put up in better quarters than his desertion merited. My wet clothes were exchanged for others, raised by general subscription, and we sat down to a dinner, which, owing to the good purveyor-ship of the sutlers, was prolonged to a later hour than was consistent with the still weak condition of our brave host.

In the beginning of February, the allied army renewed hostilities by forcing the enemy to withdraw from the right of the Adour, while Sir John Hope prepared to cross that river below Bayonne. For this purpose, a bridge of rare and laborious construction, which had been planned by Colonel Sturgeon and completed by the Staff Corps, was held in readiness to be thrown over the Adour when required.

A battalion of the guards, by means of pontoon boats, had crossed the river about two miles below the fortress of Bayonne, under cover of a battery of six eighteen pounders, commanded by Captain Morrison, and a rocket troop under the command of Captain Lane. The rockets showed less of disobedience than had been their wont at many previous experimental trials on Woolwich Marsh, preserving the straight line of duty prescribed to them, in spite of all prognostics to the contrary.

A firm footing being thus established on the right bank of the river, the bridge that had been prepared, was ordered to be thrown across, to effect which, a certain number of *chasse-marées* were sent round the coast from Passages laden with anchors, and other essentials for the foundation. The bridge itself was to be supported by the *chasse-marées,* securely anchored at equal distances across the river.

The entrance of the Adour was at all times attended with peril to craft of every description, owing to a bar of sand, over which the waves, in boisterous weather, rolled with fearful violence. On the day when the *chasse-marées* appeared at the mouth of the river, bearing the materials for the formation of the bridge, a high wind had driven a tempestuous sea over the bar, raising a mountain of surf that seemed to defy the approach of the little flotilla, that gallantly pressed forward, led by the boats of our men of war.

Having been one of the many who watched from the shore, with anxious heart, the progress of the operation, I can bear testimony to the dauntless courage of those to whom its execution was confided. The first to lead the way through the uncertain channel of the river—for the enemy had removed the buoys that marked it—was O'Reilly, the same who commanded the sailors' battery at St. Sebastian.

For a moment the boat held on, while he paused for some indication that might guide him in the course to take. During that momentary pause, which showed him nothing but the raging surf, he turned to his brave companion, Captain Faddy of the artillery, who had voluntarily accompanied him, and in a low voice told him to unbuckle his sword—a precaution he had himself taken, and which, in human parlance, saved the lives of both.

The moment's pause was over; the order "Give way, my lads," was uttered, and through the giant surf the cutter dashed, now carried to a fearful height on the summit of the waves—now borne with irresistible fury, crashing on the shore, overwhelmed by the burst of waters. The sight was appalling. Arms were stretched out from shore, as if available to save, and almost miraculously as it appeared, they were destined to do so. O'Reilly was thrown senseless on the sands, and before the rushing surge could reclaim its victim, the soldiers had linked their hands in one strong line, and running into the turbulent waters, had borne him from his perilous position. Faddy, unencumbered by his sword, had managed to swim to shore, as did also some of the crew; the rest were drowned.

Upon seeing the disastrous occurrence, the Spanish crews held back, and it was only when the wind was considerably lulled, that the attempts were renewed to cross the bar. Even then, a fine young officer of the Lyra sloop of war perished with the whole of his boat's crew. Many other valuable lives were lost; and it was left for an agent of transports, Mr. Debenham, to achieve what the most heroic efforts had failed in doing; his small boat leaping, as it may be said, over the boiling surge, in safety on the shore. The *chasse-marées* followed in the line, and thus was accomplished an undertaking, which secured a free passage for troops and war-material over that broad and dangerous river.

As soon as the investment of the citadel had been decided upon,

I received orders to prepare a battering-train of fifty pieces of ordnance for the operation—a duty of much labour and difficulty, in consequence of the local disadvantages attending it. The heavy guns and materiel were first to be disembarked from transports lying in the harbour of Passages, and transshipped into *chasse-marées* for conveyance along the coast to the Adour. From these vessels, the guns and ordnance stores were then to be disembarked, to await removal when the batteries were completed.

I received at Passages all the assistance that was in the power of Admiral Penrose to afford; but the naval force was so scantily organized, that it was inadequate even to the service for which it was stationed there; and it was only by employing night and day the exertions of working parties from the transports, a corps of Civil Artificers, and three companies of Artillery, that this onerous operation could be completed, so as to cause as little delay as possible in the contemplated operations against the fortress.

The batteries were completed under the direction of Colonel Elphinstone of the Engineers and the park of artillery, with ample supplies of ammunition, was under the command of Colonel Hartmann of the German artillery. From the undulating nature of the ground between the river and the citadel, we had deemed it impossible for the enemy to discern the site we had chosen for the magazine, which was as near as possible to the batteries, and covered by the slope of a hill.

It had been often observed that an iron cage was suspended from the flag-staff of the citadel, but beyond remarking the circumstance, no importance had been given to it, until the explosion of two shells close to the magazine drew attention to the direction from whence they were thrown. Then for the first time it was discovered that the iron cage contained a man, whose telescope commanded the whole of our position. "Jack in the box" as the soldiers called him, now became a personage of much importance, inasmuch as the hoisting up of his iron frame-work was the signal for dropping shells into the midst of our working parties. The compliment was returned on our side; and a six-pounder having been brought to the precise altitude of "Jack in the box," a few well directed shots took effect upon his hard skin, to the annihilation of his peeping propensities.

The investment of the citadel had not been effected without some hard fighting, which fell on the Germans under General Hinuber. They took possession of the Church of St. Etienne, and some houses that had been fortified by the French, who opposed a gallant resistance under the Governor, Count Thouvenot. The guards were equally successful in driving the enemy from the fortified posts he occupied in front of the fortress; and, from this period, the 29th of February, until the 6th of April, when the heavy guns were ready for removal from the park to the batteries, nothing beyond the firing kept up upon our working parties, and a few unimportant sallies from the garrison took place.

Whilst Sir John Hope was thus occupied in front of Bayonne, Lord Wellington, with the main body of the army, was moving on towards the southern capital of France. It may be said that Soult was the only obstacle to impede his progress; for the inhabitants soon appreciated the admirable regulations that insured safety to property, and respect to person, and were, if not friendly to the invading force, at least, passive.

On the 27th of February, the French Marshal made a stand at Orthes, where he was attacked by Wellington and completely defeated. The battle was bravely fought, with severe loss on both sides; and for the first time during the war, Wellington received a wound from a spent ball. While Soult, with his beaten army, retreated upon Aire and Agens, Beresford, accompanied by the Duke d'Angoulême, who had arrived at head-quarters, was sent with two divisions of the army to occupy Bordeaux. That royalist city greeted with enthusiasm the presence of a Bourbon Prince, and the *drapeau blanc* replaced the tricolour on the spires and towers of the ancient buildings.

From Agens, Soult had been forced by the allies upon Tarbes; but towards the middle of the month of March he was so closely pressed by Wellington, who had received strong reinforcements from the Spaniards, that the French Marshal, after an unsuccessful combat, marched upon Toulouse, destroying the bridges on his route. This circumstance retarded the pursuit of the allied army, and afforded the enemy time to fortify a position in front of that city. It was not until the 28th, that Wellington arrived before Toulouse, and taking up a position on the left bank of the Garonne, the hostile armies stood, the one preparing for attack, the other for defence.

CHAPTER 36

Toulouse

The great commercial city of Bordeaux was now occupied by a division of the allied army, under a British General. In sight of the southern capital of the Empire, waved the united national colours of England, Spain, and Portugal, under a British chief, whilst a formidable mass of war materiel was ready to force open the strong frontier gates of Bayonne's frowning citadel, which contained twelve thousand veteran defenders. A momentous era in the proud history of our arms had dawned, and England's sun of glory shone upon the defeat and humiliation of her foes. At this crisis, when a brief space would probably have sufficed to bring to a focus the brilliant combinations of a Wellington's genius, "a change came o'er the spirit of the dream."

Napoleon abdicated, and peace was restored to the war-sick world.

There are few things that are capable of pressing a stronger conviction of the pygmy confines to which the mind of man is limited, than the reflection that those men of war, Wellington and Soult—agents in the hands of destiny, whose only aim had been to plot, contrive, and execute means of annihilation to each other, with all the strength and energy of devoted hatred, over a series of years past, were powerless as infants to develop the events of three days before them. Had this limited prescience been granted to them, both France and England would have been spared the deplorable loss of their brave sons at Bayonne and Toulouse.

Upon this melancholy page in the History of the War, opinions will ever remain divided as to whether or not the knowledge of the events that were passing in Paris had reached the French and

British Commanders. It is an indisputable point that the armistice had not been officially communicated to the hostile parties; but is difficult to believe that either could have been ignorant that Napoleon's power was crumbled into dust, and that every day—nay, every hour, might bring confirmation of the rumour, already widely spread, of the suspension of arms.

Be this as it may, on the 10th of April, the battle of Toulouse was fought. Soult was forced from the strong position he occupied, and retired with his army into the city, which on the following night he abandoned. On the 12th, despatches arrived announcing to both armies the restoration of the Bourbons; an announcement, which, had it reached but two days earlier, would have saved eight thousand gallant soldiers, who fell a sacrifice, either to the fatal procrastination of a messenger, or to the too anxious anticipation of conquest. Nor did the useless effusion of blood end here: Sir John Hope, in consequence of the rumours that had reached him at Bayonne, delayed to arm the batteries for the attack on the citadel. Late on the 13th, he received intelligence of the armistice; but omitted on that evening to communicate it officially to Count Thouvenot, the Governor, under the conviction that he was also cognizant of its existence.

It is a most improbable circumstance that this French officer should have remained in ignorance of an event, news of which had been dispatched from Paris as early as the 7th instant, and must have been heard of by the many emissaries he employed without the citadel; for, although the fortress was invested, there was no possibility of preventing individuals from holding communication with those outside.

It is, moreover, a strongly suspicious circumstance, that during the six weeks of investment, no sortie from the citadel should have been made, until the fatal night of the 13th, when three thousand of the garrison rushed from their stronghold with no defined object in view of ultimate advantage, beyond glutting their pent-up feelings of vengeance upon the besiegers.

The roar of artillery from the citadel, and the clang of musketry summoned Sir John Hope, in the dead of night, from his bed to his saddle bow; and accompanied by the officers of his staff—amongst them the present Adjutant-General, Sir John Macdonald—he spurred onwards in the direction of the firing, for there was no other guide than sound to lead to the point of attack. While thus advancing through a narrow road, with high embankments on either side, a moving mass was heard approaching in the opposite direction. "They are the Portuguese," observed the General. As he spoke a volley was fired, and he was wounded; his horse dropping down dead at the same moment, entangled him in his fall, and as, in the suddenness of the *mêlée,* his staff had scrambled up, as best they could, the sides of the road, the General was taken possession of by the enemy.

A detachment of the guards now came rapidly up from the rear, and were firing upon the foe, when Hartmann, of the German artillery, who had himself just been wounded, called out at the top of his voice: "Don't fire, by Gott! you will kill the General." The injunction was not in time to prevent the gallant Hope from receiving a second wound from our own men in the vain attempt to rescue him. He was carried off a prisoner into Bayonne.

Among the mournful results of this wanton expenditure of human blood was the loss of the veteran General Hay; this beloved and esteemed commander had braved, and escaped the dangers of many a hard fought day in the Peninsula, and fell a victim, when the din of war was exchanged for a triumphant peace, to the savage *fanfaronnade* of a conquered foe. On that night the gallant General visited the pickets, infusing into the hearts of his old comrades in arms the happiness with which his own was inspired. "No more fighting, my lads," he exclaimed; "now for our homes, wives and sweethearts." His own family had just arrived from Lisbon, and were within a mile of the spot where he stood.

Midnight came. The stillness of that hour was broken by the musketry of the advanced posts. The General hastened with his *aide-de-camp* to the point from whence it proceeded, and concentrated his small force in the church yard of St. Etienne; the enemy had issued from the citadel, and were pouring down in numbers.

"Steady, my boys, steady," shouted the veteran Commander; "we shall soon be supported." His voice was heard no more, and a soldier, stooping in the direction where he had stood, found the corpse of his General stretched across a grave. Dearly was his death avenged; and after a carnage of several hours, the French were driven back to the very walls of the citadel at the point of British bayonets.

The morning of the 14th dawned in beauty on a ghastly scene. As nature, purified and re-freshened, follows in the track of the death-winged simoom of the desert, so seemed to burst forth the sweet serenity of a spring morning, to oppose its contrast to the ravages of the past night. Under the calm blue sky lay the stiffened corpses, and still writhing victims of the strife of man. A few hours afterwards the tidings of peace were re-echoed from thousands of tongues, and the slaughter of so many brave men in this last scene of a protracted war, left—except in sorrowing hearts—no trace on our memory beyond a passing cloud.

As soon as peace was proclaimed, active preparations commenced for the removal of the battering-train and materiel that had been collected with so much difficulty and labour before the walls of Bayonne, and as soon as all the arrangements were completed, I received orders to join the head-quarters of the army at Toulouse. After resigning my responsibilities as Military Commissary into the hands of Colonel Hartmann, I bade adieu to the gloomy fortress that reared its head, like a huge funeral monument to the memory of the slain, and accompanied by a young officer of my department, we pursued our journey on horseback to Toulouse.

The first night, we halted at Dax, an insignificant and dirty town, where we were destined to receive incontrovertible evidence that the first impressions of English childhood,—uniting frogs and Frenchmen in an indissoluble union—are not wholly founded Upon national prejudice; inasmuch as a very *appétissant* dish of these little amphibious gentlemen took a distinguished position on the supper table at the *auberge* where we alighted. A certain degree of clairvoyance enabled me to fathom the mysteries of the tempting plate; but my companion asserted that it was *a fricassée de poulet,* and treated it accordingly, with all the vigour of a keen appetite. When at length appealing to the *chef de cuisine* he was placed in possession of the fatal certainty, no wrath could equal his, and it was only with difficulty that the unreasonable propensity he had—in common with most Englishmen—of chastising others because they differed from himself in taste, could be kept in proper subjection. However, even wrath gave way to the native weakness of an English stomach, worked upon by a firmly-fixed antipathy, and the poor fellow's inside was consequently reduced to a vacuum, that rendered it most unjust that a charge for supper should have been included in his bill.

From that moment *"grenouille,"* was a word of aversion and loathing, that baffled all argument or remonstrance to overcome. Like the gentleman who fancied himself a tea-pot, or the monomaniac of more recent date, who believed himself pursued by inveterate enemies, so did my companion hear in every sound a croak, and see in every dish a delicate hind leg.

The roads in the south of France are as if designed as a wholesome restraint upon the impatient curiosity of travellers. A straight unbroken line, with trees and broad ditches on either side, forms the boundary of sight both before and behind; and when hope whispers that beyond the boundary, a turn in the road must open some changing prospect to the wearied eye, behold another line, equally straight, and apparently as interminable as the last, appears as if in mockery.

During this locomotive penance, the discordant rejoicings of millions of frogs greet the traveller on every side. In vain he seeks by spurring his horse, or urging on the postillion, escape from the sounds that assail him from the rear. Each step in advance adds to the strength of the chorus, and thus he journeys on, with senses so bewildered, that he can scarcely make out whether he is indeed flitting through a country, that has been designated *la belle France,* or through some strange place beyond the precincts of this globe, to which tormented spirits are consigned. It may be supposed that under these circumstances, my companion, during our second day's ride—the early part of it through a flat and marshy country—received no impression likely to reconcile him to his repast of the previous night, and I confess, that without having the same unpleasant recollections, I could find nothing to say in favour of *la famille grenouille.*

We had intended to reach Tarbes on the second night, but a lovely bit of Pyrenean scenery, peeping at a distance, like a pretty face intruding on one's solitude, was, as the last might be, irresistible, and we left the straight ugly road with its ditches and their noisy inhabitants, to plunge into a charming valley, rich in every production of the sweet south, and affording a shade of thick foliage that was most refreshing after a long ride in the midday sun.

The majestic barrier of the high Pyrenees, which separates France from Spain, lay stretched in the distance; its outline only faintly perceptible through the hot vapour that clouded the atmosphere. From this giant chain of mountains, others less and less conspicuous came slanting down to meet the rich valley where we stood, forming a scene, in which the sublime and picturesque were beautifully mingled with fertility. In these days, when every traveller is furnished with a guide-book of the country he is exploring, there would be little excuse for taking | wrong road, and insisting, for its beauty's sake alone, that it would lead, in due time, to the right one. But, at that time, the charlatanism of Itineraries had yet to creep from the press, and the way-farer had either to guess his course, or abandon himself to the most alluring, on the principle that, *"tout chemin mène à Rome."* Acting on the latter theory, we found ourselves still advancing through the valley, as the sun was throwing his glowing rays upon the fair landscape round us. There is nothing like hunger for dragging down the mind from the contemplation if the beautiful to the realities of creature comforts. No one ever heard of a starving philosopher. In this beautiful secluded spot of nature's workmanship, the rudest sign-post that had pointed to Tarbes, and a good dinner, would have carried off the palm even from Goddess of Beauty.

While musing whether to proceed, or to retrace our steps, a party on horseback appeared in sight, consisting of three persons. As they approached nearer, we discovered that the individual who rode a little ahead of the two others, was an elderly female habited in a dress that is still to be seen in the pictures that represent the old French costume before the Revolution of 1789 amalgamated, in one mass of anarchy and disorder, the rigidly defined classes of society in France. A cloth riding dress that buttoned tightly from her throat to the waist, differed but slightly from man's attire. She sat astride on horseback, with whip and boots that heightened her resemblance to the masculine gender, leaving her sex to be guessed at, rather than identified by the straw bonnet and grizzled ringlets that shaded her face.

It may be supposed we did not allow this opportunity to escape of ascertaining to what part of the world our "search of the picturesque," had carried us; and the courteous, but half satirical smile with which the old lady answered our inquiries by *"Messieurs, vous êtes bien loin de Tarbes,"* was very decisive as to our having deviated, not a little, from the right path.

The disappointment that our countenances must have expressed was met with the same winning manner by our new acquaintance, who congratulated herself in terms of politeness— perfectly captivating to our then inexperienced English ears— upon her own *bonne fortune,* in being enabled to carry us off to her husband's château as visitors for the night. Nothing loth, we allowed ourselves to be persuaded by this genuine specimen of *vieille noblesse;* and joining the lady's cavalcade, we pursued our way through a country even more romantic and beautiful than we had previously seen. *Chemin faisant,* our conductress informed us she was returning home with her attendants from a visit to a neighbouring château, when the beauty of the evening induced her to prolong her ride by a *détour* that brought her to the spot where we were ruminating on the chances of passing the night à *la belle étoile.*

Another league brought us in sight of the first French château of any pretensions we had seen, standing on the summit of a wooded hill. The approach was by an avenue of nearly a mile in length, skirted by tall poplar trees, ascending gradually to the iron grating of the court-yard of the chateau. Two or three old domestics, attired in liveries as ancient as themselves, that had most probably been re-assumed at the first joyful intelligence of the restoration of the Bourbons, were in waiting to open the heavy portals for their mistress.

As we advanced through the extensive court-yard to the grand entrance, I had a specimen of *les anciennes moeurs françaises,* in which there was so much more of the touching than the ridiculous—albeit there was a spice of the latter also—that I never wondered at the profound regret lavished on *le bon vieux temps,* by some of the most dispassionate and reflecting Frenchmen.

As the palfrey stopped before the hall-door, an old gentleman, with the *croix de* St. Louis suspended from his button hole, descended the stone steps, and with a *galanterie empressée* that could not have been surpassed by a devoted lover to his young affianced bride, bore his elderly partner gently in his arms from the saddle to the ground, impressing a kiss on each cheek as she alighted on terra firma. When this conjugal embrace was concluded, the lady introduced us to her lord, the Comte de S—, who welcomed us to his roof, by advancing towards us with a series of low bows; which losing gradually their profundity as the distance diminished between us, were at length terminated by his inflicting twin-kisses upon us also; an operation that almost made me fear he had mistaken the sex of his guests.

Here then, from way-faring travellers on the road side, we found ourselves welcome visitors in one of the most hospitable mansions it has been my fate to remember in any land. The supper was worthy of the high renown of *la cuisine française;* but notwithstanding the *recherché* appearance of the table, my companion shuddered as a *fricassée de poulet* made its appearance, and identifying it with the frogs of previous night, whispered to me "that is a monster."

The wines of Burgundy and Bordeaux were not only of an age and vintage that told of their patrician descent, but these valuable tenants of the cellarage were uncorked with a liberality that almost partook of profuse extravagance. At last, our host was so delighted with the homage we paid to the names of Château-Margaux, and Romani-Conti, that his hospitality seemed to increase beyond the powers of restraint.

Slipping from the room, he returned with a bottle, so closely sealed, that it might have been supposed to hold the fatal contents of Pandora's box. The cork came out loud and full; there was a moment's expectation, or rather curiosity to see if anything could be manufactured by art or time better than had been drank on that evening. A small liqueur glass of the precious liquid was handed to our hostess by her attentive spouse. *"Ah! que c'est délicieux,"* said the lady. It was soon our turn to exclaim. "By Jove! it is common rum," said my companion, with more truth than politeness.

"Oui, Messieurs," chuckled the old gentleman, his ear catching the name of the delicate beverage he seemed so much to prize. *"Oui! c'est du rhum, du vieux rhum?"*

"C'est délicieux," repeated the lady. It was some time before the worthy pair could credit the fact of *Messieurs les Anglais* preferring Château-Margaux, and Romani-Conti to rum; and as it afterwards appeared, it was solely from the mistaken notion that all Englishmen were fond of ardent spirits, that these kind people encouraged us in what they thought we liked, even at the expense of their own good taste.

At a late hour, our hospitable hostess conducted us to our sleeping apartments, and it is with astonishment that my eyes turned to the costly furniture, and elegance of taste with which they were fitted up. All previously conceived ideas of French discomforts, and unclean beds dispersed like chaff before the wind, under the gentle pressure of a delicate white satin duvet, the first I had seen; sheets of exquisite texture, and a canopy of celestial blue, that rose to an immense height above my head, supported by flying Cupids.

The superiority of the French in all arrangements that demand the exercise of taste, is now, I believe, generally conceded to them even by the most anti-Gallic; but before the opening of the continent to the class of locomotive English, strange notions were entertained of the semi-barbarism of our neighbours; therefore the excess of luxury I was enjoying, in direct contradiction to my pre-conceived prejudices, seemed like the beneficent work of some good little fairy, who held her revels amidst the wild recesses of the Pyrenees.

On the following morning we bade farewell to our kind hosts, and after the exchange of good wishes, and hopes, expressed and felt, of meeting again, we mounted our horses, and, under the guidance of a small country map, that had been brought into second existence from a dusty shelf in the old library, pursued route in the direction of Pau.

The evening was closing in, after a brilliant day of sunshine, when we reached Pau, a city that well deserves its high repute for the advantages of climate it enjoys, as well as beauty of situation. It stands on an eminence, commanding a delightful country that abounds with the necessaries and luxuries of life. The Gave meanders through its fertile plains, and a chain of lofty mountains, capped with snow, rises in the distance, forming a boundary to the attractive picture.

To the sight-seeking stranger, there are few or no objects of interest, always excepting the Castle where the gallant monarch Henri Quatre, made his first début as a fraction of frail mortality, and the tortoise-shell cradle, in which his little Bourbon eyes were wont to close in gentle slumber. The rest of this once royal residence is converted into barracks, and historical recollections are scarcely sufficient to preserve it from the degradation that time and circumstances have inflicted on it.

The beauty of the weather, the extreme comfort of the Hotel

de la Poste, and perhaps above these, the enjoyment of liberty after so many years of harness, combined to keep me some days in these seductive quarters; and at that time I could picture to myself no retreat from the cares and activities of the busy world, where man could dream away existence, forgetting and forgot, more happily than at Pau.

The political bias of the inhabitants was as yet undeclared by any public demonstration, and it is possible that their feelings and interests were so contending that it required to be developed by circumstances, even to themselves. On one side weighed the love-fostering traditions of ancestral loyalty, that warm the heart's blood from generation to generation, when cherished in the locality where they first spring. On the other side was to be placed the loss of place and power to many who had identified themselves with the existing order of things; and thus affection for the past, and satisfaction at the present, united to preserve a temporary neutrality.

La salle de spectacle has often been, both in capitals and provincial towns abroad, a chosen spot for the first ebullition of popular feeling; and it so happened that during my stay at Pau, a little dramatic scene of unstudied effect was performed, which struck a chord, that vibrated, like electricity, through a crowded audience. The performance was about to begin, when a French officer in full uniform, and surrounded by several others, called upon the orchestra from the stage-box, to play "*Vive Henri Quatre.*"

A deep silence reigned in the house, the music and the audience remained equally mute for several minutes. No voice *pour ou contre* was raised. At length the long suppressed air burst upon the ear, but in notes so low and gentle, that it seemed as if to plead an apology for its intrusion. A few voices mingled in the strain. The orchestra, emboldened by the few, burst forth with energy, and from that moment apathy was replaced by enthusiasm. From every part of the house, sobs, tears, smiles, and vociferous cheering were seen and heard. White handkerchiefs and ribbons waved from every box. Cries of "*Vivent les Bourbons!*" rent the air; and in the midst of ecstasy and joy, the restored dynasty was enshrined in the hearts of the citizens of Pau.

The country, as we approached Toulouse, was a perfect garden, rich in cultivation and in produce. The nut-brown faces of the pretty peasant girls were smiling as the blue above them. The corn and vines looked full of promise for the ensuing season; and but for an occasional military convoy that passed us on the road, we should have had nothing to remind us that the clamour and ravages of war had been carried into the very heart of this now peaceful and happy-looking land. Toulouse is a large, well-built, and in many parts a handsome town, and was at that time full of noise and gaiety. The streets and *cafés* were thronged with English and Portuguese officers, and the lounging idleness of the day was generally terminated by balls or *soirées* at night. Soult's army was cantoned at no great distance, and many of the French officers used to come over in plain clothes, to see what fun was going on, or to pick a quarrel with some unsuspecting Englishman. Now that the roar of cannon no longer broke upon the tranquillity of the plains, some of these gentlemen sought to gratify their dislike to the English by various stratagems; duels were of frequent occurrence, and several gallant men, who had passed unscathed the perils of the war, fell victims to these implacable feelings. In the *cafés,* or at the theatre, which was open every night, might be seen faces worked up for mischief; the curled lip of contempt, or glance of defiance always ready, to direct at some good-humoured group of noisy young Englishmen, who were far from being unwilling to make allowances for the mortified feelings of brave men, and therefore slow to take offence without sufficient cause.

Among many occurrences that took place illustrative of the sentiments of the *vieilles moustaches* towards the new state of affairs, may be mentioned one that placed an English officer in a position of extreme difficulty and perplexity. Major G——, of the horse artillery, having obtained leave of absence to explore the beauties of Touraine, made the selection of a quiet little town for his headquarters, where some of the French dragoons were stationed. Prudence might have suggested to an English officer, so circumstanced, the propriety of with-drawing from his helmet the emblem of Bourbon restoration—the white cockade; but the precaution was disregarded—not from a wish to humiliate others—for no such unworthy motive could have found an entrance in the honourable mind of Major G——, but from an intention to adhere strictly to the orders of Lord Wellington upon the subject.

Many were the fierce looks darted upon *la cocarde blanche* by the soldiers, as they passed this obnoxious tell-tale of many a battle lost; but it was left to a still fiercer defender of the tricolour to bring to an issue the right of a British officer to sport the detested token of legitimacy in a town where some few staunch hearts still beat for the colours under which they had bled.

It was in one of the streets of this small town that Major G— was arrested in his walk by three French officers, who, with mock courtesy, inquired if he admired the new country in which he found himself. The reply was made with the mildness that characterizes an English gentleman; but this did not suit the purpose of the Frenchmen. "You are, perhaps, come to teach us our duty to our monarch," said one of the party, pointing in derision to the white ribbon in Major G— s helmet. The latter replied, with calmness, that military man he had no alternative but to obey his General's commands.

"Your General has no power here," vociferated the speaker; and suiting the action to the word, he raised his arm and tore the cockade from its place.

The sensitive feelings of a British officer at this gross outrage may be more easily conceived than described. To chastise the offender on the spot was not in his power, for his side arms had been left at the *auberge;* and no friend was nigh, through whose medium he could seek satisfaction to his offended honour. While thus perplexed, and smarting under the sense of injury, his first idea was to bring his servant, a soldier in his troop, as *témoin* to the affair that he felt was inevitable; but second thoughts are in most cases preferable to the first impulses of excited feeling; and calm reflection pointed out to Major G— a course more in unison with his rank as an officer, and more congenial to his mind as a gentleman.

Acting on these second and better thoughts, he wrote to the Commandant, related the outrage he had received, and called on him as a soldier and a man of honour, to be his friend in bringing him face to face with the individual, who had so grievously insulted him. Between brave and right thinking men, there is a free-masonry, without its mysteries; and the Commandant of this small town in France felt the regret of a brave man, that to a brave man an affront should have been offered.

He wrote in reply that he should have been happy to have been the friend of an English officer under circumstances of so peculiar a character; but added, that such an extreme measure was no longer necessary; the offender had been placed under arrest by himself as soon as the circumstance was reported to him; and that he had already dispatched a courier to Paris for instructions how to dispose of him. Thus ended an affair that was calculated to have produced fatal results, but for the intervention of the French Commandant, whose discernment marked the difference between a calm and dignified bravery, and the blustering of an over-officious zeal.

It was during the occupation of Toulouse the British troops, that the design was formed of sending a considerable force to America, and orders were issued to prepare a military equipment for the army that was to embark for that destination under Sir Rowland Hill. This equipment devolved on myself to re-create out of the military stores that had been employed in the Peninsula. It was at Bordeaux that I commenced and completed this extensive preparation for the expedition that I had orders to accompany. The convoy was on the point of sailing, my baggage was even embarked, when it was decided that the scale of magnitude on which the expedition was mounted, should be decreased. I consequently consigned my duties to a junior officer, and returned to the head-quarters of the army which was on the eve of dispersion.

Chapter 37

To England

The moment was now arrived when the confederate armies were to break up their cantonments in France. The Portuguese and Spaniards returned to their own countries. The Commander-in-Chief took leave of his brave troops at Toulouse, to assist at the deliberations that were being held in Paris, and all the army was in movement towards home. The infantry embarked for England at the nearest ports. The cavalry and brigades of artillery traversed France by easy and pleasant marches to attain the short sea-voyage between Calais and Dover, while some of the young staff officers, with both time and money at disposal, sought the pleasures and novelties of Paris previously to their return.

It was a moment of strange excitement, this sudden transition from war to peace, from daily intercourse of men, one with another, to a separation that might be for ever. Then, appeared too, for the first time, those pantings for distinction, and petty heart-burnings that invariably follow in the train of despatches and gazettes. Many were nobly worthy of the honours they obtained; and others, who were equally deserving, were passed over for those who were not so; for, in our army, such was the nature of systematic regulations, that no man could receive a mark of distinction—however brilliant the action he might have performed—unless he came within the pale of rules framed in cold blood by government secretaries at home; for instance, an officer who had been in any kind of command at five battles, even had he peeped at them through a hedge, or showed his back instead of his front, was entitled by right, to a distinguished badge of knighthood,[1] while the most daring achievements could meet with no reward at all, because never having been of course specifically anticipated, neither could they be specifically provided for by official decree.

If the gallant Macguire had survived his chivalric leading of the forlorn hope against the walls of St. Sebastian, would any mark of distinction have been coupled with the admiration his conduct excited? The best answer will be that Colonel Jones, the young engineer, who with conspicuous gallantry led the way at the same siege, for others to follow, and who there found himself alone a prisoner on the hostile walls, who served throughout the war, a distinguished member of his gallant corps, remains, at this distant period, without one outward sign of the honour he so justly gained on that memorable occasion; but, worse than this, was the neglect of reward to the British soldier; he, the brave, the faithful, the enduring, even with the disadvantage of the cold and blighting shade under which he fights.

No hope of promotion stimulates his heart to action. No badge

---

1. (see previous page) The absurdity and injustice of this regulation was most conspicuously shown in the Royal Engineers. This distinguished corps lost, during the war, from the peculiar exposure attendant on its duties, a greater number of officers than composed its original force. No officer in command survived five battles. Consequently, although some were fortunate enough to survive four, they were debarred, by the regulations, from participating in the honours that were not only due to their meritorious services, but conferred upon many others less deserving.
2. These observations refer exclusively to the soldiers of the Peninsular war; for it appears that in later days it has been deemed expedient to strike medals in commemoration of actions, that in those days would scarcely have found their way into the Gazette. Whether modern liberality proceeds from compunction for the past, or from the rising generation requiring more active stimulants than their fathers did, is difficult to say; one thing is certain, that the veterans of the Peninsular army, who shared the dangers of their great commander on the battlefield, who encircled his brow with laurels, who gained for him, by their invincible bravery, an imperishable renown, who upheld with him the honour of their country's name, those veteran soldiers had a just and undeniable claim on their great commander, and should have obtained, through his recommendation, some special distinction that England would gladly and proudly have bestowed, at the bidding of one on whom she had lavished so many substantial proofs of her gratitude. Too many years have elapsed to render such distinctions now, conducive either to the honour of the great commander, or to the veterans who served under him. Attempts have been made, and recently, to wrench from a reluctant hand the payment of a debt which, like many others, has been annulled only by the defrauding statute of limitation; and when memory recalls the many gallant soldiers who now lie mouldering in the dust, and who, by sharing in the claims, shared also in the disappointment of their non-requital, there remains but little sympathy for the remnant that would at this late period seek justice, after thirty years' patient submission to her absence.

of honour in perspective, nerves his arm to deeds of valour; he shows bravery because it is the inherent quality of his nature—a quality that he is no more capable of divesting himself of, than he is capable of laying down his life and resuming it at will—a quality that might almost be denominated brute courage, but for the short step that divides it from heroism; and yet, to ascend that short step man's moral feeling must undergo as complete a change as that which metamorphoses brute courage into heroism. To effect this change was the study of Napoleon Bonaparte; to crush it was our military policy. Bonaparte, who owed his greatness to the power he possessed of reading the hearts of men, and rendering them subservient to his purposes, well knew that ambition is the spur to action, and therefore did not hesitate to place before the longing eyes of the drummer-boy, the glittering *croix d'honneur*, that only awaited to be won before it hung suspended to his plebeian breast. The enthusiasm thus inspired amounted almost to mental delirium, and many of the French soldiers, who, in our ranks, would have differed in no degree from the common clod-poles of the earth, were led to perform almost supernatural acts of individual heroism, under the enchanted influence of the *croix d'honneur,* whereas the British soldier, instead of wearing on his return from the wars in the Peninsula, the cross that would have linked his humble name with that of Wellington, brought back to Ins native land a thread-bare jacket, an empty purse, and a toil-worn countenance. These were the only honours that distinguished the soldier of the Peninsular war.

It was in July that I again set foot on the shores of England. London was at that time the head-quarters of the Peninsular officers, lingering for a few days in the crowded hotels, previously to a final dispersion to their respective homes. During this brief space, many were the farewell dinners that took place between friends who had shared the dangers of the war; but at these meetings, the gay hilarity of a campaigning party was wanting. Many had to mourn the breaking up of their boyhood's home, and the annihilation of the bright prospects that hope had promised on returning to it; while to others, time had touched with a rude hand affections that in the distance still wore the freshness that graced them at the parting hour. It is such shocks as these that revolutionize the heart of man; the bright dream of young life, which may be called the poetry of youth, then dies away, and a stern, harsh view of life's realities succeeds it.

It was at one of these military reunions that I fell in with Lieutenant P——, a young officer, belonging to my friend Graeme's regiment, the 89th, which had just returned from America. From him I learnt that the noble-hearted Graeme was no more; he fell on the field of honour, leaving a name that will ever remain engraven on the hearts of those who loved him. The circumstances attending his death were such as to lead the mind to contemplate, with greater reverence than we are inclined to feel on such subjects, the mystical link that unites our spirit here to its eternal abode. I wrote down, at the time, the details of what was to me so deeply melancholy an event, in the words of our mutual friend P——, who narrated it as follows:

We were in America under the orders of General Drummond, and the flank companies of the 1st and 89th regiments were sent up the interior of the country to dislodge the enemy from a position he had taken up, and strongly fortified. We commenced our march on a severe morning in the depth of winter, and I remarked that Graeme was silent and out of spirits. His heart was usually so joyous, his spirits were so exuberant with life and happiness, that I bantered him on the fit of sentimentality he had assumed, but to no purpose. He could not be cheerful, and twisting out of his cap a little bugle that ornamented it, he said to me with a sad smile: 'Here, P——, keep this for my sake.' I did take it, and I know not why, but his sadness extended itself to me. I saw he had a presentiment he should fall, and in a strange, unaccountable manner, I shared his feelings.

From the severity of the weather, and the ground being covered with snow, our march was fatiguing in the extreme, and Graeme, who commanded the light company of his regiment, had occasion to reprimand several of the men for disorderly and insubordinate behaviour, which would probably have increased to mutiny, but for the love they bore him. To one fellow, who was more unruly than the rest, Graeme sharply applied the epithet of 'coward,' alluding to a prior affair, in which some reports had been made upon this man's want of energy. The soldier looked sulkily at him, but made no remark. When we came up with the enemy's works, a murderous fire was opened on us, as we traversed the deep ravine that separated us from the heights he occupied. Every one of our officers, with the exception of Graeme and myself, had been picked off by the concealed rifles of our opponents, and we alone remained to lead on to the attack. For a moment we placed ourselves under the slope of a hill, to prepare for a desperate effort to carry the position; retreat or surrender being alike impossible. My gallant friend was rallying his men to the charge, when the poor fellow who had patiently borne the opprobrious name of 'coward,' dragged himself to the spot where Graeme stood, staining, as he moved along, the whiteness of the snow with the blood that poured from his wounds. Standing erect before his officer, he said: 'Sir, am I now a coward?' and dropped down dead at his feet.

Never shall I forget the expression of self-reproach and sorrow that poor Graeme's face wore, as for a moment he contemplated the fallen soldier who lay stretched before him. Then, suddenly springing forward, he exclaimed, 'Now, my lads, follow me!' The next moment, 'Oh God!' escaped from his lips, and he fell to the earth. A ball had struck him in the shoulder, traversed his body, and found its way out just below the hip. I rubbed his lips and temples with snow, and used every means to restore animation; but his noble spirit had fled. The rest of us, reduced to eight in number, were made prisoners by the enemy; but we were allowed to carry with us the remains of our gallant comrade; and when we stretched his lifeless corpse at a little distance from the bivouacking party, one of their officers, a rough, hard-featured man, wept, as I well remember, in contemplating the noble countenance and placid smile of that ever-to-be lamented friend. We dug for him a soldier's grave in the vast wilderness, and watered it with our tears. No monumental marble marks the spot; but as long as memory lasts, his name will there be inscribed and cherished.

Chapter 38

Ordered to America

The stirring scenes of the Peninsula had not long been exchanged for the ease and idleness of a home-life, when I received orders to join the forces in America, under Sir Edward Pakenham; and having most vexatiously lost my passage in the *Statira* frigate which sailed from Portsmouth unexpectedly, with Sir Edward Pakenham and Sir Alexander Dickson on board, only a few hours before my arrival there, the Port-Admiral recommended me to proceed in the *Swiftsure*, seventy-four gun ship, under sailing orders for Barbados with a convoy; he, at the same time, promising to send out directions to insure a passage from thence to the Gulf of Mexico. By pursuing this course, the Admiral thought it probable that I should arrive at my destination almost as soon as the *Statira*; but hopes and promises at sea are amenable to the winds and waves; and at the expiration of one month, after encountering in the channel very severe gales, the *Swiftsure* and her convoy were again anchored at the mother-bank.

At this time, fresh orders reached me from the Ordnance, with instructions to disembark, and proceed to Cork, where a force of seven thousand men were assembled, under orders for America; together with a convoy of transports laden with artillery and military stores, of which I was directed to take charge, for the same destination. For this purpose I embarked in a packet from Bristol; and after three days' pitching and tossing, we entered the Cove of Cork. Here I caught my first glance of "The Emerald Isle;" "The first gem of the sea," upon whose soil, wit and impudence luxuriate as indigenous plants, in the rich manure of ignorance and sloth.

Notwithstanding that the month of December had robbed of their green clothing, the hills that stretch to the very margin of the water, the magnificent spectacle of this fine harbour was increased by the number of men of war and transports that plunged and heaved upon its ruffled waves. Two bold headlands, strongly fortified, guard its entrance; and a number of small islands, used for military depots, rise from the surface of the waters, giving variety and interest to the scene.

The town of Cove faces the entrance to the harbour; it is sheltered by a steep hill, up the side of which it climbs, in irregular zig-zags, and was remarkable, at that time, for little but its poverty and the bustle and activity that prevail in all spots contiguous to a harbour, where Jack-tars are lying at anchor within sight.

As the packet passed Cove, which was the nearest spot to the scene of my duties, I jumped into a boat that pushed off to me from shore, and certainly thought that the whole begging population of the country had turned out to welcome me to "Ould Ireland;" moreover, that they had assumed for the occasion a masquerade variety of poverty-parading costumes.

A red handkerchief tied under the chin was, I observed, a favourite head-dress with most of the elderlies of both sexes; and to many, a sheet, a blanket, and, in some cases, coarse serge swathed round the body, performed the office of cloak in its literal meaning, of concealing what it was thrown over.

Age, ugliness, disease, and idleness, each performed its respective part, with the originality of design and earnestness of execution that I was prepared to meet in the Irish people; for in truth, I was primed with the expectation of having my ears greeted with a continuous volley of *bons mots,* talented *bullisms,* and witty repartees, discharged at the expense of the stranger's pocket, and sometimes of his *amour-propre.*

"Och! sure yer honour is come among us to lave yer good heart in the shape of a tin-penny."

"An honourable young gintleman most intirely ye are, Achrone!"

"Help a poor widdy woman with her siven fatherless childre for the love of the sweet beautiful mother that bore ye."

"Darlint, ye'll lave the light heart in my bussom, and good luck to ye."

"Dacency—dacency, don't bar up intirely his honour's way. Is it to the hootel yer honour would wish to be beguiled; faith, it is a swate illigant place for the quality, and kept by a jewel of a woman, who'll deem it an honour to be a convanience to a jintleman, quite intirely."

"Och! manners, Jim, none of yer gambolling, to fling an impedence in the face of a lone widdy, ould as she may be. Mother Broadway, good luck to her, is convanient to all gintlemen that belong to the ra'al quality and know who's who."

Amidst a little suppressed mirth, at this Hibernian introduction to the merits of Mrs. Broadway, and many groans, I made my way through the throng at the sacrifice of a few tin-pennies, and entered the little inn where mother Broadway, as she was familiarly called, presided as hostess.

"And sure yer honour is welcome, barring the dirt on yer boots," were the first words uttered as I introduced myself to a clean, buxom, elderly woman, of about sixty years of age, whose countenance offered, in the still bright complexion, grey eye, and vivacious expression, a good specimen of Irish comeliness.

"What will it plaze yer honour to axe for to ate?" was the question of a very pretty roguish-eyed little waiting maid, rejoicing in the name of "Molly."

"Anything you have got to give," was my answer.

"Why sure, anything manes nothing," said the girl, uttering a truism that nature, and not the world, had taught her—"sure the house is full of dainties, if yer honour would take the throuble jist to move yer tongue to call them."

"Have you a mutton-chop?"

"Och faith, and its thrue that the last was aten this morning by a dandified chap intirely, from the great ship yonder—a mighty dilicate appetite that could ate nothing but mate."

"Well then, give me a chicken.'

"A chicken, yer honour! Faith, the only chicken we've got is the old cock, that joys his liberty in the yard; and hard's the bit he'd make for the like of yer quality."

"I have no objection to some fish, if you have neither flesh nor fowl."

"Ochrone!" whined out Molly, in a tone of deep despair, while her eyes glanced fun all the time: "Ochrone! that ill-luck should have crept into the house jist as yer honour first made acquaintance with it. Ne'er a fish would let himself be catched this blessed week past; and Denis O'Sullivan says, they are kaping theirselves, like good Catholics, to be aten in Lent."

The debate between Molly and myself, on the subject of possibles and impossibles, appeared further than ever from conclusion; nor was I sorry when mother Broadway stepped into the council, and congratulated herself that "although her house had been unhandsomely divesticated, she allowed, of flesh, fish, and fowl, by the unmannerly spalpeens from the ships—bad luck to them—she had "a duck" she could recommend for his honour's supper."

My first introduction to Erin, at mother Broadway's Hotel at Cove, was certainly ill-calculated to impress me with an exalted view of the "iligances" of Irish life; but what a rich compensation for torn window curtains, and no bell-ropes, was to be found in Molly's native blarney, from which I received my first, my virgin impression, of Hibernian humour.

"Pray, Molly, can you get my boots cleaned," said I the next morning, after a good night's rest.

"Och, yer honour, sure ye don't mane the thing—your boots claned! Jist now put your pretty face out of the window, and see how dirty the strates are, and then 'twill be—faith—that yer honour will be axing to have yer boots claned!" Molly's logic carried the day.

On sallying forth from mother Broadway's, I was forcibly struck with the animation of the scene before me. No less than eighty men-of-war and transports were lying at anchor, the latter having on board a picked division of infantry, under the command of General Johnson. Twenty-seven of the transports were laden with field-brigades of artillery, pontoon trains, and every variety of military stores; and these, with a full complement of the field-train department, constituted the charge to which I had been appointed.

The first familiar faces I met were those of my friends Cresswell and Butcher, of the field-train—officers who had gone through the Peninsular war, and were now, like myself, on their way to America. These two gentlemanly and pleasant fellows were on board the "Nile" transport, which I, in consequence, selected for my sea-quarters; and a more united and happy little party never put their sea-stock together, than we formed.

The fleet was detained by contrary winds in the Cove of Cork for a period of nearly three months, during which time the Blue Peter was flying from the mast-head of the Commodore, as a signal to be under weigh at the first change. So many false alarms had been given during the snatches of absence we made on shore to partake of mother Broadway's currant whisky, and broiled salmon, that frequent escapes made us venturesome, and at length we depended upon the experience of an old weather-wise pilot of the harbour, and the vigilance of our scouts, and bolder grown, ventured to make excursions in the neighbourhood.

Several times we were warned of a movement in the fleet, and returned just in time to weigh anchor and to put to sea; but after tacking about some hours, we were again obliged to return into the harbour, and resume our anchorage as before.

To have quitted Ireland without visiting Cork would have shown an indifference far from being felt to a locality that is identified even more than the capital itself, with Ireland and the Irish; besides, who would forego sailing from Cove to Cork, and thanking nature for the enjoyment she has provided on the charming banks of the Lee?

To vary our excursions we sometimes "jaunted it" to the pretty village of Passage, in a "ra'al Irish sociable," a car so constructed, that two inside passengers are seated back to back, while the driver sits on a seat in front, sufficiently close to amuse his "fare," with a series of questions, answers, and descriptions; at once inquisitive, humorous, and quaint.

Not a castle but has its legend. Not a modern villa but bears the character of its owner in characters as broad and visible as the stones of which it is built, nor a dark glen that does not teem with supernatural inhabitants, through the imaginative and marvel-loving tongue of an Irish car-driver. What he has heard, he improves upon, in the ardour of his recital; and what he is ignorant of, he supplies by an invention of his own, so closely resembling what might be the truth, that it requires an intimate acquaintance with the race to detect the fraud his wit has put upon the stranger.

"What is the name of that high hill, Pat?" said one of my companions to our car-driver, whose tongue had never ceased to enlighten us with information respecting the names, properties, qualities, and private histories of every man, woman, and child we met with on the road. Pat gave a slash to the meagre flanks of the horse he drove, and gained a moment's time by the infliction.

"Was it that hill yonder, yer honour axed the name of? Don't yer honour know the name of the big hill? Och I know it well. It's called the 'ould hill,' because it's been always there."

Another of my excursions was to the far-famed Blarney Stone. Pat acted both in the capacity of driver and guide, and although it appeared very unnecessary for him to increase his share of the gift already bestowed by the talismanic property of the "Blarney Stone," Pat was of a different opinion, and reverentially kissing it, assured me with a comic grin, that "no poor man could have too much! that this world was a big ugly place for the poor, and that three halves of the rich were to be 'blarney tickled.'" After inspecting the old castle, that contains this treasure to the Sons of Erin, we returned to Cork, where McDougall's hotel afforded an excellent sample of Irish comfort and civility.

While the winds were still raging with an apparent determination lo detain the fleet within the Cove, news of the most important nature burst upon us most unexpectedly. France had extended her fickle arms to the disturber of the world's peace, and Napoleon Bonaparte was once more at the head of the French nation. For some time after this startling intelligence no change of destination was contemplated for our expedition; but, at the very moment that the weather cleared, the winds abated, and the ocean seemed to smile a welcome, the progress of the fleet was arrested by a telegraphic communication from Dublin, and soon the news spread far and wide, that peace with the United States was concluded, and that England was again about to give her blood and treasure to reinstate a second time upon the throne of France, a race that seemed pursued by an evil destiny.

Orders were immediately issued for the troops to proceed to the Netherlands, and I received directions to disembark on the Island of Haulbowline the whole of the guns, pontoons, and military stores, with the greatest possible speed, to enable the transports to fetch from America troops that had been engaged in that disastrous war. In the space of five days, with the assistance of a strong working party from the flag ship—Admiral Sawyer—and the aid of upwards of a hundred Irish labourers, the transports were cleared, and the wind being favourable, the whole fleet moved out of harbour.

During the progress of this duty I had taken up my quarters at Mrs. Broadway's, and there first learned how easily an Irish heart may be touched by the language of kindness. My intercourse with the native working class was necessarily great. I found them, at first, surly when found fault with, disposed even to be insolent, and their manner of working so deficient in method, that they impeded the progress of each other; but the moment I adopted the system of encouragement, and held out not only the golden prospect of the "poteen," when the day's work was done, but the promise of staying to share in the "farewell cup," then it was that the native character seemed to burst from the weeds that hung about it.

Each man felt his pride less burdensome, because less sorely taxed; and pride being generally the gangrene that gnaws the vitals of the Irish, when once relieved of the calamity, the brighter feelings of their hearts poured forth with freedom. The efforts of these men to deserve praise were immense. I divided them into three parties, numbering them one, two, and three; and, to suit my purpose, offered to bet upon the superiority of the party, whose services I most required at the moment.

The success of my plan exceeded my expectations, and the herculean strength and activity of one fine young fellow was beyond anything I remember to have seen. He took upon his shoulders one of the small guns, a four-pounder; and although bending under the immense weight, spurned the assistance of his comrades, and actually carried it a distance of three hundred yards, from the shore to the depot. The others would not be outdone; the heavy pontoons were hoisted from the boats, and borne on shore on men's shoulders, with a wildness of energy that it is impossible to describe.

"Who can surpass No. 1?" I called out, at seeing the sinews of the poor fellows' bare legs literally starting from the effects of their exertion.

"The boys of No. 2, plaze yer honour," was roared out by the succeeding party, and then mingling their native humour with their good will, some of them jumped into the pontoons to increase their weight, and were carried on their companion's shoulders into the depôt, where, with reckless, half-savage fun they were thrown, by the bearers, headlong among the stores, to the no small jeopardy of legs and arms.

While the Irish labourer was thus vindicating himself from the aspersion of idleness, which has been unjustly thrown upon him by those who have never seen him under the circumstances of profitable employment, mother Broadway and her little saucy-tongued waiting-maid were equally felicitous in their illustration of the open nature, and generous kindness of the Irish woman. As long as I had my companions with me, and that our boisterous parties, under the immediate inspiration of "currant whisky," partook of the nature of such meetings as generally assembled at the "hostelrie" of mother Broadway, the good dame was imperious, sharp, and often argumentative, on the propriety of allowing "a bait from the Evil One to be thrown in her strame;" but when I was left alone, and engaged in an arduous duty, the kind nature of mother Broadway's heart displayed itself in attentions as numerous as they were refined and varied.

Before the dawn of day, when I would have stolen out to my boat in waiting, without disturbing the inmates, Molly would slyly slip out of the kitchen with a cup of hot coffee, "to keep the cold from my heart, sure;" and always once a day, and sometimes twice, a little boat from mother Broadway's would push off to Haulbowline, the scene of my duties, for the purpose of bringing me some special dainty prepared by her own kind hands.

Having nothing to detain me when my duties at Haulbowline were terminated, I took my passage on board a packet that sailed from Cork, and remembering the discomforts of the last passage, I wrote to mother Broadway—we had already said farewell—begging her as we passed Cove, to send me on board some Fermoy ale, and whatever provender her larder could muster, enclosing at the same time, a five pound note to cover the expenses of my demand.

It was a fine, bright, blowing morning, when the packet started from the quay at Cork; just sufficiently boisterous to hold out a stormy prospect for the next few days; and it was with some little anxiety that I looked for mother Broadway's well-known boat, as we neared the beach of Cove. It was at the side of the packet in the twinkling of an eye; and true to the last, a well-packed hamper was hoisted upon deck.

It was late in the day before I inspected its contents, which consisted of two dozen of Fermoy ale, chickens, a ham, and smoked salmon. On the top lay a little note directed to myself, wherein I found the five-pound note I had sent, and these words:

"Sure! ye wer'nt in airnest to send me the goold, or else ye have no raal notion yet of mother Broadway's thrue Irish heart."

CHAPTER 39

To Belgium

The excitement caused by Napoleon's escape from Elba had not time to exhaust itself in speculative inquiry as to the measures that Europe would adopt; for, no sooner was the event known to the great powers of the continent, than a gigantic alliance, cemented by England, took place between them—a mighty barrier to the views of the unwelcome intruder!—that required nothing short of his mighty daring, and undiminished self-confidence to resist.

While Russia, Austria, and Prussia, were pressing forward their distant troops to the frontiers of France, England was in a whirlpool of activity, to supply, by a perfect organization of her resources, the deficiency that existed in her numerical strength. The recently terminated war in America had called away many of our veteran Peninsular troops; they had been recalled, but in the interval, the exigency of the moment required that fighting men should be sent over to the continent; and such was the requisition for artillerymen, that at Woolwich there was scarcely a sufficient number left to mount guard.

When, at length, the transports brought back our soldiers from America, they were not even permitted to land, but ordered off to the seat of war, to engage again in those scenes of bloodshed that had been their lot for so many years. Sir Alexander Dickson, of the artillery, had been only a few hours returned to the home where duty to his country had made him almost a stranger, when a messenger arrived from the Master-General of the Ordnance, with orders for him to join the Duke of Wellington's head-quarters in the Netherlands with the least possible delay: the Duke having left directions to that effect.

I was on the point of departure for that country, and, at the request of Sir Alexander Dickson, tarried a day longer to accompany him. We left Woolwich on the 12th of June for Ramsgate, where we found Sir Thomas Picton, superintending the embarkation of his horses on board a small transport that had been placed at his disposal by the government. At that time, it was generally believed among military men that this distinguished officer had reason to be dissatisfied at the manner in which his services had been recognized; and that feelings of wounded susceptibility had weakened the friendship that once united him to the Duke of Wellington.

Nothing can be more false than such an assertion; for although, under such circumstances, Picton would still have been too much the true soldier not to have felt the *prestige* of a Wellington's name, and far too noble-minded to have allowed self to interfere with the interests of the service, yet it would have been impossible for him to have paid the Duke the tribute of affection I am about to allude to, unless he had also loved the man.

The party that met at Ramsgate dined on that day together, and when the health of the Duke of Wellington was proposed, he, who had seen the sparkling eye, and heard the fervent voice of Sir Thomas Picton, as he added an emphatic "and may God bless him!" to the toast, could never have doubted the source from whence the sentiment sprung.

As soon as the tide served, on the same evening, Sir Alexander Dickson and myself embarked for Ostend with this brave man, who was destined to find a hero's grave on the field of Waterloo. As he sat on deck, closely wrapped in his cloak, his eyes were sternly fixed upon the shores that he was fated never to behold again! A melancholy shade overspread his countenance as the white cliffs of Albion faded from his sight; and never has the glorious death of Sir Thomas Picton been spoken of in my presence, without its recalling to my mind how unusually silent and subdued he was, in leaving a country that was soon to mourn his loss.

Early on the 13th we reached Ostend, where a pleasure was in store for me, in the sight of my old friend, Sinclair, of the 44th regiment. This gallant fellow was one of the *élite* of the Peninsular officers; he was in the third division under Picton, and his regiment was one of the foremost columns that advanced to the attack of Badajoz. The captain of the grenadier company having received a severe wound, the command of it devolved upon Sinclair. A sprinkling of daring spirits, such as his, was essential to the success of an enterprise, which, up to that moment, was not only doubtful, but fraught with danger to the military reputation of the great Commander who conducted it.

Sinclair led his men to the very walls of the castle, which poured upon them, from the heights, a murderous fire. Only three scaling ladders were raised against the ramparts, and at that moment of awful suspense which precedes, on such occasions, the ascent to probable destruction, of hearts beating high with life and spirit— my friend sprang to a ladder, followed by the brave soldiers of his company—for soldiers are always ready to share danger to which their commanding officer leads them. On reaching the summit, he found the ladder too short for the height of the parapet; yet, nothing baffled, he crept through an embrasure, and was one of the first who trod upon the walls of Badajoz. Closely followed by his party, a fierce contest ensued between the besiegers and the besieged. Foot to foot the ground was won and lost, and the darkness of night added to the horrors of this scene of carnage.

Although severely wounded, Sinclair still encouraged his men by his voice and example; until overpowered by a second severe wound, he sunk upon the ground, mingled with the dead and dying. In this state, he lay trampled under foot by the combatants, who successively advanced or retreated, as the tide of success ran with or against them. Yet, still as the glare of light flashed from the fire-arms around him, and allowed him to distinguish his gallant followers, still did his voice animate them on, until nature became exhausted, and he sunk into insensibility. It was not until the invincible intrepidity of our troops had surmounted an every obstacle, and driven the enemy from his posts, that my friend was discovered at day-light in the place where he had fallen.

This gallant soldier, at a later period, was one of the foremost who escalated the fortress at the unfortunate attack of Bergen-op-Zoom, and was by the side of the lamented Colonel Carlton, when fighting hand to hand, that officer received his death wound;

and yet, Sinclair, whose name is dear to all who knew him as a soldier—whose name is dear to all who know him as a friend, quitted the service of which he was an ornament—a subaltern!

On the evening of the 14th, Sir Thomas Picton, attended by his three *aides-de-camp*, Captains Tyler, Chamberlain, and Price, Sir Alexander Dickson and myself arrived in Brussels. Who could have imagined, in viewing the gay aspect of that city, that the desolation of war was concealed behind the brilliant scene, or that any thought, save that of pleasure, could intrude on minds apparently so eager to enjoy it? And yet, at the very time, Napoleon's formidable army, under his own experienced generalship, was concentrated on the Sambre ready to advance on the capital of Belgium.

Early on the morning of the 15th the French commenced hostilities by attacking the Prussian outposts at Thuin and Lobez; and after gaining a decisive advantage, advanced upon Charleroi, while the Prussians fell back upon Sombref. The first intelligence of the outbreak of the enemy reached the Duke of Wellington through the Prince of Orange, at about four o'clock on the same day.[1]

The Duke was at dinner when the Prince rode into the courtyard of his hotel in the Rue Royale, and without dismounting from his horse, communicated the intelligence to his Grace, who immediately afterwards issued orders to the several divisions of the army in their respective cantonments, to be in readiness to move at a moment's notice. But no stir or bustle accompanied the important arrangements that were going on. The town was yet in ignorance of the events that had occurred; and such was the tranquil demeanour of the experienced officers, to whom the Duke's orders were given, that hence may be supposed to have arisen the absurd and fabulous report of the Duke of Wellington having been surprised by the enemy, while philandering away his time at a ball given, on the night of the 15th, by the Duchess of Richmond.

Long before the Duke and his staff joined that memorable *fête* every preparation had been made for an immediate movement of the army; and Bluchers despatch, which arrived towards midnight,

---

1. This information was given to the author about an hour afterwards by Sir Alexander Dickson, who was dining with the Duke of Wellington, when his Grace rose from table to receive the Prince.

bearing the intelligence of the enemy's nearer approach, only hurried the conclusion of the arrangements that had been quietly, yet actively progressing for some hours previously.

At that late hour the 5th division, quartered in Brussels, was summoned to arms. This division was under the command of Picton, whose first inspection of the gallant regiments that composed it, may be said to have taken place in the testing presence of the enemy. Even before the sounds of the drum and bugle had called the troops to the rendezvous, groups of persons were gathered in the streets, to gain some more defined intelligence than the rumours that were beginning to circulate through the town. Nothing positive was known, but everything was feared, and the indistinct hum of voices breaking on the stillness of the night, sounded ominously, like the distant murmur of convulsed elements, that precedes the storm at sea. When, at length, the drums beat to arms, and the troops poured forth from their quarters towards the Place Royale, where they were ordered to assemble, the truth could no longer be concealed, and the night was passed in feverish anticipation of the morrow.

Before the break of day, the rifle corps, headed by the gallant Sir Andrew Barnard, and followed by the brave regiments of Picton's 5th division, and Brunswick's "black horsemen" issued from the gates of Brussels on the road to Quatre Bras, where the left of the Anglo-allied army was menaced by the enemy.

The 1st and 2nd corps of the French army were under the command of Marshal Ney. This division was intended to attack, in detail, whatever allied troops might present themselves from Brussels, while Napoleon carried the strength of *la grande armée* and the magic influence of his name and presence against the Prussians under Blucher. Had Ney concentrated his troops at Frasnes, which, by using great exertions, he might have done by the morning of the 16th, history would probably have had a very different tale to record of the events of that day. Had the French Marshal even employed the strength he had, of eighteen thousand men, well supported by cavalry and artillery, instead of allowing them to slumber away the night of the 15th on the heights of Frasnes, he might still have carried out the designs of his great master, by attacking the Belgic-Dutch brigade, which formed the extreme left of Wellington's army, and sweeping it from its position before Quatre Bras. The same night his head-quarters would have been at Gemappe. On the 16th, his columns would have been concentrated, and the 1st, 2nd, and 5th divisions of the Anglo-allied army would have been attacked in detail, or forced into a retrograde movement.

On the 17th, Napoleon, who, on that day, forced the Prussians to retire upon Wavre, would have operated upon Wellington's left, and before the concentration of the allies could have been effected, Brussels would have been the head-quarters of Napoleon, and the Belgian army, although at that time no great prize to any monarch, would have ranged itself under the French *tricolour*.

This was the scheme of Napoleon; and that its execution failed, must be ascribed to one of those inexplicabilities in the tide of Fate that no human discernment can solve. As already stated, Ney's disposable force bivouacked on the night of the 15th at Frasnes, and it was only at about one o'clock on the following day, that the French Marshal, uncertain, it is true, of the strength of the enemy before him, shyly advanced some of his light troops in the direction of Quatre Bras, a position that was held by a division of the Dutch, under the command of the Prince of Orange. Not withstanding the superiority of the enemy, this Prince chivalrously maintained his ground until the arrival of Picton's division; and it ought to be one of Belgium's proudest recollections that her hereditary Prince, so young in years, yet old in the experience of a soldier, should have struck the first blow against the violators of her liberty.

The appearance on the field, of the British regiments was the signal for the opening of a tremendous fire from the enemy's batteries. The enemy mustered strong, even from the first, in artillery and cavalry, whereas we were most deficient in both, having of artillery only two batteries—British and Hanoverian— of six guns each; and of cavalry—to be depended on in the hour of need—the "Brunswickers" alone.

This it was that made the battle of Quatre Bras so fatal to the brave fifth division, which had to sustain the furious charges of the French Cuirassiers and Lancers, in addition to the sweeping havoc of artillery from the enemy's heights; yet such was the determined bravery that was opposed to these unequal odds, that every charge was repulsed at the point of the bayonet, and every murderous gap filled with the same steady coolness that might have been displayed on a field-day.

As if it had been the caprice of Fate to test to the utmost the endurance of the 'superb division,' the already preponderating force of Ney's cavalry was increased by the arrival of two thousand of Kellerman's heavy cavalry division, while no reinforcement of the British troops came to cheer the hearts of the devoted men, who were nobly upholding their old Peninsular fame.

Nothing henceforth could have sustained this fearful conflict, but the unconquerable spirit of the lesser number. That spirit, unflinching, unshaken, never for a moment flagged during the unequal contest. It animated the men to die rather than to yield an inch of the contested ground; but, as the instruments of carnage mowed down their ranks, Wellington watched, in anxious suspense, for the arrival of the more distantly cantoned troops to reinforce the devoted band.

By six o'clock the first and third divisions, under General Cooke and Sir C. Alten, and a strong reinforcement of artillery, had relieved the exhausted fifth division; but the enemy's strength had been also materially increased by fresh troops, and the fierceness of the combat raged the more intensely, from the renewed vigour of the combatants.

Although severely fatigued by a long day's march, the allies resisted, with indomitable bravery, every effort of the enemy to force the position of Quatre Bras, and finally, Ney, conscious that further attempts would prove equally unavailing, withdrew his troops to the heights of Frasnes, and night threw a veil of darkness over the field of blood.

CHAPTER 40

Hard Fighting

The footing so gallantly maintained at Quatre Bras was effected at a fearful loss to the Anglo-allied force, and at the price of many valuable lives. The Duke of Brunswick nobly fell at the head of his brave "black horsemen," while cheering them on to avenge a father's death and a country's wrongs.

The veteran Colonel Macara, of the 42nd Highlanders, was sacrificed, with two companies of his regiment, to the furious onset of a body of the enemy's Lancers. This charge was with such startling rapidity, that there was not time to include the flank companies, as the regiment formed square to receive it, and direful was the result to these brave fellows. Macara had served in India and throughout the Peninsular War with distinction, and was peculiarly adapted for commanding the hardy clansmen of the 42nd. His stalwart figure and martial countenance were well in character with the mountain-clad warriors he had so often led to victory; and such was the love he bore the regiment that he used to say, he would rather head it to confront the French, than be made the General of a division, in which it played no part. Mortally wounded, the veteran fell amid a host of his own brave soldiers, and right nobly was his death avenged by the survivors of the 42nd, under their next officer in command, the gallant Colonel Dick, who was himself soon afterwards severely wounded.

Some of the regiments of the fifth division were reduced to nun skeletons of their former strength; but gained a glorious compensation in the undying renown their devoted valour won. Maitland's guards and Barnard's riflemen showed, by the consummate skill with which they took advantage of every change of circumstance, that their practical knowledge of warfare had been acquired in the training school of the Peninsula; while our faithful allies, the Germans, asserted, as they ever have done, by their conspicuous gallantry, their right to participate in the laurels of the British soldier.

While Ney's division was engaged with the allied troops at Quatre Bras, Napoleon was in fierce contest with the Prussians, under Blucher, at Ligny. This battle was one of the most sanguinary of modern times, and waged with unabated fury, from three o'clock till nightfall; both armies bringing to the encounter a hatred that could only be extinguished in death. No quarter was asked or given. The advantage of position was on the side of the French, and although the numerical strength of the two was slightly in favour of the Prussians, yet such was the preponderating influence of the enemy's cavalry, which nearly doubled that of Blucher, and the superiority of his artillery, that it may impartially be affirmed, that in strength, the French army predominated. To render it still more effective, Napoleon sent orders for the first corps of infantry, and Gerard's division of the second corps to march from Frasnes to join *la grande armée*. Of this ill-judged movement, so fatal to the enemy, and so fortunate to the allies, Ney complained, in bitter terms, at a later period, when unjustly reproached for, at best, a cold adherence to his master's cause.[1]

The Prussians fought with an infuriated energy that sprung from the recollection of past humiliation and grievous injury, and the veteran Blucher himself, during the fierce conflict, performed prodigies of personal valour, leading his troops, sword in hand, into the thickest of the fight.

The carnage was terrific on both sides, but greatest on the side of the Prussians, resulting from the disadvantages of ground. At length, unable to withstand the concentrated assault of the whole of the enemy's cavalry, including the veterans of the Imperial Guard, Blucher drew off his army, unmolested by the enemy, who had also suffered severely, and re-forming it at a distance of a mile from the scene of action, retreated under cover of night, and in admirable order, upon Wavre.

The heroes of Quatre Bras bivouacked the night of the 16th

---

1. Vide Marshal Ney's letter to the Duc D'Otrante, dated Paris, June 26, 1815.

upon the ground they had so valiantly made their own; and it was not until the following morning that Wellington, apprised of Bluchers retreat, decided on a retrograde movement, to facilitate the junction of the allied and Prussian armies. This retreat of the troops concentrated at Quatre Bras was effected with so much secrecy, that the greater part of the infantry was beyond molestation, before the enemy was aware of the movement; and it was only when the cavalry of the rear-guard, under Lord Uxbridge, moved off from the ground, that a large body of French cavalry and lancers was sent in pursuit. From that time, a continuous skirmishing was kept up between the hostile cavalry, with little or no results, with the exception of an affair at Gemappe, where the rear-guard, closely pressed by a regiment of lancers, received Lord Uxbridge's orders to charge them. This was done with much spirit, but with ill success, by the 7th Hussars, who, in their turn, received the spirited charge of the lancers, and suffered considerable loss. Major Hodge, commanding the leading squadron, was slain, and the regiment thrown into great confusion.

It was soon manifest that the hussars, notwithstanding the gallantry they displayed, were unequal to the part assigned them. Neither men nor horses were fitted to cope with the novelty of lances and flags; and it was injudicious to order light horsemen to charge the solid wall of bristling lances that was opposed to them. So the result proved. The horses fell back in alarm at the flags that flapped in their eyes; and although several desperate efforts were made to re-form, and the attack was renewed by the hussars, it failed to make any impression on the enemy. Lord Uxbridge then withdrew them from the unequal combat, and ordered the 1st Life-Guards to charge the increasing masses of cavalry that menaced the rear.

Headed by Major Kelly, these gigantic horsemen rushed down the hill upon their opponents, sweeping before them, like an avalanche, every object in their course. Nothing withstood the shock of that magnificent charge. Men and horses, lancet and flags, were trampled in the dust together; and driving the enemy to a respectful distance from the retreating columns, the Life Guards thus secured a free and uninterrupted passage for the allies to the plains of Waterloo.

It was growing dark on the evening of the 16th, when a wagon, filled with our wounded men, slowly descended the road that leads from Quatre Bras to Brussels through the Forest of Soignies. The rain was pouring down in torrents from the dark and angry skies; the thunder growled heavily, and the lightning illuminated, at intervals, the gloomy depths of the forest.

It was a fearful storm, and every living creature had sought shelter from its violence, when two females were seen approaching from the direction of Brussels. The youngest was tall, and of a commanding figure, though fatigue and anxiety seemed to have bowed her down, as the lily by the passing blast. Her complexion was white and pure as marble, and the perfect regularity of her Grecian features rivalled the *chef-d'oeuvre* of a Canova; but there the resemblance to inanimate nature ceased, and the fevered lip, and anxious eye told of the mockery of art.

No bonnet covered the long dark tresses that fell, matted with the rain, in crazy disorder on her shoulders. A thin white dress was the only protection against the torrents that came rattling to the earth. It seemed as if some horrid vision, some fearful presentiment of evil had beckoned forward this fair being, to meet a fatal certainty. Her companion was of humble class, and her bronzed complexion, and thick cloak of scarlet cloth, spoke of old campaigning habits, acquired under a warmer sun than shone in the skies of Belgium. Mary Gifford looked, and was—the soldier's wife!

In spite of the increasing storm, the two walked on—their silence only broken by the deep-drawn sighs that burst from each, when their attention was arrested by the wagon already mentioned, which approached, slowly jolting over the rough and rutted road.

"My God!" exclaimed the soldier's wife, whose experienced eye could not be deceived as to the purpose of the vehicle before her; "they are bringing off the wounded. Heaven help us, young lady, this is not a sight for the like of ye."

"Oh, mind me not!" murmured faintly her companion; "but ask—ask what news of the 28th regiment." She could say no more, but sank fainting by the road-side.

Mary Gifford, whose feelings, although deeply rooted, were become less excitable, from long acquaintance with the dangers of a soldier's life, advanced to seek the dreaded information.

The irresistible eloquence of grief was not to be misunderstood.

"Whom seek ye, poor woman," said the driver, mechanically stopping his horses as she laid her hand inquiringly on his shoulder. The name—the nearest—dearest, trembled on her lips, but could not escape them.

"I seek," she replied, while her dark complexion assumed a darker hue, as she spoke: "I seek tidings of the 28th regiment."

The driver shook his head.

"Poor fellows, they have been sadly cut up, I hear; but none of them are with me;" and so saying, the wagon jolted onwards in the direction of Brussels.

With anxiety, swelled to agony, the unhappy woman returned to the young lady, who still lay insensible on the bank, where she had placed her. The cold air of approaching night, however, at length revived her to a sense of the mission she had undertaken to accomplish; and with faltering steps, she again endeavoured to advance. Another, and another wagon dragged slowly its sad burthen over the uneven road, and again and again was hailed by the poor wanderers; but night had closed upon this day of trial, and the groans of the suffering wounded as they approached and receded from the spot, stifled the women's feeble efforts to attract attention. Long and dreary was that night; and stretched on the cold damp earth, lay the sinking form of the young and fair Emma C——, who had placed herself under the protection of a soldier's wife, to seek, on the field of the dead and dying, a beloved and only brother.

The morning of the 17th dawned; and with it returned the anxious restlessness of those devoted beings to advance towards the scene of the previous days' combat. Wagon after wagon passed, bearing the mangled victims at the shrine of glory; and into each sad receptacle of mortal suffering, the stern soldier's wife bent a piercing look of inquiry, in which hope and fear were strangely blended. Another appeared in sight—it was open; and the countenances of all within were distinctly visible. A very young man, in the uniform so dear to Mary Gifford, and whose fair hair was dyed in the stream of gore that flowed from a severe sabre wound in his head, raised himself to bend over the side of the wagon as she approached.

"Well, Molly," he said, "we ar'nt quite so cock-a-hoopish just now, as we were yesterday morning."

"And, John?" demanded the woman in the husky voice of deep emotion.

"Hit—badly hit," answered the young soldier. "I saw him on the ground last night very much hurt."

The poor woman groaned aloud, and returned with rapid strides to her young companion. In another hour they were in the midst of the horrors and confusion of the field of Quatre Bras.

Surrounded by the dead and dying, Mary Gifford left her weaker companion to the care of some soldiers' wives, who were assembled round the brandy flagon; and moving forward to a group of men, clad in the well-known uniform, she found herself led, almost unconsciously by a kind supporting arm—for Molly was the favourite of the regiment—to the presence of her wounded husband.

Extended on a litter of straw, and covered with a blanket, lay the gallant Sergeant Gifford; and one look sufficed to tell the distracted wife that all would soon be over with the veteran. A kind smile of welcome flitted over his dying features, at this last proof of devotion from his faithful help-mate.

"Molly," he faintly whispered, as she leant in bitter, but silent grief over him; "this is like you—like what you have ever been to me—the best of human beings. Molly,"—she bent down to listen to his faint voice, "they have shot off both my legs!"

The wretched woman heard no more, but fell senseless on the mutilated form, that one short day before had displayed in a remarkable degree, the strength and health of vigorous manhood.

The wounded man made an effort to raise the devoted wife, who had fallen, without consciousness, on his bosom. A blessing on her head struggled with the parting breath of life, and the British soldier was no more.

When Emma C— was placed under the care of the rough followers of the camp, the excitement of her mind bordered upon frenzy. A flush of crimson overspread her usually pale complexion, and the pensive cast of her large expressive eyes had changed to a feverish and unnatural brilliancy. With vacant stare, she met the inquiring looks of those around her, and gazed, with apparent indifference, on the appalling scene of the previous day's carnage, where the slain were stretched in the stiffened shroud of their own gore. Some she passed unheeded by; others she examined with intense interest.

At length an object arrested her attention; she sprung towards it, clapped her hands, laughed, and throwing herself upon the lifeless form of a young officer, whose uniform was of the gallant 28th, she kissed with frantic fondness the eyes and lips that death had for ever sealed.

"William," she joyously exclaimed, "I have found you at last, and we will part no more. Dearest brother, hearken to that waltz; do you remember that we danced to it at the ball last night?"

Can it be—that the young brother and sister—on whose graceful movements an admiring circle gazed but a few short hours before, as one encircled the other, in all the pure freedom of fraternal love—are here stretched a loathsome spectacle of death and madness?

Short-sighted mortals! look again, and in the picture trace the mercy that Providence has shown to both. To the young soldier who died in the arms of victory, was spared the disappointments, the heart-gnawing evils that as surely attend on after-life as death attends its close.

On the young girl, the loss of an only brother fell gently; for her mind was unconscious of the bereavement, and her disordered fancy created images of past and future happiness. Images that knew no change, and which the cold realities and conventions of the world had no power to destroy.

Chapter 41

Waterloo

Historians have celebrated, and poets sung, the Field of Waterloo; and as far as it has been possible, have dilated upon the beginning, progress, and result of that eventful battle, until nothing has been left to add to the many glowing pictures they have transmitted to posterity. It is true that all have been subjected, more or less, to the charge of incorrectness, on some particular point or another, and have given rise to contradiction and controversy, nor is it possible that it should be otherwise, when it is considered that information on the details of battles must necessarily be gleaned from individuals, whose individual feelings are interested, and consequently are to be gratified. Leaving therefore such points as admit of dispute to those who have already met on the hostile ground of controversy concerning them, it will perhaps be more interesting to look back upon the plains of Waterloo through that prism only, whose faithful accuracy time has tested; and which brings them to the view of all, as plains hallowed by the life blood of the brave: as plains, on which thousands of deep embedded recollections linger still.

Vain indeed would be the efforts of the human pen, accurately as it might delineate the leading features of the contest on the plains of Waterloo, to trace even the faintest outline of the feelings that flowed from that vast fount of human suffering. How many have found refuge in the grave from the intensity of sorrow, that mingled with the name of Waterloo. How many have withered in the chill blight of memory, unable to force the sap of life from its strong tenement, and thus dragged on a miserable existence!

Others again—like the sapling that bows to the earth its young head as the raging storm sweeps over it, escaping annihilation by bending to the stroke—were laid prostrate by the sudden wrenching in twain of ardent affection. Sorrowing in deep despair over the field of Waterloo, their grief found at length extinction, in its own violence.

On the morning of the eventful 18th of June, the allies rose from their bivouac on the wet earth—for the night had been a tempestuous one—and prepared to face the formidable enemy that lay stretched, in masses of cavalry and infantry, along the opposite heights. This army, headed by Napoleon, numbered eighty thousand men, and was supported by a well-equipped artillery of two hundred and fifty guns. Moreover, it possessed the immense advantage of being composed of men of one nation; men, bound together by the pride of country, as well as by an enthusiastic feeling towards their sovereign and leader. Whereas, of the allied army under Wellington's command, although but slightly inferior in point of numbers to the French, twenty-five thousand only were British soldiers. The rest were foreign troops; some of which were nobly brave—others were rendered useful auxiliaries by the power of good example; while others again were to be trusted so cautiously, that their absence from the field would only have been felt as a security against treachery

The hostile armies occupied heights running nearly parallel with each other. The distance that separated them was about twelve hundred yards, and the intermediate ground, or rather valley, formed by a gentle declivity on either side, was richly covered with luxuriant corn.

The allied forces stretched across the high roads that lead to Brussels from Charleroi and Nivelles, having in their rear, at a distance of about two miles, the Forest of Soignies. Their led extended to the hamlet of Ter la Haye, from whence a road leads to St. Lambert by which a communication with the Prussians was maintained. In front of their left centre stood the farm house and gardens of La Haye Sainte, and towards the centre of their right, the Château of Hougoumont.

The enemy's attack on the latter position at about eleven o'clock a.m., on the 18th, was the commencement of the battle of Waterloo.

At about that hour, a numerous host of tirailleurs advanced close to the wood and orchard of the chateau, followed by two massive columns of the 2nd corps of the French army, under Jerome Buonaparte. Pressing rapidly through the waving corn, these columns were next seen as rapidly pressing up the slopes that led to Hougoumont; but here they had to deal with British and German valour, and while a detachment of the guards that occupied the house poured upon the assailants a fire calculated to impair the ardour of the assault, the opening thunder of the battle pealed through the air from Cleeves's battery of nine-pounders, stationed on a height, at a distance of about three hundred yards to the left, and a little in advance of the front line.

The leading column was seen to lose its firmness, and to hurry onwards, when a second roar of artillery, from the battery of Captain Sandham, posted on a height that nearly faced the advancing foe, stopped its progress, by laying low the front ranks. Before the rear could fill up the gaps, Cleeves's guns were again at work, and as the two batteries threw, with deadly aim, their showers of spherical and case shot on front and flank, the columns wheeled round, and retired in precipitation and disorder.

Thus commenced the battle of Waterloo; a battle that differed from all others in the sacrifices demanded and conceded during its long continuance, of nine hours. Wellington had taken the best position left to him. It covered the capital of Belgium—it communicated on the left with the Prussians. The undulating nature of the ground was favourable for acting on the defensive until the arrival and co-operation of Blucher, and upon strict adherence to the defensive, the safety of Wellington depended.

Here then was no field for the display of skilful generalship, and tactical knowledge. The one great essential to a Commander so placed, was firmness, and fortunately for the allies, Wellington possessed that attribute in no small degree. The one great essential for soldiers so placed, was blind obedience—which is a habit rather than a principle—and was so rigidly inculcated in the British army by the Duke of Wellington, that he well knew how far he could depend upon its practice in the field.

Necessity demanded that the position of the allies at Waterloo should be maintained, though rivers of blood should flow from its defenders. And more than this; necessity demanded that brave men should stand passively to be slain, nor slay in turn, until, like automatons, their faculties were put into movement by a superior power. This it was, that made the bloody field of Waterloo one, over which angels might have wept. No retaliation was offered by the brave, the young, the haughty, as mutilated and bleeding, their comrades fell in heaps around them. The flashing eye and panting heart, told what the spirit longed to do; but confidence in their leader, and blind obedience to his will, were stronger even than revenge, and like lambs they stood the slaughter, until the word of command roused them to be lions.

During this contest, the French varied their modes of attack, sometimes by advancing columns of infantry, flanked by cavalry, and under cover of a powerful artillery. At such times, our gunners, posted on the rising ground, would throw their missiles, with tremendous effect, among the closely wedged masses, and if driven from their guns to seek shelter in the squares, our heavy cavalry rushed down the slopes, and, with their powerful horses, rode down the mailed squadrons of the foe; while our infantry deploying into line—generally only two deep—would steadily ascend the slope that sheltered it from the enemy's batteries, and facing the advancing mass, until within sometimes only twenty yards, would greet them with a well directed volley. The next moment, the order to "charge" would be responded to by a true British "hurrah," and before the enemy could fly back to his position, the guns, that had been momentarily abandoned, were again at work. Our infantry would then steadily resume its place behind the slopes, often lying down to avoid the fire; and the cavalry having driven back to their own territory the French squadrons, would resume its station, ready to repulse, in the same manner, similar attacks.

At other times, the French cuirassiers advanced in heavy masses, covered by their artillery. As they boldly ascended the slopes, exposed to a murderous fire from the batteries, our gunners were again driven to seek shelter in the squares, or under the limbers of their guns, where many were lanced and sabred.[1] The bold horsemen would then advance, at furious speed, until within a horse's length of our firm and close-knit squares; here they would brandish their long swords in impotent defiance, and often strike the bristling bayonets that stood as barriers to their further advance. Imprecations, screams, and even jests were levelled at the impassable obstruction. Carbines and pistols were discharged in mock revenge; but not a trigger returned the challenge until the word "fire" ran clearly down the line of the menaced square. Then down went the front men and horses of the leading squadron. A well directed fire from the next square threw the rest into confusion, and our cavalry would effectually complete their rout.

Such were the leading features of the day's engagement, in which both armies displayed a desperate valour, that has never been surpassed. The position of Hougoumont was as vigorously sought for by the enemy, as valiantly defended by the allies; and if victory could have found space for one laurel more, in the thickly-entwined wreath assigned to bravery on that celebrated spot, she would have added it, in honour of the British guards, under the command of the gallant Colonel Hepburn.[2]

Among other most conspicuous instances of corresponding gallantry may be named the repeated brilliant charges of the two regiments of Life-Guards, in which their gallant Colonels Ferrier and Fitzgerald were slain. The matchless conduct of the Royals, the Greys, the Inniskillens, headed by the brave Ponsonby, who yielded up his life in this glorious struggle for Europe's freedom, the intrepid advance against nine thousand of the enemy, of Kempt's brigade, led on by one, whose name is his eulogy, the loved, the chiv-

---

1. (see previous page) Had the squadrons of the cuirassiers been accompanied by a few mounted artillerymen, each provided with some common spikes of four inches in length, and a small hammer—with which the French and English field-batteries are always supplied—they might have been employed during the few moments that the cuirassiers were in possession of our guns, with much advantage to themselves and injury to us. It would not have occupied the space of half a minute for these artillerymen to have introduced a spike into the vent of a gun, and with a sharp blow from the hammer, to have broken it off flush with the metal—the spike being in cast steel. This simple operation would have placed our guns *hors de service,* and the result would, in all human probability, have been fatal to the allied army.
2. This officer's name was omitted by the Duke of Wellington—in reference to the defence of Hougoumont—in his Grace's dispatch of the battle of Waterloo, and the name of a junior officer substituted for it. The mistake—which doubtless it was in the first instance—was never rectified, and in consequence every writer upon Waterloo securely firm on the authority of the Duke himself, has failed to render justice to the memory of a gallant officer, and honourable man, by mentioning him as the officer in command on that memorable occasion.

alrous Picton, who was struck from his horse a lifeless corpse, just as the word "charge" had rung from his lips in a loud and animating tone—the bright example set to the sons of Belgium by the Prince of Orange, from the first opening of the day of strife, until within a short period of its glorious close, when severely wounded, he was carried from the field, where he had so nobly sustained his early frame—these are some of the recollections of Waterloo, that cast a hallowed light over its dark field of carnage; and of such reminiscences, none are of a more lofty character than those inspired by La Haye Sainte. This farm, immediately in front of our left centre, was occupied by five companies of the 2nd light battalion of the German Legion, under Major Baring, and was vigorously assaulted by the enemy. The defenders barely numbered three hundred men, and yet heroically repulsed four desperate attempts of the enemy to gain possession. The walls had been loop-holed for musketry, and from these apertures, as well as from a loft, commanding the road, the marksmen of the Legion committed murderous havoc on the assailants. Officers were the principal objects of their aim, and numbers of these were stretched under the walls by the unerring shots of the Germans. A lull of some minutes usually succeeded the unsuccessful efforts of the enemy to force an entrance, and it was during one of these cessations, that a French cuirassier, for the purpose of ascertaining the real strength of the party within, showed a self-devotion that was very remarkable.

The road to La Belle Alliance passes directly under the walls of La Haye Sainte, and at a distance of about one hundred yards, sinks into a hollow, invisible from the house. The entrance from this road to the garden of La Haye Sainte was defended by an abbatis, constructed of loose timber, and guarded by a detachment of the legion under Lieutenant Graeme—a young and gallant Scotchman. The firing had for some time ceased, and the road—as far as it could be seen—was clear, when a French cuirassier was seen upon the ridge of the descent slowly advancing towards the position, round which the dead and dying were thickly strewn.

No aim was taken at him as he approached, for who could guess at the fearless purpose that brought him there? And from the point of his sword being studiously lowered to the earth, during his slow progress forwards, it was supposed he was a deserter. The defenders of the abbatis challenged him as he neared the post; and as no answer was returned, his silence confirmed the supposition that he had deserted from the enemy. As he reached the abbatis, Graeme summoned him to surrender; when the bold intruder replied to the demand by quietly raising himself in his stirrups, until he could command an entire view of the party within, and its defences. He then aimed a terrible blow at Graeme's head, and turning his horse round, galloped off at lightning speed the way he came. Such was the surprise created by the audacious daring of the man, that although every musket was turned upon him, and he had fully one hundred yards to ride, before he could be screened by the sinking of the road, he escaped in safety to the French lines.

Reduced in number, and with ammunition exhausted, the gallant Germans could maintain themselves no longer in the ruins, to which La Haye Sainte was reduced; and when at length the French infantry, supported by artillery, poured into its walls, the assailants looked round in astonishment at finding barely thirty men to welcome them with their last round of ammunition.[3]

This gallant remnant, that had so nobly obeyed Major Baring's orders to defend the position to the last, was furiously assailed by the enemy; and even the wounded that lay stretched upon the floors, were cruelly bayoneted. The young officer, Graeme, whom the chance of war had left uninjured, rushed through the throng of French soldiers, who were glutting their vengeance upon his dying comrades, and miraculously effected his escape through a passage, which led

---

[3] It was not owing to the difficulty of communicating with the gallant men, who defended the farm of La Haye Sainte—as it has been asserted—that the failure of their ammunition is to be attributed, but to the exhaustion in the field depots, of that particular cartridge adapted to the German rifles. Fresh supplies of ammunition had been issued by the Field-Train throughout the entire line, at different periods of the battle, which responsible branch of the service was conducted by the Author of this work. Some regiments expended more than others, and particularly the three battalions of the old 95th; whose calibres differed from the other regiments of the line, and were the same as those of the 2nd light battalion of the Germans. Towards the close of the day, the last round of this species of ammunition had been issued. There can be no doubt, however, but that La Haye Sainte required for its defence a reinforcement of men, far more than of ammunition. Before the position was taken by the enemy, its defenders were nearly all slain. Ergo, fresh supplies of ammunition would have been of little service to them. Had a battalion of men, and a couple of howitzers been posted within its enclosures, La Haye Sainte would have maintained itself against any assault, as Hougoumont maintained itself, to the close of the day.

into the open ground upon the right. Perceiving the remainder of his regiment, headed by the gallant Baring, posted behind a stunted hedge at a short distance, he sped towards it through a shower of musketry, and had just reached it, greeted by a shout of welcome from his comrades, when he was struck down with a severe wound.

Thus fell La Haye Sainte, the stout defence of which position, by so inadequate a force, through a long period of the day of strife, reflected on that battalion of the German Legion engaged in its defence—an honour that might well have been commemorated by the name of "La Haye Sainte," appearing in conjunction with that of Waterloo, upon the banners of its regiment.

The softened light of evening had succeeded to the broad glare of day; and how stood the hostile legions that survived the uncompromising advance of time? Still on the one side, flashed the presumptuous daring that attack inspires. Still, on the other, was displayed the same passive submission to a leader's will; but, over both, time had thrown a spell that weighed most heavily on the weaker side; and strong as the spirit still remained, the physical energies of Wellington's soldiers were almost exhausted by protracted endurance of the frightful contest.

The slopes that at morning's dawn had worn their covering of freshest verdure, were at evening's close, heaped depositories of dead men's bodies. The corn that had waved in rich luxuriance, was now trampled to the earth from whence it sprung, staunching with its heavy fruitfulness, many a stream that flowed from the death-gaps of the brave. The clearness of a summer sky was screened by a thick and lurid atmosphere that pressed upon the field of carnage, as gloom presses on the hearts of men, who think themselves sacrificed in vain. And such was, for a time, the thought of many who lived to see the evening hour on the field of Waterloo.

It was nearly seven o'clock, when a thrill of renewed hope and joyful excitement revived the fagged and drooping spirits of our diminished squares and exhausted squadrons. The hour had at length arrived when fortitude and forbearance were to meet with their reward; and as Blucher's guns boomed in the distance, each man felt that the signal of revenge was given in that glad sound. On Napoleon's ear, the echo fell as the knell of departing glory. One hope and one alone remained. The Imperial Guard had never yet been vanquished.

This veteran band of fifteen thousand men, which had taken little part in the contest of the day, was now ordered to charge the British line; and with noble intrepidity, these renowned warriors, headed by the chivalrous Ney, rushed with fresh and unimpaired vigour to our slopes.

As they advanced, a tremendous fire from our artillery poured destruction into their ranks; yet, still pressing forward, they gallantly made their way to the ridge that concealed the British guards. The fate of Europe hung upon the crisis; and fortune held in reserve for Wellington, at that moment, the proudest distinction of his military life.

"Up, guards, and at them," are words that will thrill through the hearts of men, long after who spoke them, and they, who responded to them, are passed away. The guards sprung up from their recumbent position at the welcome command, and poured a volley into the advancing column that stopped effectually its progress. Panic-stricken, the Imperial veterans staggered, as a second well-directed fire took fatal effect among them; and as the British guards charged with overwhelming fury down the hill, these old soldiers durst not meet the shock, but turned and fled in wild disorder, pursued by the victorious guards and Adam's light brigade.

Vainly did some of the *vieille garde*, in reserve at the bottom of the descent, try to reform the routed columns. Our cavalry, headed by the noble Uxbridge, dashed among them, driving them onwards into the thick confusion, that now began to envelope, in every direction, the French army.

By this time, the Prussians were pressing heavily on the right flank of the enemy; and Wellington, no longer restrained by the stern necessity of prudence, which had been so dearly practised throughout the long day of tumult and anxiety, ordered his whole line to advance upon the foe.

The brave allies, forgetting past tribulation in present glory, advanced with loud cheers to the attack; and the last effulgent rays of a setting sun shone on the conqueror, Wellington, as he led the general charge. With desperate valour, the warriors of the Imperial guard endeavoured to check the tide of victory by making a stand worthy of their high repute. Vain effort! Onwards, like a tempestuous torrent rushed the victorious allies, sweeping before them, in one blended mass, a confused and broken multitude, while the Prussian cavalry, animated by a spirit of deadly hatred, followed up the pursuit with eager ferocity, repaying with interest, upon the flying remains of *la grande armée,* their long standing debt of revenge.

On the ground where stood, on the morning of the 18th, this formidable army of Napoleon, the junction of the allies with the Prussians was consummated at close of day, by the meeting of Wellington and Blucher, and by the mingling together of British and Prussian voices in one heartfelt cry of "victory."

It was dark when I turned my horse's head in the direction of Brussels, in obedience to orders I had received from Sir George Wood, the commanding officer of artillery, to proceed to that place, and to send forward without a moment's delay, fresh supplies of small arm ammunition for the troops in the field, and the materiel necessary for the re-equipment of the brigades of artillery, after the rough handling they had sustained during the contest.

At a very critical period of the battle, I had brought up to the German batteries, under the gallant Hartmann, the last of the howitzer ammunition that remained in reserve on the field; and it was, therefore, of the first importance that a fresh supply should be obtained with all possible expedition, to replenish the exhausted limber boxes of the guns, as well as the cartouch boxes of the soldiers.

The battle was won, but the sweeping overthrow of the French army by the rapid and indefatigable pursuit of the Prussians was not then known to its full extent; and it was very essential that the thinned tanks of our matchless army should be provided with the means, of making a stand worthy of themselves, in the event of the enemy rallying.

The road that led from the field of battle was so densely thronged, that it was a matter of difficulty to thread a narrow pass through the moving crowd. In some places, carts and wagons, filled with dead and dying, stood wedged so tightly together, that many minutes would elapse before they could be disengaged, while the groans of the sufferers within them, the oaths of the drivers, and the entreaties for help from those wounded soldiers who had managed to crawl into ditches for temporary shelter amidst the confusion, combined to create a scene that can never be forgotten by those who witnessed it.

The long straggling street of the village of Waterloo presented a curious appearance. Every house, even to the most lowly, was a blaze of illumination, from the number of candles that flared within, and each window disclosed a crowd of shadowy figures gliding to and fro behind the humble curtains. In those rooms where the wounded lay, might have been seen suffering, in all its sad hues of gloomy colouring, from the young and impetuous soldier—whose leading star had been ambition for distinction, and whose young dream of glory was still lingering on the threshold of memory, even while the cold damps of death were settling upon his brow—to the veteran of many battlefields, in whom age and experience had blotted out those dreams of youth, and whose thoughts, on the bed of death, were turned to the loved home, and desolate hearts of those he left behind.

During the day's engagement, I had seen an officer struck from his horse by a cannon ball, and on going up to him, recognized the gallant Colonel, Sir Alexander Gordon, whom I had known in the Peninsula. Only a few minutes previously I had seen and spoken to Dr. Hume, the head-quarter surgeon; and it was with no small gratification that I assured the poor sufferer that assistance was at hand. By great good fortune, I found Dr. Hume on the spot where I had left him, and his valuable services were quickly afforded to this distinguished officer, who was placed in a blanket, and carried to the rear.

At the village of Waterloo, I inquired with anxiety his fate from an artillery surgeon that I met. Poor fellow! he had just expired, after undergoing amputation of the leg, leaving behind him a bright fame as a soldier and a gentleman.

A little further on, continuing my road, I came up with an artillery cart, in which lay an officer, stretched upon a blanket. My anxiety for many in that gallant corps, caused me to inquire his name, and I learnt with sorrow, deep and true, that young Robert Manners—the gay, the handsome, the brave—was lying a corpse in that wretched conveyance. I knew that he had lost his leg in the early part of the day; but I little expected to meet him on that dark road, his eye as dark, his joyous voice silenced for ever. I laid my hand upon his breast—it was cold as marble. I pressed his hand, which for the first time, gave no pressure in return, and turned away more sick at heart than words can well express. It was doubly mournful to reflect that this fine fellow might have been saved by remaining where his leg was amputated; but, removed at his own request, too soon after the operation, haemorrhage came on, and his young life ebbed away in that dark, cheerless vehicle, as it jolted over the rough *chaussée* that traverses the gloomy Forest of Soignies.

As I continued my way onwards, the confusion seemed, if possible, to increase. Groups of intoxicated soldiers were congregated on the sides of the roads, adding to the general dismay and alarm, by recklessly firing off their pieces, upon every passing object. Some of the commissariat wagons had been deserted by their drivers; and the empty barrels that rolled upon the road, displayed the means by which liquor had been obtained by the soldiery.

On approaching nearer to Brussels, the inhabitants of that city were thronging forwards to hear tidings from the scene of action—tidings that might be depended on; for so varied and contradictory had been the reports throughout the day, that it was impossible to extract a rational conclusion from so many conflicting falsehoods. The first face I recognized, under the broad glare of a lamp in the Faubourg de la Porte de Namur, was that of Admiral Sir Pulteney Malcolm. The anxiety of his countenance was very great.

"The battle is won. The Duke is safe," were my first words.

"God be praised for both," said the veteran sailor, with an "onction" that could not have been surpassed by his holiness, the Pope; and at the moment, I really believe that we could, though we did not, have hugged each other, à *la française,* for joy. Sir Pulteney Malcolm had been sent by the Admiralty to Ostend, to be in readiness for any emergency that might require his aid. Like a true British blue jacket, he could not endure being kept so far from the scene of action; therefore, leaving his ship, he came to Brussels to obtain the earliest information of what was going on. Having heard my news, the Admiral started off again, with the same zealous impatience to be the first to announce the great victory of Waterloo to his gallant crew.

My jaded horse dragged his weary legs, at a slow pace, through the crowded streets of Brussels, seeming little to participate in the triumphant feelings that were beginning to assume a decided ascendancy. Had victory been on the side of the French, it is probable that the demonstrations of joy evinced by the populace, at the success of the allies, would have been equally vehement, and more sincere. The events that have since occurred in Belgium justify such an opinion, by proving how ready she would have been to incorporate herself with France, had Europe so consented. But leaving that as an uncertainty, it will be admitted by all, that greater enthusiasm could not have been displayed, than when tidings of the victory of Waterloo were received. Nor in the annals of war were the inhabitants of Brussels ever surpassed in the humanity and tenderness they exhibited towards the distressed wounded of all nations, that assisted in the glorious result.

At that late hour, women of the highest rank were hastening to the hospitals, with lint and necessaries for the sufferers. Some even took upon themselves to assist the surgeons in their painful duties, and watched with gentle assiduity by the pallets of the wounded soldiers, throughout that long night of agony to so many. Each hour added to the noise and confusion of the town. The arrival of vehicles of every description, bringing in the wounded from the scene of the day's battle, appeared endless; and the cheers of the mob, as our soldiers came galloping in, with some proud trophy of the victory, mingled in strange discordance with the laments of women seeking among the wounded, their relatives and friends.

After having communicated with the field-train officer, in charge at Brussels, upon the object of my mission, I retired to my quarters; but sleep, I can well believe, visited the eyelids of few, who returned that night from the field of Waterloo. Time seemed to have made a leap that placed a chasm between the events that had occurred before the opening of the battle, and those that had since happened, leaving memory in possession only of the latter. It was impossible to believe that the day which was past, and the night which was passing, were limited, by the hand of time, to so short a space; for within the first, an eternity of feeling had been concentrated, which the latter was reflecting with a shadowy, but painful accuracy, and the shouts of men, the clang of arms, and battle's thunder, that had prolonged the day to an immeasurable length, were scarcely more exciting in their reality than was the repetition of them, by a fatigued imagination, throughout the night.

Such sensations did not fall to my share alone. I have heard others describe the turbulence of their dreams on the night of the 18th of June, 1815; but, when another rising sun dawned upon the world, it brought with it an invigorated healthfulness to the mind; and exultation, and joyful gratitude, that victory had again crowned her favoured Wellington in the great cause of freedom on the field of Waterloo.

CHAPTER 42

The End of My Military Life

The tempest which had threatened the world was hushed, and the dawn of a lasting peace seemed to have risen from its scattered elements. France, with apparent sincerity, called upon her legitimate Ruler to resume his position, and he, in turn, admitted past error, and promised that experience should be his guide for the future.[1]

The army still adhered with faithful tenacity, to the name of Napoleon, and even after an abdication, which resembled the mock-heroic *denouement* of a stage performance, a host of gallant men held together, under the banner of the tricolour. The towns and fortresses of France were garrisoned by these troops, and while Wellington and Blucher pursued their victorious route towards the capital, levelling whatever obstructions impeded their progress, the second corps of the Prussian army, under the command of Prince Augustus of Prussia, was directed to reduce the northern frontier fortresses of Maubeuge, Landrecy, Philippeville, Marienbourg, and Rocroy; a powerful and well-equipped battering train—to the charge of which I was appointed—having been placed by Wellington at the disposal of the Prussian Prince, to effect these operations.[2]

---

1. Vide Louis XVIII's proclamation to the French nation, dated Cambray, June 28, 1815.
2. On the morning that succeeded the battle of Waterloo, the author was specially appointed to the charge of the battering-train, placed at the disposal of the Prussian army, for the reduction of the French frontier fortresses. This battering-train, which was on a scale of extraordinary magnitude, consisted of two hundred and forty-five heavy guns and mortars; two hundred and eighty-eight thousand rounds of shot and shells; nineteen thousand barrels of gunpowder, with a pontoon train, and other heavy stores. From this immense park of artillery, which had been collected and equipped for service at Brussels, seventy-five heavy guns and mortars were transported over cross roads, measuring a distance of two (*continued overleaf*)

The frontier fortresses were all well garrisoned, and in a good state of defence. Philippeville and Landrecy had received reinforcements in the fugitives from Waterloo, and the gallant stand they made against the formidable armament brought to reduce them, showed the fidelity of the French soldiers to their flag, even after it had ceased to represent the power of the extraordinary man who had adopted it as his own. Yet it is just to the Commandants of these fortresses to observe, that they were not desirous of an unnecessary effusion of blood, for when summoned in succession to surrender, by Prince Augustus, each replied, that he was ready to open the gates intrusted to his keeping, upon receiving orders to that effect, from whatever government existed, at the time being, in Paris. No such orders were given, nor indeed was sufficient time allowed for receiving them; and consequently the fortresses were consigned to the unnecessary horrors of bombardment, which was the mode of attack adopted by the Prussians, to the great injury of the inhabitants and houses, especially at Philippeville, where conflagration destroyed nearly half the town.

Each fortress was taken in succession: Maubeuge was the first attacked, and held out five days. Landrecy was the next, and was reduced after a period of two days. Philippeville suffered severely from the town being bombarded and set on fire in many places, and surrendered on the fourth day. Marienbourg capitulated after a bombardment of three days, and lastly Rocroy, which made a stout resistance of five days.

After the capitulation of each fortress, the garrison marched out with the honours of war, dispersing immediately in every direction, with a celerity that was marvellous. Not a French soldier tarried behind to witness the ingenious method adopted by the Prussians to maintain an army at little cost, or rather to ensure to themselves a remuneration for the trouble of coming so far from home, to return the visit made by the French to them in Prussia.

The first step taken by the Prince, on entering the captured town, was to call upon the civil authorities to provide quarters for himself and staff, suitable billets for the Generals and other offic-

---

(from previous page) hundred and ninety miles to the scenes of warfare. Three thousand horses of the country were required to move this ponderous train from one point of attack to another. Six companies of British artillery accompanied this expedition under the command of Sir Alexander Dickson.

ers, and billets and rations for the troops, on a scale of quantity and quality designated by himself; exacting also that the best provisions and wine should be supplied at the same economical ratio, to every officer, Prussian and British, who accompanied him.[3] Nor was this all. These snug little towns contained hoards very precious to the army, of cloth, linen, and leather. A strong hand was laid upon them also; and it was required of the inhabitants, that not only these articles should be appropriated to the wants of the troops, but that all the tailors, sempstresses, and shoemakers that the town could muster, should be employed day and night to replace, by their handicraft, the wear and tear occasioned by the long marches that were necessary to bring the Prussians to these forest fastnesses.

The pursuance of this course was considered by Prince Augustus as perfectly justifiable, when carrying on war in an enemy's country, repressing on one side all excesses and cruelty in the troops under his command, and exacting, on the other, that they should be supplied with every necessary they stood in need of; and when the blood-stained route of the French army through Prussia is remembered, the moderate and equitable demands made on the inhabitants of the French towns, on this occasion, stand forth in honourable contrast.

The discipline of the Prussian troops during this short campaign was admirably maintained, and displayed to advantage the qualities of the Prussian soldier, which are—high courage, an exalted love of country, patience under privation, and devotion to his officers, who are, in themselves, well worthy to inspire a feeling that tends very materially to the high organization of the Prussian army.

---

3. After the capture of Marienbourg, Prince Augustus issued orders for the defences of the town to be destroyed, and directed that the inhabitants should furnish the working parties for the purpose.
On the same day, Sir Alexander Dickson and myself dined with the Prince in the fortress, when His Royal Highness jocosely asked me, what I thought of his method of making war. I answered that I had every reason to consider it the best method I had yet witnessed. "*Comment cela,*" said the Prince, "you have served under Wellington in the Peninsula and at Waterloo." "True, your Royal Highness; but in those countries I was obliged to spend my money, and here I keep it, and am much better lodged and fed into the bargain." "Ah!" said the Prince, laughing, "*L'Angleterre est plus riche que la Prusse, et plus généreuse aussi.*»
There was a sly sarcasm in his manner, that lent an interpretation to his words, as the moral does to the fable.

On the morning that preceded the capitulation of Rocroy, I was returning from a mortar battery to the park of artillery, to forward fresh supplies of ammunition, when perplexed by the many cross roads that intersect the forest of the Ardennes, I chanced, most inopportunely, to take one that led me to a French piquet. The surprise of the French soldiers at the appearance of an English officer among them was great; but my chagrin was greater still at being taken prisoner at that eleventh hour. Chagrin and regrets were, however, alike unavailing, and I was marched off into the fortress, with many a *mauvaise plaisanterie* to beguile me on the way. The interior of the garrison showed the feelings of the French military at that moment. The capitulation of this last fortress, on whose walls still proudly waved the tricolour, was hourly expected, and the excitement of the soldiers, at the necessity of surrendering to the Prussians the banner under which they had fought and conquered at Jena, amounted to savage frenzy.

My reception, as I passed through a crowd of half drunken soldiers, was none of the most friendly. Execrations on England and the English greeted me on every side, and it was only when I found myself in the presence of the Commandant that I considered my life in security from the inflamed passions of the soldiery. At an early hour, the officers of the garrison sat down to dinner, and I was invited to join this meeting, that was looked upon as the last, in which they were to be assembled in the brotherhood of arms. The turbulence of that party can only find an excuse in the conflicting feelings that waged fiercely in the breasts of men, peculiarly susceptible by their national character, to the humiliation of defeat. The room was crowded beyond what it could hold with any degree of ease, and wine flowed with a freeness that soon took effect upon imaginations already over-heated.

The drinkers, from enthusiastic, became literally mad, and shouts and oaths, mingled in one furious uproar with uncorking of bottles, and smashing of glasses against each other, to the health of the Emperor Napoleon. Spurred on by the uncontrollable frenzy of the moment, the Commandant turned suddenly and fiercely upon me, insisting that I should drink to "*L'Empereur.*" I declined the honour, as in duty bound, when this *officier supérieur,* no longer able to withstand the dictates of hatred that were urging him on to wreak his vengeance on an Englishman arose, and with his sword unsheathed, swore with a tremendous *"Sacré nom de Dieu,"* that I should not leave the table until I had complied with his demand.

If it be true that *"in vino veritas"* the French character was nobly redeemed by what followed. A simultaneous rush was made towards me by a phalanx of brave fellows, whose countenances spoke eloquently their indignation at conduct so unchivalrously and ungenerous towards a prisoner. Nor was their example lost upon the aggressor, for throwing his hostile weapon at a distance from him, he rushed to embrace me, at the risk of excoriating the sides of my face with a stubble beard of at least a ten days' growth. The remainder of the day was passed in riot and uproar, and on the following morning terms of capitulation were sent in by the Commandant to Prince Augustus.

That morning was one of proud and yet painful feelings. Seated on his beautiful charger, Prince Augustus surveyed his well-dressed, well-disciplined troops, as they marched past him, their fine bands playing the martial airs, of their liberated country, while the triumph of conquest imparted a proud confidence, which was perceptible in their whole appearance. The last sound of the cannon had been heard which had revenged the wrongs of Prussia; and as memory retraced those wrongs, and with them the sorrows and humiliations to which Prussia's beautiful and high-minded Queen had been exposed, a sigh of regret arose that she had not been spared, to witness the regeneration of the land she so dearly loved.

Such was the picture presented by the Prussian troops, as they filed past their Prince; nor was it less interesting to behold the garrison of Rocroy, as with defiance still marked upon their faces, the veterans marched out with the honours of war, and piled the arms that had so often been victorious, upon the glacis of the fortress. How was it possible not to think of Friedland, Austerlitz, and Wagram, on seeing the groups that now congregated together to take a last farewell. Distinctions of rank had been cast off with the arms they bore, and officers wept, and grasped the extended hands of privates, with the affection that men feel, who have been bound together by the tie of mutual danger, and the comradeship of military life.

As soon as the French garrison had dispersed, Prince Augustus made known his wish of taking leave of those British officers who had taken part in the recent campaign.

Dismounting from his horse, and surrounded by his staff, his Royal Highness placed himself on the ramparts of the fortress, on which the Prussian Eagle now floated in the breeze, and addressing us in English, he dwelt with noble enthusiasm, on the restoration of liberty to nations, and peace to Europe, through the instrumentality—in a great degree—of England and of Prussia. He spoke of the curse of war, as too dearly proved by years of insolent aggression on the part of France; and gave it, as his firm belief, that Germany—integral Germany, the heart of Europe—undivided in her policy, and united to England by the adamantine chain of mutual confidence, might defy all future efforts to disturb her peace.

The Prince then returned us, individually, his thanks for our services; and as a mixed group of Prussian and British officers stood on the glacis of Rocroy, exchanging heartfelt assurances of kindly feeling, and regret at parting, each felt an honest pride at having contributed his share to the conclusion of a war, that in ages yet to come, will shine among the most glorious in the page of History.

ALSO FROM LEONAUR
AVAILABLE IN SOFTCOVER OR HARDCOVER WITH DUST JACKET

WELLINGTON AND THE PYRENEES CAMPAIGN VOLUME I: FROM VITORIA TO THE BIDASSOA *by F. C. Beatson*—The final phase of the campaign in the Iberian Peninsula.

WELLINGTON AND THE INVASION OF FRANCE VOLUME II: THE BIDASSOA TO THE BATTLE OF THE NIVELLE *by F. C. Beatson*—The second of Beatson's series on the fall of Revolutionary France published by Leonaur, the reader is once again taken into the centre of Wellington's strategic and tactical genius.

WELLINGTON AND THE FALL OF FRANCE VOLUME III: THE GAVES AND THE BATTLE OF ORTHEZ *by F. C. Beatson*—This final chapter of F. C. Beatson's brilliant trilogy shows the 'captain of the age' at his most inspired and makes all three books essential additions to any Peninsular War library.

NAVAL BATTLES OF THE NAPOLEONIC WARS *by W. H. Fitchett*—Cape St. Vincent, the Nile, Cadiz, Copenhagen, Trafalgar & Others

SERGEANT GUILLEMARD: THE MAN WHO SHOT NELSON? *by Robert Guillemard*—A Soldier of the Infantry of the French Army of Napoleon on Campaign Throughout Europe

WITH THE GUARDS ACROSS THE PYRENEES *by Robert Batty*—The Experiences of a British Officer of Wellington's Army During the Battles for the Fall of Napoleonic France, 1813.

A STAFF OFFICER IN THE PENINSULA *by E. W. Buckham*—An Officer of the British Staff Corps Cavalry During the Peninsula Campaign of the Napoleonic Wars

THE LEIPZIG CAMPAIGN: 1813—NAPOLEON AND THE "BATTLE OF THE NATIONS" *by F. N. Maude*—Colonel Maude's analysis of Napoleon's campaign of 1813.

BUGEAUD: A PACK WITH A BATON *by Thomas Robert Bugeaud*—The Early Campaigns of a Soldier of Napoleon's Army Who Would Become a Marshal of France.

TWO LEONAUR ORIGINALS

SERGEANT NICOL *by Daniel Nicol*—The Experiences of a Gordon Highlander During the Napoleonic Wars in Egypt, the Peninsula and France.

WATERLOO RECOLLECTIONS *by Frederick Llewellyn*—Rare First Hand Accounts, Letters, Reports and Retellings from the Campaign of 1815.

AVAILABLE ONLINE AT
www.leonaur.com
AND OTHER GOOD BOOK STORES

ALSO FROM LEONAUR
AVAILABLE IN SOFTCOVER OR HARDCOVER WITH DUST JACKET

CAPTAIN OF THE 95th (Rifles) *by Jonathan Leach*—An officer of Wellington's Sharpshooters during the Peninsular, South of France and Waterloo Campaigns of the Napoleonic Wars.

BUGLER AND OFFICER OF THE RIFLES *by William Green & Harry Smith* With the 95th (Rifles) during the Peninsular & Waterloo Campaigns of the Napoleonic Wars

BAYONETS, BUGLES AND BONNETS *by James 'Thomas' Todd*—Experiences of hard soldiering with the 71st Foot - the Highland Light Infantry - through many battles of the Napoleonic wars including the Peninsular & Waterloo Campaigns

THE ADVENTURES OF A LIGHT DRAGOON *by George Farmer & G.R. Gleig*—A cavalryman during the Peninsular & Waterloo Campaigns, in captivity & at the siege of Bhurtpore, India

THE COMPLEAT RIFLEMAN HARRIS *by Benjamin Harris as told to & transcribed by Captain Henry Curling*—The adventures of a soldier of the 95th (Rifles) during the Peninsular Campaign of the Napoleonic Wars

WITH WELLINGTON'S LIGHT CAVALRY *by William Tomkinson*—The Experiences of an officer of the 16th Light Dragoons in the Peninsular and Waterloo campaigns of the Napoleonic Wars.

SURTEES OF THE RIFLES *by William Surtees*—A Soldier of the 95th (Rifles) in the Peninsular campaign of the Napoleonic Wars.

ENSIGN BELL IN THE PENINSULAR WAR *by George Bell*—The Experiences of a young British Soldier of the 34th Regiment 'The Cumberland Gentlemen' in the Napoleonic wars.

WITH THE LIGHT DIVISION *by John H. Cooke*—The Experiences of an Officer of the 43rd Light Infantry in the Peninsula and South of France During the Napoleonic Wars

NAPOLEON'S IMPERIAL GUARD: FROM MARENGO TO WATERLOO *by J. T. Headley*—This is the story of Napoleon's Imperial Guard from the bearskin caps of the grenadiers to the flamboyance of their mounted chasseurs, their principal characters and the men who commanded them.

BATTLES & SIEGES OF THE PENINSULAR WAR *by W. H. Fitchett*—Corunna, Busaco, Albuera, Ciudad Rodrigo, Badajos, Salamanca, San Sebastian & Others

AVAILABLE ONLINE AT
www.leonaur.com
AND OTHER GOOD BOOK STORES

ALSO FROM LEONAUR
AVAILABLE IN SOFTCOVER OR HARDCOVER WITH DUST JACKET

THE JENA CAMPAIGN: 1806 by *F. N. Maude*—The Twin Battles of Jena & Auerstadt Between Napoleon's French and the Prussian Army.

PRIVATE O'NEIL by *Charles O'Neil*—The recollections of an Irish Rogue of H. M. 28th Regt.—The Slashers— during the Peninsula & Waterloo campaigns of the Napoleonic wars.

ROYAL HIGHLANDER by *James Anton*—A soldier of H.M 42nd (Royal) Highlanders during the Peninsular, South of France & Waterloo Campaigns of the Napoleonic Wars.

CAPTAIN BLAZE by *Elzéar Blaze*—Elzéar Blaze recounts his life and experiences in Napoleon's army in a well written, articulate and companionable style.

LEJEUNE VOLUME 1 by *Louis-François Lejeune*—The Napoleonic Wars through the Experiences of an Officer on Berthier's Staff.

LEJEUNE VOLUME 2 by *Louis-François Lejeune*—The Napoleonic Wars through the Experiences of an Officer on Berthier's Staff.

FUSILIER COOPER by *John S. Cooper*—Experiences in the 7th (Royal) Fusiliers During the Peninsular Campaign of the Napoleonic Wars and the American Campaign to New Orleans.

CAPTAIN COIGNET by *Jean-Roch Coignet*—A Soldier of Napoleon's Imperial Guard from the Italian Campaign to Russia and Waterloo.

FIGHTING NAPOLEON'S EMPIRE by *Joseph Anderson*—The Campaigns of a British Infantryman in Italy, Egypt, the Peninsular & the West Indies During the Napoleonic Wars.

CHASSEUR BARRES by *Jean-Baptiste Barres*—The experiences of a French Infantryman of the Imperial Guard at Austerlitz, Jena, Eylau, Friedland, in the Peninsular, Lutzen, Bautzen, Zinnwald and Hanau during the Napoleonic Wars.

MARINES TO 95TH (RIFLES) by *Thomas Fernyhough*—The military experiences of Robert Fernyhough during the Napoleonic Wars.

HUSSAR ROCCA by *Albert Jean Michel de Rocca*—A French cavalry officer's experiences of the Napoleonic Wars and his views on the Peninsular Campaigns against the Spanish, British And Guerilla Armies.

SERGEANT BOURGOGNE by *Adrien Bourgogne*—With Napoleon's Imperial Guard in the Russian Campaign and on the Retreat from Moscow 1812 - 13.

AVAILABLE ONLINE AT
www.leonaur.com
AND OTHER GOOD BOOK STORES

ALSO FROM LEONAUR
AVAILABLE IN SOFTCOVER OR HARDCOVER WITH DUST JACKET

LIGHT BOB by *Robert Blakeney*—The experiences of a young officer in H.M 28th & 36th regiments of the British Infantry during the Peninsular Campaign of the Napoleonic Wars 1804 - 1814.

NAPOLEON'S RUSSIAN CAMPAIGN by *Philippe Henri de Segur*—The Invasion, Battles and Retreat by an Aide-de-Camp on the Emperor's Staff

SWORDS OF HONOUR by *Henry Newbolt & Stanley L. Wood*—The Careers of Six Outstanding Officers from the Napoleonic Wars, the Wars for India and the American Civil War. Illustrated.

HUSSAR IN WINTER by *Alexander Gordon*—A British Cavalry Officer during the retreat to Corunna in the Peninsular campaign of the Napoleonic Wars.

THE LIFE OF THE REAL BRIGADIER GERARD VOLUME 1 THE YOUNG HUSSAR 1782 - 1807 by *Jean-Baptiste De Marbot*—A French Cavalryman Of the Napoleonic Wars at Marengo, Austerlitz, Jena, Eylau & Friedland.

THE LIFE OF THE REAL BRIGADIER GERARD VOLUME 2 IMPERIAL AIDE-DE-CAMP 1807 - 1811 by *Jean-Baptiste De Marbot*—A French Cavalryman of the Napoleonic Wars at Saragossa, Landshut, Eckmuhl, Ratisbon, Aspern-Essling, Wagram, Busaco & Torres Vedras.

THE LIFE OF THE REAL BRIGADIER GERARD VOLUME 3 COLONEL OF CHASSEURS 1811 - 1815 by *Jean-Baptiste De Marbot*—A French Cavalryman in the retreat from Moscow, Lutzen, Bautzen, Katzbach, Leipzig, Hanau & Waterloo.

RIFLEMAN COSTELLO by *Edward Costello*—The adventures of a soldier of the 95th (Rifles) in the Peninsular & Waterloo Campaigns of the Napoleonic wars.

AVAILABLE ONLINE AT
www.leonaur.com
AND OTHER GOOD BOOK STORES

www.ingramcontent.com/pod-product-compliance
Lightning Source LLC
Chambersburg PA
CBHW031615160426
43196CB00006B/148